Bhopal Nama
Writing a City

Dedicated to the people of Bhopal –
Past, Present and Future.

CONTENTS

Section 3
Magnificent Matriarchy in a Century of Anarchy

Section 4
Feudalism and Modernity

Section 5
A Janus-Faced City - The Past in the Present

FOREWORD

It is very clear that when I speak of an urban edge, it is not merely a physical demarcation or design proposition, but a 'thick' socio-cultural, economic, historical, methodological and political construct in space and time. It has as much to do with emotion as with the practical and the so-called 'real', which can be counted and measured. At least for me, to define this edge would be to decipher a code or to be able to understand the secret which weaves magic, of which I do not find myself capable enough. The real and the imaginary concoct a vision which surpasses any practical reality that I can visualise or see for myself. Confusing, I know, very confusing at times, distressful to the extreme, but that is what, according to my personal experience, happens when we begin to see life in its three avatars – the past, the present and the future.

I will speak of my experiences as a fiction writer and my relationship with the place I belong to – Bhopal, where I was born and brought-up and have spent most of my life. At the time I was born, India had achieved freedom from British rule and had gone through the trauma of being partitioned into India and Pakistan. That Bhopal was a Pathan Muslim State, one of around 600 such states of different denominations, was handed down to me as a bit of history, when history was a subject in my school, making only slightly more sense than religion, which was never meant to be understood. History tried to rationalise the happenings which made our past. A strange and intriguing past. It talked of Aryans coming down to India from far-off and becoming the rulers and in the process it also talked of Muslim invasions of India, Mahmud Ghaznavi, Mohammad Ghouri and Shershah Suri, and the Pathans. A certain Pathan who laid down the foundation of the Bhopal State, long back, sometime after the death of the Mughal, Aurangzeb. The Begums of Bhopal who cultivated friendship with the British and were able to rule despite heavy odds. Aid it successfully to the last, when the State finally had to merge with independent India.

To begin with, it was difficult for me to believe that I was not a son of the soil, but an offspring of a Pathan who came from the frontiers, many years after the State was formed. But honestly speaking, by the time I was able to see and think, I found that there was not much difference between us and the various kinds of other, of our class of citizens.

My first memory of Bhopal is that of a walled city, with a number of 'gentle' hills (Nirmal Verma's term for the hills of Bhopal) and water bodies. The city walls were soon to be brought down and a process of change was to begin, which has left the city almost an alien to me. The younger generation calls it more beautiful, better planned, liveable etc., which it must be when compared to the old that has wholly turned into a ghetto. But I have memories of the days when it was not the ghost it has turned into. I live with a number of impressions of the same place, some narrated, others read and many more disappearing and giving way to newer ones that I have watched with wonderment and apprehension. It is a strange mix of a familiar and never seen or imagined future that co-exists in the name of my present birthplace.

The city of Bhopal, perhaps the city as existed even before I was born, has been crystallised in my mind through its inextricable linkages from the innumerable stories one heard, and from such autobiographical novel as *Voh Aadmi* by my friend Fazal Tabish, who has described the emerging as a human being, absorbing the breath and shadows of the people and the city of his time. The depths of this city which Fazal has tunnelled into, can only be lived through his eyes and his perception as a poet and aficionado of culture. For such a personality, the city opened up and offered myriad opportunities to discover her. There is a different vocabulary of Bhopal and the street languages are quite far from the grips of the script. It has its own tonality with its typical vernacularism.

Even the poets and thinkers who came to Bhopal were mesmerised by its pristine beauty and quivering past. I remember an instance when, in 1981, a poet temptingly wrote an impromptu couplet that captured the essence of Bhopal's past. Fazal Tabish in his capacity as the Secretary, Urdu Academy, had invited a number of poets for an All India Mushaira. Prominent among them were Shaharyaar and Mohammad Alvi from Ahmedabad. I was assigned the task of escorting them and showing them the walled city. Alvi Saheb kept on asking me about the city's past and how it emerged as a Pathan kingdom. After we returned, I suddenly found Alvi Saheb becoming pensive and aloof even amongst a group – which is typical of creative people. He withdrew himself to a corner and began to jot something down on a piece of paper. When I got up to leave, he pushed that crumpled piece of paper into my hand and said, 'my impressions of Bhopal.' I read and then re-read the note, and all of a sudden, as a young man I was overwhelmed by that feeling I have often described by using a word I was introduced to by my favourite writer Orhan Pamuk – *'Huzun'*. Let me share this couplet here, which became oft quoted lines by newspapers and literary magazines of those days:

'Ek shaksh bhatakta hua aaya hoga
Chillake pahadon ne bulaya hoga

Usne bade pyar se talaabon ke soye huye paani ko
jagaya hoga
Bhopal usne tujhe badi hairat se
Paani par larazta hua paya hoga.'

The urban has extended far into the rural sprawl, the old places have either gone or are about to go and new colonies to house the burgeoning citizenry have been built where thick forests once existed. The priorities in life have changed and so has the road map. The old villages have been welded into the urban areas and now they are prominent urban zones. The change has been too fast and too comprehensive. There are plans: everything is given due consideration, but the pace at which things seem to be changing leaves much more to be desired. There is talk of a hyphenated urban-rural planning. The shift in the urban population and thereby shift in the definition of urbanity, planning according to topographical and geographical suitability and demands.

Urban is gradually becoming a comparative term, less or more urban, or with an ambiguous degree of urbanity. Except, of course, the areas that are presently out of reach. For me, my urban edge has gradually become my own threshold, the ones that I cross while I am on the streets of the city each time I find it to be a new world to encounter. When I return, I am with the old, the gone, the going – I dream of the old walled city of the lakes and its peaceful environs – knowing that I am closing my eyes upon so much that must have been most undesirable.

Honestly speaking, the world as a globe also doesn't hold much charm for me. It seems more like a Sunday Bazaar than a place to live in with one's likes and dislikes. In our times how would I define or plan a city to live? To what extent would I like it to grow and what facilities extended to the citizens? I find myself too old and tired to think of, and tell a story with a happy beginning, happy middle and a happy ending... it would be too cynical. Kindly do not take my bitterness as aggression; there are times in life when one is unhappy with what unfolds before him, as also, when one is unable to suggest an alternative.

In the recent years, because of the profusion of some high profiled contemporary events, Bhopal has attracted a lot of attention. Books by Abida Sultan, Shaharyar Khan and Claudia Preckel have, in their own ways, fulfilled the parameters of historical writings on the city. As a matter of fact, there are certain specialities about the history of Bhopal which set it apart from the rest. Apart from history, its geography, its 'gentle' hills, its weather and a pulsating syncretic culture that bloomed during the Princely State days. The remnants of this are still visible in its transformed shape and in its continuously changing profile, almost 70 years after the Merger, which gives it an exclusive relevance.

Bhopalnama – Writing a City, by Vertul Singh is a challenging work if one looks at the many other books on Bhopal. Any writing on the city is like treading a really dangerous path, particularly when the writer claims to symmetrically join the dots from the scattered pieces of information and come out with an all-inclusive portrait of the hubbub of a city's life. However, when one goes into the choice of topics and the mundane life that have been described along with the historical anecdotes, narrated by the author, they are collectively enthralling. Most of them were known to us, the older generation of Bhopal, in the form of folk-lore or sometimes as a ballad. It is therefore praiseworthy that they have been sequenced in a single book, and would otherwise have been languishing in the archives or in digitally restored online libraries, or would have simply been forgotten – since there are no storytellers anymore and the conversational places of olden times – the *'Pattias'*, have all been gobbled up by the ferocious pace of expansion.

Although many aspects of the city have been lost, but at the same time, many an antiquated mien have not only been preserved, but their charm has been augmented many folds. It is important therefore, that the younger generation have some reference points from where they can piece together the complexities and the vibrancy of the city which they have chosen to stay in. I hope *Bhopalnama,* in many ways, will meet up to their expectations. Since the writer of this book also happens to be a fiction writer, one can glimpse flashes of creative writing in his articles.

– Manzoor Ahtesham

Manzoor Ahtesham is a well-known literary figure and the author of five novels, several short story collections and plays. He is a recipient of the *Bharatiya Bhasha Parishad Puruskar, Shrikant Verma Smriti Samman, Virsingh Deo Award,* amongst others. He was honoured with the *Padma Shri* in 2003.

INTRODUCTION

In the past few years, there has been a spurt of books on Bhopal. Although only a handful of them are good and most of them are of uneven quality, this interest in Bhopal's culture and history is indeed welcome, because generally, the Bhopali character is marked by a self-effacing and laid-back trait topped with self-deprecating cynicism. Although a true Bhopali is not inclined to blow his own trumpet, Bhopal, certainly is a city whose unique history and character deserves to be documented and celebrated.

The Bhopal we know today is largely a city of migrants, just as all state capitals of modern India are. The original Bhopal established by Dost Mohammad Khan and his successors, is but a small part of this sprawling and ever-expanding city. The first modern wave of migrants came just after the Partition of India, mostly from Sindh. A few got assimilated in old Bhopal, and many of them settled in the World War II cantonment barracks of Bairagarh. But the migration that really changed Bhopal's demography happened only after 1956, when Bhopal was made the capital of the newly reorganised state of Madhya Pradesh.

A large settlement named after the great freedom fighter Tatya Tope was established, people from all parts of the new Madhya Pradesh – from Malwa, Bundelkhand, Baghelkhand, Mahakoshal, and Vidarbha (now part of Maharashtra) – came to Bhopal to work for the Madhya Pradesh government.

Their initial attitude towards old Bhopal, or the 'city', was that of unfamiliarity, suspicion and some amount of contempt. Their native places were Nagpur, Indore, Rewa or Damoh, where they would regularly go on long summer and winter holidays. The majority of Bhopal's population today consists of the second and third-generation descendants of these migrants.

For these second and third-generation migrants like us, the attachment to the native places was not that strong, and almost unknowingly, in a very silent, unobtrusive way, Bhopal became a part of us. The beautiful hillocks, lakes and minarets became part of our inner landscape. The history and culture of Bhopal became our own history and culture. The laid-back and unassuming ways of Bhopal made inroads into the inner landscape of the migrants. That is the beauty of Bhopal.

Vertul Singh came to Bhopal even later, as a student in the 1980s. He left Bhopal after hardly three or four years, and his career – first in the Army and then with the CISF – took him all over India and abroad, from strife-torn Kashmir to Kosovo in the Balkans. Yet, he kept coming back to Bhopal. It was Bhopal with which he could feel a special bond.

This book is a labour of love for, and enchantment with, the city of Bhopal. Vertul has the advantage of being an insider, as well as an outsider at the same time, which gives him a unique perspective. Thus, he provides fresh insights into the Bhopali mind, which, for outsiders, will become a well-rounded introduction to the unique history of the magical city of Bhopal. The content in this book was originally written as articles for a weekly newspaper column, and I hope that, in the form of a book, it will provide a more comprehensive and well-structured picture of Bhopal. This book is certainly a welcome addition to the chronicles of Bhopal.

– Rajendra Dhodapkar

Rajendra Dhodapkar is an independent journalist, cartoonist and columnist who started his career with the Indian Express Group. He has published a collection of poems and two plays. He is the recipient of the *Bharatbhushan Agrawal* Award for poetry, besides several awards for journalism.

PREFACE

It is said that a city grows on you – either momentarily, or forever. Bhopal's grip on me has been everlasting. I first came here as a teenager in 1983. Since then, much as I have tried to unshackle my bonds with this city, it has only grown deeper – not just in the form of fond memories, but also as a space to decipher and a subject to be pondered over and philosophised. Naturally, the culmination of all this had to be a tangible sublimation – and this book is the outcome.

The term *Bhopalnama* was first used by the satirical poet (*tanz-o-mazah*) and veteran Communist leader, GM Naghmi, as the title for his collection of *nazms* on Bhopal. Popularly known as Ghurru Miyan, a term of endearment for his nom de plume, *Ghazanfar,* he, in one of his *nazms, Guzra Hua Zamana,* bemoans the lost glory of Bhopal, and essentially narrates the various facets of life in the old city of Bhopal. The Welsh word, *hiraeth,* which means homesickness for a home to which you cannot return, a home which, maybe, never was – the nostalgia, yearning and grief for the lost places of your past – closely describes the heartbreak which most old-time denizens of Bhopal are afflicted with, particularly those who have migrated to Pakistan.

The incidents and historical snapshots carried in this book have been culled from many sources. The contemporary relevance of the anecdotes and vignettes may not be as relevant as it was when they appeared in the newspaper column by me (*Bhopalnama, a weekly column in the now defunct daily published from Bhopal – The DB Post*), but their topicality remains the same. Even if we were to dismiss history as a 'fable agreed upon', the quirkiness of Bhopal's history, the typicality, peculiarities and clichés of its evolution, culture and customs – and about the city itself – is succulently delectable.

I have not tried to rewrite the history of Bhopal, and in no way do I claim to be an expert or a scholar on Bhopal's past. However, I have endeavoured to research the dates and occurrences of the incidents narrated here. To the best of my knowledge, they remain undisputed, barring a few instances, where some historians who, maybe rightly, feel that due recognition has not been given to some ancient and early medieval historical personalities. In doing this, I have also tried to include those aspects of history which were overshadowed by the towering Pathan era. In doing so, I have taken into account the recent archaeological findings and research on Raja Bhoj and the Ashapuri temple complex.

For the benefit of the readers, irrespective of the dates of publication of these articles in the column, I have sorted them out in their historical chronology, with a separate section on the miscellaneous. Occasionally, readers may find some of my references unrelated to the main topic of an article. I wish to humbly state that they have been inserted to make the article more interesting and salubrious. I could not help being slightly autobiographical, without being judgmental or conceited, in my mentioning the events of the '80s and '90s. I feel it adds to the passion and love with which I hold this city so close to my heart. But, again, my attempt has been to put into words the collective feelings of the Bhopalis of my generation. The prominent Urdu poet and intellectual, Izlaal Mazid, often quotes an unknown Bhopali poet:

'Yaadein hain apne shahar ki ahl-e-safar ke saath;
Sahraa log aayein hain deewaron dar ke saath.'

These words aptly surmise the essence of my generation.

'Colonial Bhopal was one of hundreds of princely states, together covering a third of British India, whose rulers were promised support and internal autonomy in return for loyalty. The British, out of strategic considerations, not only preserved the Bhopal dynasty, but subsequently opted to support four women rulers for more than a century, beginning in 1819. Such matriarchal succession was a complete anomaly among the princes and wholly unprecedented among the Afghan Pathans, or Pashtuns, the rulers' ethnic group of origin,' writes Barbara Metcalf in her scholarly book, *Islam and Power in Colonial India: The Making and Unmaking of a Muslim Princess*. It is quite appropriate then to quote here the famous couplet on Bhopal:

'Riyasat-e-Bhopal ki nishaani hain char;
batua, chuneti, begum aur taal.'

The sheer force of willpower, persistence and awesome personality, augmented by an unimpeachable strength of character, the *Begumat* steered the history of Bhopal, which is astounding and unparalleled. So, I thought it would be fair to devote a chunk of the narrative to incidents that occurred during the Begums' rule, which not only make for interesting reading, but also let us know those human stories that have mostly remained buried under mundane lessons in conventional history, or as punctuation marks in narrations by court historians. Thus, the section on the Begums also has a poignant piece on the suicide by Waheed Mian, the eldest son of General Obaidullah Khan, which has been beautifully worded by a 'family source' and given to me to be included in this book.

The phenomenal leap of culture and urban development that the city has taken in the past seven decades, post-independence, has overtaken the laidback and somewhat snail-paced cultural progress it had managed to make during the 107 years of the Begums' rule.

It would be incorrect to attribute this progress to a single individual. Rather, it was wrought by a new way of thinking that struck roots in the gradually evolving society of Bhopal under the combined impact of Nehruvian ideology and the full-throttled energy unleashed by the dawn of Independence. This radically changed the dynamics of the city, ushering in an urban culture. Although this may be perceived as being Janus-faced, but in being so, it also continues to quietly imbue this city with a refined cadence which makes it more alluring as a whole.

In its formative years, Bhopal was looking forward to the realisation of Nehruvian dreams, and at the same time, was caught in the shackles of the feudal era of Raj colonialism and the Begums. The Bhopal which was anointed as the capital city of the newly formed state of Madhya Pradesh in 1956, though apparently very different from the Bhopal of the Begums, metaphorically and literally remained a conjoined Siamese twin. Both the old city and new Bhopal have a symbiotic relationship and both are sustained by the nourishment they provide each other culturally, politically, economically and socially.

Modernistic trends had already started budding since the last Nawab, Hamidullah Khan's enthronement in 1926. His contribution to infusing urbanity in an otherwise mofussil town of Bhopal is extraordinary. His daughter has mentioned that way back in the late '20s, Bhopal enjoyed all the amenities of a modern European city – complete with electricity, tarred roads and a municipality to cater to its upkeep and cleanliness. The city's elite enjoyed flush toilets, running hot and cold water, refrigerators, cars and customised railway saloons, modern medical facilities and so forth.

Hamidullah invited a host of forward-looking Leftist liberals from outside the state, particularly his Aligarh Muslim University cronies, who usurped the best administrative posts available in the Bhopal state, much to the chagrin of the ruling elite – the Jalalabadis and the Baqi Khels, as well as the Barru Kat Pathans, the British and, interestingly, even his own mother, the indomitable Begum Sultan Jahan. These AMU alumni were steeped in modern Islamic trends with an overdose of Leftist liberal political thinking, and all of them idolised such leaders as Jawaharlal Nehru, Kemal Ataturk Pasha of Turkey, and the Soviet Communist model of government etc.

But, like Skandgupt, Bahadurshah Zafar and Wajid Ali Shah before him, Hamidullah Khan intuitively knew that he would be the tail-ender of his dynasty. The English were not going to be here forever and the end of the Princes' rule could clearly be seen looming over the horizon. He had twice been Chancellor of the influential third block of governance of the Raj era, the 'Chambers of Princes', and had honed his political skills by his active participation in some of the underground political movements during his AMU days. He had thoroughly internalised Leftist liberal thinking, but was constrained in its implementation owing to his being a member and the head of a feudal order. By being head of the quasi British-controlled administration, Hamidullah Khan, obviously, never encouraged any fissiparous political activities in his State. But at the same time, he never came down too heavily on his detractors. Let us not forget the extremely brutal and ruthless manner in which the Nizam dealt with freedom-fighters, creating a militia known as the 'Razakars', who, till date, are a dreaded and hated lot in the Telangana and Western Maharashtra areas. In fact, 'Vilinikaran Andolan' leaders, such as Shankar Dayal

Sharma got a scholarship from the Bhopal government and was a respected figure amongst the feudal gentry of Bhopal.

I must candidly admit that most of the articles on the nawabs and begums have been inspired by their account in the popular and seminal books by Princess Abida Sultan and Shaharyar Khan, the daughter and grandson respectively, of Hamidullah Khan. Had Shaharyar Khan continued to live in India, he would have been the titular Nawab of two erstwhile principalities, Kurwai and Bhopal. I have liberally quoted from both of them.

Also, in my writings on the miscellaneous hubbub of city life, I have relied heavily on hearsay and oral tradition. Both these have always had very deep cultural moorings in the description of India's past. Right from the days of the Śrutis of the *Vedas*, to the Smriti of the *Puranas* and then, from the metamorphosis of the Buddha into Vishnu in the *Jatak Kathayein*, upto the humanisation of animals in the *Panchtantra*, we have a plethora of tales as told by the seers. I have also used the information, particularly about life in and activities of the old city from books by Khalid Mohammad and Shyam Munshi (please see Bibliography).

In addition to this, long conversation sessions with the city's most-loved intellectuals like Manzoor Ahtesham Saheb, Izlal Mazid Saheb, Rajendra Dhorapkar, and Mumtaz Khan etc., brought up innumerable topics worth pondering over. I remain indebted to them, particularly Manzoor Saheb, who has been my friend, philosopher and mentor. He has guided me in narrating occurrences with the soul of a fiction writer and dissecting and analysing them like a scholar. Mumtaz, a renowned fashion designer, on my request has also drawn the sketches of erstwhile Bhopali libaas for this book.

I, however, request erudite readers not to equate this book with the great and famous books on the past of cities, such as

City of Sin and Splendour: Writings on Lahore, by Bapsi Sidhwa, or *Guzistan Lucknow,* by Abdul Haleem Sharar, or *Dilli Jo Ek Shahar Hai,* by Maheshwar Dayal, and many more. These are scholarly works based on long research and the authors' own deep and personal association with the cities. In my case, the latter is true, but certainly not the former.

Even before the advent of Google, the information was there, but it was dispersed in archives, oral tradition, mythological books and the like. The only difference is, now, one can cull out facts much faster and most of them from one source – the Internet. But this has its pitfalls in terms of authenticity, accuracy and chronological order. What has been my own contribution is that, from the many sources of available information – which include Google, nevertheless – I have only collected the raw material to build upon and create the edifice for my muse. Often, I have related that to contemporary events, as well as their relevance to historical chronology. My effort has been to make the narrative more readable and thought-provoking.

The persistence and threats with which Jema (my wife, Smita Singh) began Fridays of each week, lasted until I finally submitted the article which had to appear on the fourth page of *Sunday DB Post.* This book would not have been possible if I had reneged on that! Along with her, I also wish to thank the readers of my column who encouraged me to write on many other aspects of Bhopal's past. This gave me an added impetus to continue with my writing.

The very idea of this book was first discussed with Vikas Rakheja, my publisher, who not only encouraged me to go ahead with it, but also introduced me to his colleague, Manoj Kulkarni, who further articulated the concept of the book and, with great finesse, sculpted, edited and refined the articles for them to be able to come out in book-form. I tender my sincerest gratitude to Vikas and Manoj. Dada (Anshuman Bonnerjee, News Editor at *The DB Post*) mercilessly chopped off the (perceived) verbosity in my articles for the newspaper column, but left the articles more enriched and more lucid at the same time. An adherent to chaste Victorian English, he has embellished my writing style. I thank you Dada for bringing me back to 'the Queen's English'! My dear mother, even with her smattering of English, diligently read and commented on all my articles. Our daughter, Boond, and our two furry wonders, Tsar and Pepa, continued to be pleasant distractions.

I also wish to thank my household staff, Kamal, Manjhi, Nirmal and my cooks, Ramjivan Yadav and Biju Das, who kept me free from the encumbrances of the daily humdrum and gave me the time and space to ruminate on my chosen topics.

– Vertul Singh

RULERS OF THE BHOPAL REGION

Era of Early Rulers

- Raja Bhoj (1010–1055 A.D.)
- Jayasimha
- Yasovarman (1055–1180)
- Ajayavarman
- Laksraivarman
- Vindhyavarman

Era of Medieval Rulers

- Udayvarman (1180–1210)
- Dark Age (1300–1500 approx.)
- The Gonds and the Rajput Principalities (1500 to 1707)

Era of the Bhopal Nawabs

Dost Mohammad Khan 1672–1728	Founder and first Nawab	1709–28
Yar Mohammad Khan 1709–1742	Second Nawab	1728–43
Faiz Mohammad Khan 1731–1777	Third Nawab (under the *de jure* rule by Mamola Bai)	1744–77

Hayat Mohammad Khan 1735–1807	Fourth Nawab (under the *de jure* rule by Mamola Bai)	1777–1807
Ghous Mohammad Khan 1767–1827	Fifth Nawab and titular Ruler	1807
Wazir Mohammad Khan 1766–1816	Sixth Nawab	1807–16
Nazar Mohammad Khan 1791–1819	Seventh Nawab	1816–19
Qudsia Begum 1801–1881 age 80	Regent and eighth Nawab	1844–68
Jahangir Mohammad Khan 1816–1844	Ninth Nawab	1837–44
Sikandar Begum 1816–1868	Regent and tenth Nawab	1844–68
Shahjehan Begum 1838–1901	Eleventh Nawab	1868–1901
Sultan Jahan Begum 1858–1930	Twelfth Nawab	1901–26
Hamidullah Khan 1895–1960	Thirteenth Nawab	1926–60

SECTION ONE

The Myth of Gondwana

ONE

THE SEARCH FOR OUR HUNTER-GATHERER ANCESTORS

Yuval Noah Harari, in his *New York Times* top 10 bestseller book, *Sapiens – A Brief History of Humankind*, makes a keenly observed but scathing statement that agriculture is the most devastating discovery made by mankind. He proposes a rather provocative and rebellious theory that the earliest hunter-gatherer humans were far more superior and smarter than the later communities of pastoral and agriculturalist sapiens. He analyses, with challenging consilience, the lives and social patterns of the hunter-gatherers with the aid of their cave paintings and burial mounds along with other sociological, anthropological, and evolutionary evidence.

Reading Harari's engrossing book tempted me to find out about the interest of and the efforts made by erstwhile rulers of the princely state of Bhopal towards discovering and documenting the pre-history and history of the land they ruled. Particularly, the Begum Nawabs, who were far more enlightened and erudite rulers than most of their male counterparts elsewhere in the subcontinent during the British Raj.

I discovered that, sadly, for them, history began with the arrival of Dost Mohammad Khan, and ended with their staid

Bhimbaithika

accounts of the state of administration, the almost fawning, eulogistic descriptions of the British Viceroys of the time, and the King Emperor's visits to India. Prime examples of this are the voluminous *Taj-ul Ikbal Tarikh Bhopal (The Crown of Prosperity – the History of Bhopal)* by Shahjehan Begum; *Hayat-iI-Qudsi (The Life of Nawab Gauhar Begum)* by Sultan Jahan Begum, and her own autobiography *Gauhar-i-Iqbal (The Pearl of Prosperity)*, and *Akhtar Iqbal (The Star of Prosperity)*. None of these have any mention of the earliest settlers in this land, or earlier rulers other than those with whom they had some score to settle.

There seem to have been no serious efforts by the Nawab Begums to find out or promote research about the early history of Bhopal. Surprisingly, it was the British officers who, alongside their professional responsibilities, showed deep interest and inquisitiveness about early settlers in the region, and delved painstakingly in the pursuit of researching, collating and preserving various pre-historic and historic sites here. The documents which these amateur historians and archaeologists have left behind are still considered to be the most authentic reference sources for all future studies of this nature.

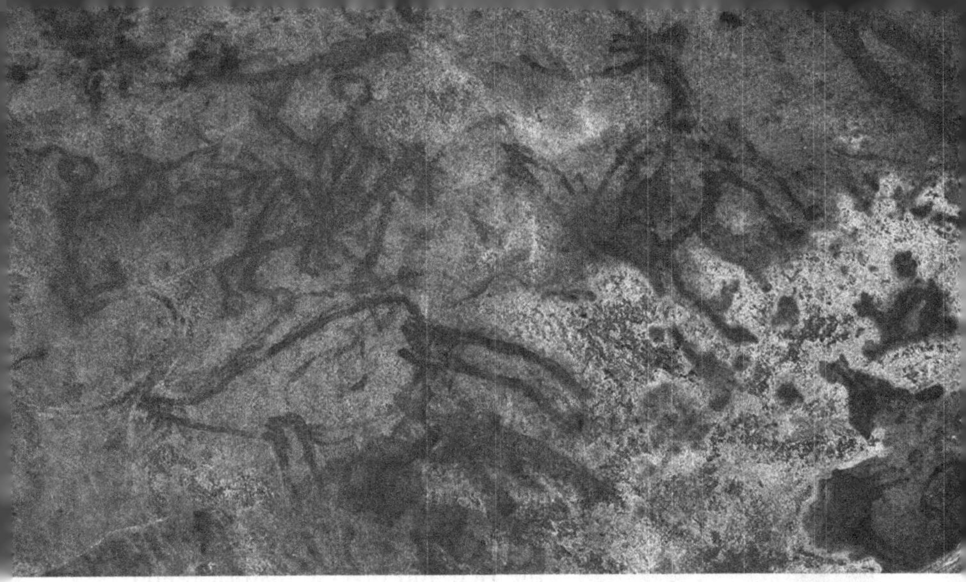

Bhimbaithika

Consider the pre-historic cave paintings at Bhimbaithika in Madhya Pradesh, which are in continuum with the existence of hunter-gatherers and grain-eaters who had not yet learned to plough the earth, but knew the value of grains. Bhimbaithika was first mentioned by Colonel W. Kincaid, the British political agent in Bhopal during Shahjehan Begum's reign. In a scholarly paper he wrote in 1888, Kincaid presented detailed references of the existence of archaeologically and historically precious caves in the Satpura mountain range, and of a much bigger lake in Bhojpur. But in spite of his thoroughness, he too, for the lack of precise scientific techniques like carbon dating at the time, had to rely largely on the oral tradition of mythological accounts of the local *adivasis* or vernacular literature, and as a result, wrongly classified Bhimbaithika as a Buddhist site!

Wilkinson Lancelot, another serious scholar and also a political agent during Sikandar Begum's rule, was, unbeknown to the chroniclers of the history of Bhopal at the time, a Sanskrit scholar as well. He authored a book in Sanskrit, titled *Siddhanta Siromani (The Ancient System of Hindu Astronomy).* He lived in the township of Sehore near Bhopal, where he ran a Sanskrit

Colonel William Kincaid

school which put special emphasis on the study of cosmological *siddhantas* (principles).

That said, it would not be fair to blame the Nawab Begums wholly for this lack of historical enterprise. It can be presumed that the knowledge they could have garnered from discovering the rich and diverse historical and cultural heritage of their land, would probably have augmented their own administrative acumen more profoundly.

TWO

THE MYTH OF GONDWANA AND THE EMERGENCE OF THE MALWA PLATEAU

We have all heard of the Gondwana Praja Party and the Gondwana Gantantra Party, who have been demanding a separate state called 'Gondwana'. The name Gondwana elicited in me a desire to find out its connection with the eponymous geological term. We have all come across this term during geography class in school, when we were being taught the contentious continental drift theory. For any astute explorer of the city of Bhopal, understanding the history behind the geography of the hills, rock formations, rivers and the beautifully undulating contours surrounding it – the word Gondwana evokes a strange yet intriguing familiarity.

Geologically, Gondwana or Gondwanaland was a supercontinent that existed between the Neoproterozoic Era (about 1000 to 554 million years ago) until the Carboniferous Period (about 359 to 299 million years ago). Why then has a political party named itself after a supercontinent that existed millions of years ago? Is this in some way connected to the predominantly aboriginal population of the Gond tribe, or with their kingdoms which were systematically destroyed or subsumed by the marauding Moghuls, Marathas and Rajputs? Is this a movement to correct the wrongs of history? Many such questions need answers.

The term Gondwana came into popular lexicon only after Afghan traders started using it in the region south of the Vindhyas, sometime around the 11th century CE. The word originally has a Telugu root – *konda* meaning hills and *vana* meaning forest, combined together to mean – 'people of the hills and forests.' Some linguists also attribute it to the originally Sanskrit word 'Gondvan' – 'land of the mountain people.' Actually, the region of Gondwana covers a vast area north of the Godavari and east of the Narmada valley that falls mainly in the three states of Madhya Pradesh, Maharashtra and Chhattisgarh. But if it refers to the land of the Gonds, then they are spread over seven states of present-day India.

The geological term Gondwana was a name given by H.B. Medlicott and W.T. Blanford, two British geologists who are credited with using the term 'Gondwana System' for the first time, in 1879. They conducted comprehensive research on the fossilised rock formations of the Satpura ranges and in the hills of western Orissa, where this term was used to refer to some rock shelters and ranges. They published their work, that ushered in the 'great Gondwana era,' on which research and studies are still being undertaken. It is just a coincidence that the Gonds specifically live in the areas which happen to have had the oldest rock formations. Later, the German geologist Eduard Suess suffixed the term Gondwana with 'land.'

In fact, after the great tectonic shift millions of years ago, the Gondwana land-mass splintered into what became the continents of Africa, South America, Australia, Antarctica, and the Arabian and the Indian peninsulas. It is the central, hilly Malwa plateau which houses the Satpura and Vindhya ranges that further branch-off into the Mahadeo and the Mahakal hills,

W.T. Blanford

H.B. Medlicott

and the hills of Bhopal that are formed out of the Palaeolithic rocks and glacial sedimentations.

Let us specifically focus on the Bhopal geographical region as it existed during early Medieval and Medieval period and its Gondwanaland genesis. Its boundaries flanked Malwa, with the *subah* of Berar in the south of the Satpura ranges. East Nimar, along with Khandesh, formed its western part in the Narmada Valley. It was flanked by the Rajput Umatwada region and Khichiwada with the river Pārbati forming a natural boundary.

The Bhopal region was fed with three major rivers: Betwa, Pārbati and Narmada. Its prominent water bodies like the Bhojpur Lake built by Raja Bhoj and destroyed by Hoshang Shah in the early fifteenth-century, were inundated with numerous catchment areas, as the Vindhyan ranges provided a natural watershed source. The countless rivulets emanating from the hills of the Satpuras also recharged them. The Betwa, (called Vetravati in the ancient times) originated at Kumri, with the Kaliasot as its most important tributary. Kaliasot remains the perennial source for the Bada Talab (Upper Lake) in Bhopal. River Pārbati spurts somewhere south of Ashta, with Ajmal and Papnes as its chief tributaries. The Narmada is the largest and the most important river which has its source in the south eastern region at Amarkantak. Denva and Tawa are the major tributaries of Narmada.

The Gonds, by virtue of their being the oldest inhabitants of 'Jambudweep', have unwittingly stamped a romantic inflection to Gondwanaland which continues to occupy the imagination of the lyricists, poets and the scientists, somewhat like the utopian lost city of Atlantis! It has been adopted by the Australian Cultural institutions, particularly those that are related to the studies on the aboriginals. Books like *The Greening of Gondwana* by Mary E. White, and *Gondwana to Greenhouse*, by V.A. Gostin etc. have unhinged a series of creative endeavours. There are even choirs and bands named after it, like 'The Gondwana Voices'. The most famous of them all is the popular novel by Craig Robertson: *Song of Gondwana*, which has many bands by its name, from Namibia to India.

THREE

THE LEGEND OF RAJA BHOJ

Once, when Mirza Ghalib was passing through the streets of Chandni Chowk in Delhi, he heard a Sufi *fakeer* singing a beautiful verse which had a metaphysical undertone to it:

> *'Patta patta boota boota haal hamara jane hai;*
> *jane na jane gul hi na jaane, baag toh saara jaane hai.'*
>
> (Every leaf and every bud in the garden knows the state of my being, as does the garden itself; But alas...it is only the flowers that feign to be unaware).

Upon hearing this, Ghalib was alarmed, because by then he was the most established and well-known Persian and Urdu poet in Delhi, and vainly believed that his were the only verses popular enough to be chosen by the likes of mystics and courtesans to sing. So, he asked the *fakeer* as to who exactly had written this particular verse. The *fakeer* revealed that it was Mir Taqui Mir's ghazal that he was singing. Taken aback and humbled, Ghalib is said to have composed one of his most famous verses, almost as a rejoinder to Mir's talent:

> *'Rekhte ke tumhīñ ustād nahīñ ho 'Ghālib',*
> *Kahte haiñ agle zamāne meiñ koī 'Mir' bhī thā.'*

> (It seems you are not the only virtuoso of the verse, 'Ghalib',
> they say someone called 'Mir' also lived in years bygone).

There appears to be a similar rethinking going on amongst thinkers, historians and academics who are rediscovering the lost empire of Raja Bhoj in the context of the city of Bhopal.

Empirically, there seems to be a stand-off between archaeologists and historians, who each base their arguments on available written texts and the mythologies surrounding Raja Bhoj. For example, D.C. Ganguly, author of *History of the Paramara Dynasty* (1933), which remains the most comprehensive and authentic account of the dynasty, writes:

> '...an inscription, dated 1199–1266 CE, of Udayavarman's reign, has been discovered in a field at the village Uljamun, in the Bhopal State. It records that, after bathing in the river Reva (Narmada), at a place called Guvadaghatta, he granted the village of Gunaura, to a Brahmin named Malusarman, the son of Yajnadhara.'

An English officer posted in the Bhopal State has identified Gunaura with the modern village of 'Ganora', seven miles south-west of Hoshangabad. The Bhopal grant thus seems to be at the time when Udayavarman, the great-great-grandson of Bhoj, was ruling over the Hoshangabad district which formed a part of the Bhopal State.

Bhoj was to succeed his uncle Munja as the ruler, but there is an interesting legend around this. The 14th century Jain historian Merutunga's *Prabandha-Chintamani*, a Sanskrit text which he authored in 1306 CE, mentions that a horoscope drawn at the birth of Bhoj, stated that he would rule for fifty-five years. This prediction made Munja conscious of the fact that his own son would never ever be able to succeed him.

So he ordered Bhoj's execution, once Bhoj had attained the age of ascension to the throne. Bhoj is said to have sent the following sarcastically existentialist verses to the king and to have requested the executioner to wait until the king replied:

> *'Mandhatr, that lord of earth, the ornament of*
> *the Treta age, passed away;*
> *Where is that enemy of the ten-headed Ravana,*
> *who made the bridge over the ocean?*
> *And many other sovereigns have there been,*
> *Yudhisthira and others, ending with thee, O king;*
> *Not with one of them did the earth pass away;*
> *I suppose it will pass away with thee.'*

When Munj read this, he is said to have been so overcome by his own pettiness that he handed over the throne of Malwa to Bhoj, along with the Garuda and Snake seals, the sovereign emblems of the Paramaras.

Here, Mertunga's story is contested by Ganguly, who says that Munja was succeeded by his younger brother, Sindhuraja, who was followed to the throne by his son, Bhoj.

Al-Biruni, the legendary Islamic scholar and traveller, with his observation corroborated by some other epigraphic evidence as well, mentions that:

> '...in 1030 CE, Bhilsa was the eastern limit of the Malwa kingdom, the following being the outline of the Paramar dominion, over which Bhoja ruled in the early part of his reign; it extended on the north as far as Banswara and Dungarpur, on the east to Bhilsa, on the south to the upper courses of the Godavari, Khandesh and Konkan, and on the west to the modern Kaira district. "...A moon to the lotus which was king Bhoja."'

The second-half of Raja Bhoj's rule was fraught with unabated wars with the neighbouring Chalukya rulers of Gujarat, and by 1044 CE, Malwa was overrun by Somesvara, a minor king of a rogue state, forcing Bhoj to abandon his dearest city of Dhara Nagari (modern-day town of Dhar). By the second-half of the 12th century, the Parmar dynasty and their seat of power, Dhara Nagri, were completely subjugated by the Chalukya kings of Gujarat. Bhoj, now growing old, had not somehow been able to groom anyone well enough to be capable of defending and running the behemoth he had inherited and expanded.

Eventually, two legendary generals of the day, Bhima and Karpa, formed an alliance against Bhoj and crushed his already weakened and dejected army once and for all. Bhoj could never recover from this shock, and died a disheartened man, still trying to put up that one last fight in the hope of saving his kingdom.

How does the soul of a city find utterance under such a plethora of conflicting claims and counter-claims? How can the narrative of a civilization manifest itself tangibly under such ambiguous influences?

One amongst many endeavours by nation-builders has been to build a superstructure of a great hero, whose actual existence is very often either created on the basis of folklore or mythology, either historically chronicled or simply just invented. Thus, the city of Rome has a mythical account of the brothers Romulus and Remus. After the New World – the Americas – was discovered, its nation-builders scoured through the names of cities of antiquity, and more than a hundred cities on the North American continent came to be named after Greek and Roman legends and heroes.

The evolution of a city is first defined by the group or community of initial settlers with a common thread connecting them to it with their rights and obligations.

The emergence of the *Polis* in Greece and the *Civitas* in Italy was a result of an extended cultural churning, which started sometime in the eighth century BCE. The self-awareness of the new citizens expressed itself through mythical stories about the origins of their cities. At times, aboriginal theories were propagated, and many a time, diaspora theories were put forth, as in the case of the popular theory on the migration of the Aryans to India.

Unless well-researched and properly documented, it is difficult to separate the grain from the chaff. This would mean distinguishing folklore from empirically established ancient historical events and occurrences. Whatever be the attempt at manipulation, the intrinsic desire was not just self-affirmation of the people, but more often than not, it was also the desire for self-glorification of the ruling elite.

The origin of the city of Bhopal was very much like the *Polis* in Greece and the *Civitas* in Italy. Bhopal, though, has been '...more of a "melting pot" than a "salad bowl"', to paraphrase Ashish Nandy. A popular theory on the city's origin is that of Raja Bhoj who built the 'Bada Talab' in order to collect water from 365 rivers to cure himself of a skin ailment. The lake was called Bhoj-taal, around which a settlement came up which was called Bhojpal. Therefore, it can be said that, unwittingly, the original founder of the city was Raja Bhoj.

This has been contested by those who claim that the original taal built by Raja Bhoj was near the present day Hoshangabad, and was drained of water by the ruler of Malwa, Hoshang Shah, in his greed for acquiring more arable land, after Bhoj's death. Bhoj ruled the Malwa region around 10th century CE. To quote Ganguly:

> '...He himself was a great poet, and spent his days in the company of erudite scholars. He was beloved by all the literary men of his age, and his unbounded liberality gave

> them fresh encouragement to pursue their work. Bhoj's activities in the field of architecture also deserve special notice. The *Udaipur Prasasti* credits him with the building of a large number of temples. Bhoj was well-known for his munificence and liberality.
>
> In his Modasa plate inscription, he lays down the following maxim, which seems to have been the motto of his life:
>
> *'Of wealth, this is as fleeting as a flash of lightning or a bubble of water; there are two good fruits or uses, and only two: one is its employment in charities and the other is the maintenance thereby of other men's fame'.*
>
> All this speaks for the broadness of his mind. As a conqueror, as a poet, and as a builder of architecture, he deserves a high place amongst noteworthy sovereigns of ancient India. As a benevolent monarch he had hardly any parallels. He left behind him an abiding impression that survives even to this day.'"

It is also a fact that around the same time, many local warlords named themselves on mythical figures. In all probability, the taal near Hoshangabad was indeed constructed by Raja Bhoj, but the story of the Bada Talab has more to do with the local Gond kings than with Raja Bhoj. This helps another theory gain some credence: that the name Bhopal can also be attributed to a Gond king, Raja Bhupal Shah. Many old-timers still recall that the name of the Bhopal Railway station used to be Bhupal. In Sanskrit, the word 'Bhupal' means a king or a prince, but more precisely, it means 'guardian of the land'. This, thus, negates the theory that Bhopal derives its name from Bhoj-taal or Bhojpal.

Similar attempts have been and are still being made to claim the classical antiquity of this city. The legend of Raja Bhoj has provided another dimension to the theories of the origin of the city, one of which is that it was founded much later by Dost

Mohammad Khan, the Pushtun mercenary. This has rekindled interest in the more distant past of the city.

Amidst all of this, true to its conscience, the soul of the city, with its rich narrative of heterogeneity and amalgamation of different religions, cultures and schools of thought, continues and will hopefully continue to resonate by its name – Bhopal.

FOUR

THE ASHAPURI TEMPLE COMPLEX - A COMPLEX CONUNDRUM

Gabriel Garcia Marquez has said, '*True histories seemed like phantoms, while false histories were so convincing that they replaced reality.*'

This stands true for some of our historians, who have unjustly given rather disproportionate space, and perhaps not so schrolarly analysis of historical bits and pieces passed on by invaders and rulers of the past. They have deliberately glossed over some of the authentic and glorious achievements, as well as the profound contribution of the magnificently indigenous cultures of ancient and early medieval India.

As not so career-conscious young students, way back in the late eighties, skipping classes was a style statement for us. During such breaks, we would invariably drive towards Bhojpur (on a moped, of course), passing the newly constructed campus of Bhopal University (now renamed Barkatullah University). Often, we would come across broken statues and large remains of unfinished sandstone sculptures strewn all along on the banks of the Betwa river, on a mule track heading towards Goharganj. Little did we realise then that we were treading on mounds of the remnants of an ancient and a spectacular era

Ruins of the Ashapuri Temple Complex

in our history, which had been lost due to a variety of factors, both natural and manmade.

Just 35 Kms from Bhopal, lie the ruins of the once stunning Ashapuri temple complex. Comprising of 26 complexes, this impressive temple complex was being built during the heyday of the Parmar-Pratihar rulers (900–1300 CE), whose kingdom stretched from the borders of modern-day Gujarat to as far as the modern-day Sehore. Many aspects of ancient temple architecture, which hitherto were mere speculations, have come to the forefront through the discovery of this magnificent temple complex.

'Ashapuri' as the Hindi word implies, must have been an ambitious project signifying hope and prosperity. The intricate lattice work and projections is in the quintessential Malwa style of temple-building known as the 'Bhumija' style. The splendour of this style can be seen in the Bhootnath (Shiva) temple within the complex and also in the nearby Bhojpur temple. Not far from the Bhootnath temple is the Billota temple, again dedicated to Lord Shiva. It has a massive Shivlinga outside the temple, which has an astonishing combination of numerous small shivlingas carved on it, known as the 'Sahastralingas'.

The complex also has the remnants of elaborate and beautifully carved sculptures and building parts exhibiting the various *avatars* of Vishnu. For example, there is a dismembered but exquisitely carved Vishnu Dasavatar pillar which has Varah, Narsimha, Vaman and Parasuram – all avatars of Vishnu, carved on its four sides. This ostensibly means that the rulers though Shaivites themselves, nevertheless, encouraged Vaishnavite motifs – a very tolerant aspect, considering the polarisation that existed between these two sects at that time.

Another unique aspect of this temple complex is that apart from the site of construction of the temple, it also ran a training school for the art of temple building. This was not unusual, given the strong *Guru-Shishya* tradition, through which all esoteric crafts were passed on from the exponent to dedicated and diligent disciples.

Remains of a pillar with the Vamana Avatar of Vishnu carved on it

What then exactly happened to this glorious temple and the unique concepts it embodied? Many attribute its destruction to the great earthquake that shook the region sometime in the late fifteenth-century. Others ascribe it to the typical victimisation theory, which accuses the medieval Islamic fetish of idol-destroying and desecration of Hindu places of worship.

Remains of the Bhootnath Temple in the Ashapuri Complex

The most plausible and logical reason could however be the constant involvement of its Parmara sponsors in debilitating wars and in defending the land from regular onslaughts of marauding hordes, ubiquitous during that cusp of history. This may have drained their resources, resulting in paucity of funds and moral patronage. One only needs to see the partially carved stones which still have masonry marks on them and the half-

Varah Avatar of Vishnu carved on a pillar of a temple in the Complex

built parapets supported by pillars with unfinished carvings to realise this.

Today, due to the assiduous efforts of the state government and the Archaeological Survey of India, we have a treasure trove of priceless heirloom, which could open up the chances of further unearthing of our fabulous riches and could possibly solve the conundrum surrounding this unique temple complex. As Cicero eruditely cautions us:

'Not to know what took place before you were born is to remain forever a child.'

FIVE

AFTER RAJA BHOJ AND BEFORE DOST MOHAMMAD

Not much is known about the important events that marked the Bhopal region in the period between the end of Raja Bhoj's reign and the beginning of the Nawab era. Raja Bhoj never ruled the actual settlement of Bhopal, but his empire did extend to the periphery of Bhopal, right upto Bhilsa (now Vidisha), and the present-day Bhojpur and Raisen.

Strategically though, since ancient times, the geographical centrality of Bhopal was always the keystone for empire builders, military planners, local warlords and mercenaries etc. One of the most travelled ancient and early medieval route from Shravasti to the Deccan, criss-crossed through the Bhopal region and important forts like Raisen, Chaukigarh and Ginnaurgarh remained impregnable bastions for a very long time. However, quite unlike its more prosperous, culturally and socially thriving neighbour – the Malwa region – the Bhopal region continued to stagnate and remained relegated to the background.

In historical analyses and debates, the Malwa perspective invariably gets superimposed on the narrative of the Bhopal region. There were no go-getter rulers or chieftains in this region who could have galvanised the people and lifted them

Ruins of the Raisen Fort

out of their general primitiveness and stupor. The Malwa region was fortunate to have had some daring Rajput rulers who had migrated from Rajasthan and had established principalities which gave new vigour and vivaciousness to the Malwa region after Raja Bhoj. Some of these survived right up to the merger of the princely states to the Union of India post-Independence. Notable amongst these were small kingdoms of the Deora Chauhans of Jagdishpur, the Khinchis of Raghogarh, the Solankis of Mangalgarh, the Rathores of Sitamau, Ratlam, Jhabua, Alirajpur and Sailana, the Pawars of Dewas, the Rawats of Piploda and Narsinghgarh, etc.

After the death of Raja Bhoj, his successor Jayasimha could not get a hold on the marauding bands of various petty warlords. However, some detailed accounts that have been discovered, mention that the predecessors of the main branch of the Parmar dynasty of Dhar continued to rule over parts of the Bhopal region like Hoshangabad and Raisen. Two branches of these Parmar chieftains with the title of 'Mahakumars' emerged. Their names were Yasovarman, Ajayavarman, Laksraivarman and Vindhyavarman. However, their rule was not very significant.

Ruins of the Ginnaurgarh Fort

The most notable amongst the Mahakumars to rule over a part of the Bhopal region was Udayvarman of the original Parmar dynasty of Dhar (circa 1180–1210 CE). He and his successors continued to rule this region for another eighty years. It is also recorded that Udayvarman's wife, Rani Shalmali, built a temple and a significant seat of research and learning, somewhere on the western bank of the Bada Talab in Bhopal. The services of over five hundred Brahmins were commissioned to run this colossal institution named 'Sabha Mandala'. If this is true, then Bhopal must have been a large town, comparable to the larger early medieval towns like Dhar, Shravasti, Kannauj, Kumbhoj, etc. By the end of the thirteenth century, the imminent decline of and the beginning of the dark ages for the central Indian kingdoms reduced this institution to a mere subsistence-level settlement, inhabited largely by aboriginals and a few pastoral and agriculturalist communities.

The Imperium In Imperio - Empires Within an Empire

Such scenarios have always attracted chaos and upheaval, where even small mercenaries and petty opportunists lay siege to once thriving and dominant empires. At one time, the Bhopal region must have been thickly populated, but as the British historian, Sir R. Jenkins points out:

> 'It would appear, from ancient records and travels of old towns, forts, villages and water-tanks to be met within the jungles, that the country was formerly much more populous than at present day.'

But, by the beginning of the 18th century CE, the region had long been forgotten and obliterated in memory and historical accounts, until just before the arrival of Dost Mohammad Khan. The central agency and in particular, the Bhopal region, witnessed the rise of Rajput kingdoms and parallel Gond principalities. The latter mimicked many aspects of the administrative procedures, royal ostentations and more significantly, the cultural subversion of their antecedents. There was much intermarriage between the Gond rulers and the Rajputs. Thus, there emerged an elite ruling and religious class from amongst the otherwise egalitarian Gond community. They were known as the Rajgonds and the Rajpurohits, respectively. The latter was an amalgamation of the brahminical and the animist orders as practiced by the Gonds.

For the Mughals, whose rule at the time extended to most of northern and central India, this region was the last priority and they generally preferred to let the Rajputs and Rajgond local rulers to run errands for them. Colonel Willis commenting on the state of Central Province stated that:

> 'Gondwana was too poor to be worth inclusion in the regular administered territories of the Empire.'

The powerful Gond principalities included the Garha, Deogarh, Chainpur Bari and Ginnaur. In the twilight years of the Mughal empire, their nobles still held large states and *sanads*, mostly in

A close-up view of the Raisen Fort

the northern region of Bhopal. For example, a Mughal noble, Taj Muhammad Khan, held the *jagir* of Berasia, from whom Dost Mohammad would later lease it out to himself. The Marathas invaded this area, first under Krishna Sawant in 1699, and later with a much bigger force under the command of Nima Scindia in 1703.

To the south of Bhopal, the fort and town of Hoshangabad was under the Sultan of Malwa – Hoshang Shah Ghori – who had to frequently bear the brunt of the Gond raja of Ginnaur and the Solanki Rajput kings of Mangalgarh and Parason. Interestingly, the Rajputs and Gonds were dedicated and tough fighters, whose main profession was soldiering. But as is evident and rued by most of the present-day observers, they continuously kept fighting amongst themselves, usually on petty issues, and some or rather most of them, even collaborated with the invading foreign armies of the Pathans and the remnant Mughal chieftains to harass their neighbours. For example, the Deora Chauhans of Jagdishpur lost their kingdom to Dost Mohammad Khan, and the Rajput chieftains of Parason rebelled against the chief of their own clan, the Solanki Queen of Mangalgarh. Again, it was the rivalry between the Rajgond families of Chainpur Bari and Ginnaurgarh, which Dost Mohammad took full advantage of.

SECTION TWO

Birth of the Royal House of Bhopal

ONE

THE ANTECEDENTS OF DOST MOHAMMAD KHAN – THE FOUNDER OF THE ROYAL HOUSE OF BHOPAL

After the smashing success of the movie 'Bahubali 2' in 2017, the word 'Pindari' has come back in our collective memory. The terror of the Pindaris has been brilliantly exploited by the filmmaker – albeit in a historically irrelevant and chronologically misplaced context.

The Pindaris are thought to be descendants of fighting and warmongering clans, and were mercenaries or irregular fighters, who allied themselves to various dynasties and principalities that ruled Northern and Central India. Infamous for their shrewd planning and manoeuvres, and their brutal and indiscriminate implementation of these, they were aberrations largely shunned by society. After the collapse of the Mughal Empire in the early eighteenth-century, they were left to fend for themselves by pillaging and plundering, and came into their own.

The Pindaris had a ferocious image and were cruel and ruthless marauders and rioters, who could be hired as mercenaries by anyone who was willing to pay them for

Dost Mohammad Khan (Courtsey Wikipedia)

their services. Comprising primarily of foot-soldiers and cavalrymen of mostly Afghan and Jat descent, they also had a small number of generals and onetime *sanad*-holders from noble families, who had been defeated and stripped of all honour. The Pindaris' trust, loyalty and cooperation was purely based on materialistic foundations, and they were very much capable of dishonouring their allegiance and turn traitors to their patrons without batting an eyelid, whenever political or military exigencies appeared to be tilting in their favour.

The Pindaris' success was derived from their opportunism in those chaotic and highly divisive times. They could be sublimated only by granting jagirs or fiefs as footholds. They never accepted any remunerations during war, but claimed a hefty portion of the plunder afterwards.

Their main patrons were the Maratha chieftains and Rajput kingdoms of Central India. Though the Pindaris were a band of assorted and mismatched comrades who did not have any overall authority on the land or its people, they had a common aim of looting and plundering. But they had a tacit and unwritten code of conduct, which entailed camaraderie during raids and when sharing the booty of war. No one particular person was the designated leader of the pack, but depending on the situation they were up against, anyone amongst them could be chosen to lead, depending on such skills as knowledge of local terrain and language, sense of direction, better fighting gear, etc. Their operating procedures were loosely the same as those of the 'Thugs' – a cult of thieves and murderers who were successfully eradicated by the British by the 1830s.

The Bhopal royal family chroniclers have evaded to use the word Pindari in the documented history of the city. Shaharyar Khan, a scion of Bhopal royalty, has used such phrases for his forebears as: '*...through courage, charisma and abundant treachery...*,' but has not addressed the question of descent. Down the ages, the appellation Pindari has become deprecatory and uncomplimentary. The generally acceptable euphemism is a mercenary offering his services as a warlord, a 'Mukhtar' (guardian), plunderer, etc., but never a Pindari.

Consider the circumstances and the resultant conduct of Dost Mohammad when he first arrived in Bhopal penniless and with a handful of his brigands, who, in the adverse atmosphere of deceit and treachery, did everything it took to survive and, eventually, thrive. He became a 'predatory forager' in the jungles in the area, heading an unscrupulous band of guerillas, who offered his services to a host of Rajput, Maratha and Muslim warlords and feudal barons for their protection or to fight their internal wars. He served the Raja of Sitamau, Mohammad Farooq – the Mughal governor of Bhilsa, the Rajput Diye Bahadur who was the Mughal deputy governor of Malwa, and subsequently, Raja Anand Singh Solanki of Mangalgarh. Needless to say, he served his term with utmost loyalty and devotion while he was in service with each one of them... but at a later juncture, did not shy away from fighting wars against almost all of them.

It was only after he leased a small piece of *mustajiri* (leased land) in Berasia in 1709 from a Muhgal fief-holder, that he actually started a settled life. Then again, the analysis of his

The Tomb of Dost Mohammad Khan

being a descendent of the Pindaris gains more credence because the royal houses of Jaora in Western Madhya Pradesh and Tonk in Rajasthan were both founded by the erstwhile Pathan Pindari marauders!

In final assessment, who exactly was Dost Mohammad Khan? Was he really an Empire builder? Or was he a just a megalomaniac or, worse still, a non-conformist opportunist? In all fairness, in the great churning that was going on in Central India after the death of Aurengzeb – when even established royalties sometimes had to become warlords and petty brigands in order to benefit from the general chaos and confusion, Dost Mohammad can be said to have been simply riding the wave. He was eventually formally recognized as a 'Sardar' with the title of 'Diler Jang' bestowed on him by the Mughal emperor Farukhsiar. This was for the support he gave to the Mughals in the battle of Khandwa against the combined onslaught of the Nizam and the Peshwas.

There were many instances when he ostensibly destroyed his one-time saviours, though when he was on good terms with them, he never reneged on his commitment to them and ensured this period of amiability was spotless from any misdemeanour against his benefactors. The historical reason on which the premise of the Bhopal royalty being descendants of the Pindaris stems from, is the observation that Dost Mohammad Khan, the founder of the Bhopal State fulfills almost all the attributes that the Pindaris possessed. Dost hailed from a Sardar family, his father being the chief of the Mirazi-Khel clan of the Orakzai tribe, and so, was of a noble descent, but he certainly did not have any royal lineage whatsoever.

There are many other references in history of the early Nawabs, taking either clandestine or even overt support of the Pindaris to strengthen their hold on the still nascent but steadily growing State of Bhopal. During the reign of the fourth Nawab, Hyatt Mohammad Khan, two Pindari leaders – Hiru and Barun – who were brothers, offered their services to save him from the advancing Marathas and also from the palace intrigues and machinations of his own nobles. However, the dithering Nawab was unable to decide. This dilemma almost cost him his kingdom, as Hiru and Barun were soon lured by the Bhonsles of Nagpur and readily went on to join them. A Pindari called Karim Khan is even said to have tried to lay claim on the Bhopal State by masquerading as a prince by flaunting looted treasures and cavalry in an extravagant display of wealth!

However, the most famous instance by far of a Pindari helping a Nawab was when the sixth Nawab, Wazir Mohammad Khan was aided by a Pindari leader, Namdar Khan and his band of three thousand men. This was during the terrible siege of Bhopal. Wazir Mohammad was able to deter and drive back the mighty combined forces of the Scindias of Gwalior and the Bhonsles of Nagpur. This ill-famous siege lasted for an agonising

Remains of the Fatehgarh Fort

nine months from October of 1812 to July of 1813. Namdar Khan later deserted the Nawab and continued his random forays for territorial expansion and plunder, until he was tamed by the British and made to settle down with his people in Pindarwad (the settlement of Pindaris), roughly located in an area near the present Bhopal railway station and the Central Library, which is sometimes still addressed by the same name.

TWO

RANI KAMLAPATI – THE FORGOTTEN GOND QUEEN

> *'Age cannot wither her, nor custom stale Her infinite variety',* wrote Shakespeare of Cleopatra. Alas, we did not have someone like the Bard who could immortalise our own Cleopatra – Rani Kamlapati, the forgotten Gond queen, who may have been instrumental in founding this city. There are, however, some fleeting descriptions of her in the Gonds' oral tradition in which she has been described to be more beautiful than a fairy, more graceful than a doe, and more delicate than a rose. Legend has it that Kamlapati, who lived in a lakeside palace, would swim in the lake held afloat on a lotus flower with 500 of her hand-maidens following her in boats. The Rani is said to have drowned herself in the lake along with all her worldly possessions after her husband, Nizam Shah – a powerful and influential Gond warlord, was treacherously poisoned to death.

Shaharyar Khan, in his erudite book *The Begums of Bhopal: A Dynasty of Women Rulers in Raj India*, mentions Kamlapati to be:

> 'A woman of luminous beauty and unmatched talents.

> She was not only lovely in appearance but was educated, refined and superbly talented in the arts.'

The palace of Rani Kamlapati was said to be seven-storied and was situated between two lakes – the Upper and the Lower lakes (around the present day Kamla Park).

Like Cleopatra, apart from her beauty, Kamlapati was also known for her astute, keen and farsighted political and military acumen, and she is said to have often given advice on administrative matters to her husband. This is said to have inspired and emboldened Nizam Shah to seize the almost impregnable fort of Ginnaurgarh.

A limerick, popular to this day, goes as noted below:

> *'Rani theen toh Kamlapati, aur sab hain gadhayyen;*
> *Garh hai toh Ginnaurgarh, aur sab hain garhaiyyen.'*

After her husband Nizam Shah was poisoned to death by his nephew, a distraught Kamlapati is said to have sought protection and help from Dost Mohammad Khan to save her kingdom from rivals. Theories abound regarding this decision of hers. But much unlike the romantic involvement of Cleopatra and Marc Antony, legend has it that Rani Kamlapati tied a *Rakhi* on Dost Mohammad's wrist and acknowledged him as her brother.

She also presented him with the village in which he would later lay the foundation for Bhopal. Through this intrinsically Indian, albeit rather soap operatic act, she had the wily Afghan mercenary bound by this Hindu custom. Dost Mohammad, to his credit, loyally followed the tradition for over a decade.

But after Kamlapati's death, Dost Mohammad seized the fort of Ginnaurgarh from her son Nawal Shah. History, though, has not been fair to Rani Kamlapati, or for that matter, to the erstwhile Gond kingdoms as a whole. To cite a modern-day example, many people still wrongly presume Kamla Park in

Bhopal to be named after Kamla Nehru, the wife of Jawaharlal Nehru!

The Gond kingdoms which straddled much of Central India eventually faded into oblivion, and the existence of a queen who may have been one of the founders of the city of Bhopal, turned into a legend and a fairy tale with incredulous and often historically incorrect conjecture. No statue, or painting, or any other kind of representation of Kamlapati has ever been found, and her abode is now just an archaeological site with only some ramparts and parts of the facade remaining.

THREE

DHĀI SEEDHI KI MASJID

'*The mosques are our barracks, the domes our helmets, the minarets our bayonets and the faithful our soldiers...*,' when Recep Tayyip Erdoğan, the serving President of Turkey, said this in a speech in 2014, it was as if he was articulating what could have been the thought process of Dost Mohammad Khan, the founder of the Bhopal State. A similarity can certainly be drawn, because when Dost Mohammad Khan started constructing the Fatehgarh fort around the city in 1716, he also laid the foundation for what would become the first mosque to come up in Bhopal – a very small alcove in the parapet of the fort – with just enough space for only a few soldiers to pray in at a time.

Strategically, the mosque also functioned as a watch-tower and must be the only mosque with hollows in the turrets and embankments for guns, bearing testimony to the eerie similarity between the words of Erdoğan and the thought-process of Dost Mohammad Khan, about three hundred years earlier. The overlap of spirituality and strategy is also a grim reminder of the use of religion as a political tool during constantly ongoing strife and the struggle to hold on to what had been conquered. But at that time, religion was certainly not a factor to be considered for soldiers to be loyal. Dost Mohammad laid the foundation of this mosque with his own hands as an act of benediction.

Only a few decrepit portions of the ramparts of the Fatehgarh fort survive today, but the Dhāi Seedhi Ki Masjid symbolising the tough exterior for the city of Bhopal, echoes the history of battles fought – whether lost or won – and still offers solace to the faithful.

The Dhai Seedhi Ki Masjid, as it stands today

The mosque was named 'Dhāi Seedhi', because originally, there were all of two-and-a-half steps to access it! Today, the steps are more in number and more comfortable to climb, and lead to a prayer hall of about sixteen square metres in size, which according to Daniel McCrohan of *Lonely Planet,* makes it the smallest mosque in the World. It is located in the periphery of Gandhi Medical College near Hamidia Hospital and is a well-known tourist attraction today.

Dhāi Seedhi Ki Masjid is also a testimony to the perpetual battle to control the mind and the struggle to survive. A soldier is not just a symbol of the power of the state; he also becomes

Present day interior of the Dhai Seedhi Ki Masjid

A scruffy signboard outside the Dhai Seedi Ki Masjid

a part of the greater war against the devil within us that is corroding our souls.

FOUR

DOST MOHAMMAD AND HIS TROJAN HORSE TRICKERY

The classical story of the Trojan Horse from ancient Greek literature bears an uncanny parallel in Dost Mohammad Khan's life and times in medieval Bhopal. The Greek story describes how Greek soldiers were finally able to conquer the city of Troy after a futile ten-year long siege. They achieved this by entering Troy by hiding in a giant wooden horse, supposedly left at the gates of the city as an offering to the goddess Athena. The idea of using a wooden horse came from the Greek general – Odysseus, and the effectiveness of it altered the course of warfare and brought into play another strategic dimension to the history of warfare – *Deception.*

Many anecdotes underlining the unambiguous courage and also, quite paradoxically, the appalling treachery and ruthlessness of Dost Mohammad have come to the fore. There are four daring instances of pure military brilliance and cold-blooded ambition of his that incite both admiration and disgust for him at the same time. In all of these instances, a tweaked version of the Trojan Horse epic was re-enacted during the consolidation of a nascent Bhopal State, after almost two thousand years of the fall of Troy. Only, now, the part of General Odysseus was played by Sardar Dost Mohammad Khan.

The first instance was when the Mughal governor of Bhilsa, Mohammad Farooq imprisoned many of Dost's men against his word of honour. A battle ensued between the 40,000-strong troops of Farooq, who was aided by the Marathas, and Dost Mohammad's loyal Pathan and Rajput soldiers numbering a paltry 5000. Dost, quite obviously, did not stand a chance. His army was trounced and fled the scene. But Dost Mohammad did not give up. He, along with a handful of his most loyal soldiers who had stayed with him, hid in the nearby jungles from where they could observe the army of Farooq celebrating their victory. When the merrymaking army neared his hideout, Dost made a most audacious move – he ingeniously dressed himself and his men in the uniforms of dead soldiers from the winning side, disguising their faces with helmets and scarves.

Then, under the cover of darkness and amidst the din of drums and intoxicated cheering, he stealthily approached the elephant on which Farooq was seated. He managed to sneak up to the *howdah* on the elephant and after killing the lone guard, thrust a dagger into Farooq's gut, killing him instantly. He then kept Farooq propped up with his strong arms, so that the dead man would appear to be sitting normally to any onlookers on the ground, until the elephant reached the gates of the Bhilsa fort. A large crowd had gathered at the gates to welcome their hero, Farooq, but then suddenly and ingloriously, Dost Mohammad hurled Farooq's corpse out from the *howdah* into the crowd, and declared himself the victor. His loyal men surrounded him and anointed him as their leader in front of the masses. Dost Mohammad, thus, literally snatched victory from the jaws of defeat with phenomenal intrepidity!

The second instance was when Dost Mohammad resorted to a combination of Trojan Horse-like tactics and plain coercion, was in his pursuit of expanding the territories of the Bhopal State, sometime around 1723, after the death of Rani

Kamplapati. Along with traits like treachery and craftiness, Dost Mohammad did possess certain attributes which are the hallmark of a seasoned statesman. For instance, he never went back on his word, always upheld the soldier's ethical code of conduct, and ensured implicit loyalty of his men.

The story of the *rakhi* diplomacy which Rani Kamlapati displayed after her husband's murder by poison, when she tied a *rakhi* on Dost's wrist and recognized him as her brother and how Dost, in turn, ensured that her honour was not compromised, and she and her kingdom remained protected while she was alive, is well-known.

But nothing stopped the shrewd Pathan from expanding the territory under his control whenever he smelt an opportunity brewing. Ginnorgarh, near the present Obaidullah Ganj, was Rani Kamlapati's most important and tactically situated fort. The keen militarist that he was, Dost Mohammad was aware that whoever controlled the Ginnorgarh fort would have control of the entire tract of South-Central India.

After Kamlapati's death, her son Nawal Shah inherited her property. But, free from the shackles of his allegiance to Kamlapati now, Dost let it be known that he had given his word only to the Rani, and was now free to pursue what he wanted. He sent veiled threats to Nawal Shah, emphasizing the rules of the game – lest he be accused of reneging on his word.

Raw and inexperienced, Nawal Shah failed to read the writing on the wall. Dost continued to put up a façade of allegiance but was already planning his next move. Ginnorgarh was absolutely impregnable, with the only entrance to it heavily guarded and armored. Dost dressed up about a hundred of his soldiers as women and arranged for 'palkis' (palanquins) to be carried by the rest of his men posing as 'kahars' (palanquin bearers). In those days, 'palkis' were routinely used to carry women, children and the sick in and out of forts and walled-cities. The guards at the gate therefore allowed the spurious palanquins in without smelling a rat. Nawal Shah and his soldiers were caught completely unawares, and in an easy manoeuvre thereafter, Nawal Shah was killed and Dost Mohammad took over the strategic fort of Ginnorgarh. Apart from the fact that the strategy was truly innovative and undoubtedly brilliant, what is baffling is how Dost Mohammad would have convinced the virile and masculine Pathan and Rajput soldiers to don women's attire – could it have been his out-of-the-box creative thinking and glibness that had saved the day for him?

Almost a century later, in another experiment with the Trojan Horse-like trick during the great Siege of Bhopal in 1812–13, Dost Mohammad's great-great-grandson, Nawab Wazir Mohammad would do just the opposite – dress up the women-folk of the city in soldier's fatigues, to augment the number of his gravely depleted manpower, in order to fool the Marathas!

Dost Mohammad left no stone unturned to usurp lands to establish his empire on his own terms and conditions. For this, he did not shy away from changing goalposts willfully and frequently. In an era of chaos and confusion, Rajputs and to some extent, even the Mughals, strictly followed a code of conduct during battle, which was respected and adhered to by both the warring factions. It was Dost Mohammad, who, like the Marathas, used the mercenary services of the Pindaris, to change the rules of the game and ensure that his enemies were completely decimated.

The third Trojan Horse-like manoeuvre that Dost Mohammad ruthlessly carried out was when he was in the service of the Rani of Mangalgarh. The Rani's son, Raja Anand Singh Solanki had died of a battle wound, and petty Rajput chieftains, who used to pay obeisance to the Raja earlier, upon sensing that the kingdom was vulnerable without a strong leader, had decided to harass the dowager Rani by jointly rebelling against her. Dost Mohammad decided to take them on in a fierce battle that raged on well beyond its expected duration. Dost Mohammad, though new to the customs and traditions of the Hindus, agreed to pause the ongoing battle at Parason (located north of Bhopal), to let the Rajput chieftains celebrate the festival of Holi.

The cunning Pathan knew that the predominantly Hindu soldiers of the Rajput chieftains would be celebrating the festival in a state of complete inebriation, and would have no control over their minds, let alone weapons and fortifications. He first sneaked in a spy dressed as a beggar into the enemy camp to gauge the degree of their drunken torpor. He then dressed his frontline posse of soldiers as beggars and instructed some of them to act drunk, melt into the crowd, and then surreptitiously separate the leaders from the soldiers. This accomplished, Dost Mohammad struck in full-force with his regular army, and destroyed the Rajput forces completely.

Narsingh Rao Chauhan, the Rajput Chief of Jagdishpur, was jubilant that Dost Mohammad had finished off most of his adversaries. He wanted to have peaceful coexistence with the new power center in the making, and maybe even to share the booty. He agreed to meet Dost Mohammad along with sixteen of his advisors on the outskirts of his territory on the banks of the river Thal. This was to be the fourth major Trojan Horse-like deception which Dost would flawlessly execute. Unknown to the excited and gushing Narsingh Rao, Dost Mohammad, under the pretext of arranging a scrumptious lunch feast for his guest, had a devious and macabre plan to put into effect.

He had already instructed his soldiers, who were hiding in the jungles surrounding the encampment, to attack the tent once he himself had stepped out to fetch the customary offering of paan and itar for the guest at the end of the luncheon. During the meeting, to the utter astonishment of Narsingh, Dost agreed to all his offers and even gave him a bear hug. After the lunch, as planned, he stepped out of the tent and signalled his soldiers, who pounced upon the gullible and defenseless Rajputs and slaughtered them in sheer cold blood. The gruesome sight of this massacre is said to have shaken even the most hardened Afghans in Dost Mohammad's army.

It could have been, presumably, one of these witnesses to this sanguinary blood-bath, who must have renamed the Thal as the Halali river. Today, very few would know that the now popular picnic spot near Bhopal, the Halali dam and the area around it, has such a grisly past.

Dost Mohammad also lay claim to the fort and all the territory of Narsingh Chauhan, and renamed Jagdishpur as Islam Nagar, which remained the capital of the Nawabs of Bhopal for the next eighty years.

FIVE

THE RAJPUT CONNECTION

What happens when two races, whose valour, sense of honour and commitment are the stuff of ballads and paeans, join hands? The Pathans and the Rajputs both possess very similar military and leadership traits, and have produced legendary empire builders galore. Both communities trace their ancestry to ancient Greek, Hun, Scythian, Kushan and Bactrian lineage. Both are brave, honest, truthful and fiercely loyal to anyone who they have given their word to.

So striking are the similarities that Khaled Ahmed, a reputed Pakistani journalist, has quoted an Indian-born British doctor Henry Walter Bellew, who, in 1864, said that most Pakhtun tribal names were actually Rajput names which had undergone changes over time. This actually gave rise to a theory that Hindus had occupied the region called Afghanistan before 'foreigners' took it over.

This theory may certainly be debatable, but the very foundation of the Bhopal State hinged on the close association between the Pakhtun founders of Bhopal and the Rajputs. Dost Mohammad Khan's forays as a mercenary seeking to capture new territories in Central India were channelised when the Raja of Sitamau, a Rathor state, gave him a stable job. Khan worked as a tehsildar under the Raja, and was later able to put this experience to good use as a revenue officer-cum-troop-commander under Anand Singh Solanki, the Rajput chieftain of Mangalgarh. His fierce loyalty and wise statesmanship were recognised when, after the death of Raja Anand Singh, his mother appointed Khan as the mukhtār of Mangalgarh in 1708.

Dost Mohammad later went on to marry a Rajput princess from this family, who was renamed Fateh Bibi. Khan's first fiefdom of Berasia was financed by Fateh, and she was also the one who paid ransom to secure Khan's release when he was held captive by his own troops while on a raid in Gujarat. Jai Kunwar was the third wife of Dost. As is evident, she was presented to him by the Rajput zamindar of Kliakheri as conquered booty from the spoils of petty wars that abounded in the region. Mamola Bai, the wife of Yar Mohammad Khan, the son of Dost Mohammad, also came from a branch of royal Rajput stock.

To quote Shaharyar Khan:

> 'The Rajputs treated war as a sport, like cricket, to be played according to established traditions of the game.'

This compliment to the Rajputs was to prove true in an interesting turn of events. Once, Dost Mohammad was defeated by a Rajput chieftain by the name of Diye Bahadur, and severely battle-scarred and unarmed, was taken captive. But, although a prisoner, Dost was treated very well by the Rajputs and was given all medical aid necessary, as per the prevalent Rajput code of conduct.

In fact, his captor Diye Bahadur was so impressed with Dost's bravery that he offered him a high-ranking position in his own army. But Dost, as was his wont, audaciously declined the magnanimous offer. At this, Diye Bahadur asked him what he would do if he were to be set free? Dost contemptuously shot back that he would fight Diye Bahadur again.

Anyone would expect certain death for such a display of

A representation of Rajput warriors of the time

ingratitude and arrogance. But here again, Diye Bahadur's sterling character shone bright in a touching display of battlefield sportsmanship, and he set Dost free! History, alas, has it that Dost Mohammad again fought a battle against Diye Bahadur and defeated him.... Dost Mohammad's flagrant hubris and the subsequent large-hearted reaction by Diye Bahadur only validates the dauntlessness of spirit – whether generous or inglorious – of these born fighters.

It is also a historical fact that Dost Mohammad did take up arms again this eventual benefactors – the Mughals – when the Mughal army was sent to quell the Rajput rebellion. He sided with and fought alongside his trusted long-time companions, the Rajputs.

Years later, during the great siege of Bhopal of 1812–13, it was Wazir Mohammad Khan's comrades, the faithful Rajput zamindars, Ratan Singh and Aman Singh, who ferried grain and other essential supplies through dense jungles and unloaded these near the Fatehgarh fort. The nearly starving population of Bhopal was thus able to successfully resist the combined might of the Scindias and the Bhosles.

Wazir Mohammad Khan's second wife was a Rajput princess whose two sons, Amir Mohammed Khan and Nazar Mohammad Khan, subsequently became claimants to the title of Nawāb, but in a complex power struggle, Nazar Mohammad became the Seventh Nawāb of Bhopal.

Thus, it can be surmised that the royal bloodline of the Bhopal Nawābs also had royal Rajput blood in it... a living proof of the 'Ganga-Jamuni *tehzeeb*' that the city of Bhopal boasts of to this day.

But for this collaborative and symbiotic relationship that existed between the Rajputs and the Pathans during those times, the history of the Bhopal State would have been very different.

SECTION THREE

Magnificent Matriarchy in a Century of Anarchy

ONE

THE LEGENDARY QUEENS AND BEGUMS OF BHOPAL

> 'Colonial Bhopal was one of hundreds of princely states, together covering a third of British India, whose rulers were promised support and internal autonomy in return for their loyalty. The British, out of strategic considerations, not only preserved the Bhopal dynasty, but, subsequently, opted to support four women rulers for more than a century, beginning in 1819. Such matriarchal succession was a complete anomaly among the princes and wholly unprecedented among the Afghan Pathans, or Pashtuns, the rulers 'ethnic group of origin.'
>
> Barbara Metcalf writes in her scholarly book, *Islam and Power in Colonial India: The Making and Unmaking of a Muslim Princess.*

The Epitome of Motherhood

The inborn maternal instincts of a woman can be summed up as the ability to nurture and protect, farsightedness and wisdom, calmness and patience under trying conditions, the ability to be an undemanding provider, the insight to compromise rather

Qudsia Begum

than risk life and property. These and many more such traits of a woman's personality proved to be the building blocks for the future nineteen-gun salute deserving state of Bhopal, which was indeed a jewel in the British Crown, complete with an outstanding Coat of Arms emblazoned with the motto *Nasr Minullah.* The founding of the Bhopal state has been attributed to two erstwhile queens. Its consolidation thereafter, has been largely attributed to the astute statesmanship and wisdom of the first two Begums. Its eventual cultural, social and economic enrichment and development as a civilization and as a well-knit, functioning administrative unit is credited to the last two Begums, who completed the tasks undertaken by their predecessors towards establishing Bhopal as a matriarchal and matrilineal empire.

In British history, when Lord William Burghley once condescendingly commented on the womanhood of Queen Elizabeth-I, that: 'Forgive me, Madam, but you are only a woman...,' the queen had firmly interjected, saying, 'I may be a woman, Sir William, but if I choose, I have the heart of a man!' Just like Elizabeth-I faced serious opposition and aspersions on her ability to govern because of her being a woman, the Begums of Bhopal must also have, undoubtedly, faced similar hurdles. But ironically, the very traits that are perceived as weaknesses and flaws in a woman's personality, nourished the marrow which made Bhopal state a cohesive, unimpaired and unbroken dynasty for over two centuries.

When the Gond queen of Ginnorgarh tied a *rakhi* on Dost Mohammad Khan's wrist in the 1720s, she had already foreseen his inherent qualities as a potential empire builder. Once she had secured her own kingdom with his help, she gifted Dost Mohammad the village Bhopal, as a symbol of her gratitude. This was an opportunity for him to kick-start his ambition of becoming a ruler. But Dost, for some reason, continued with Islam Nagar as his capital. It was his wife, the Rajput princess of Mangalgarh, Fatah Bibi, who pointed out to him the strategic and sustainable centrality of Bhopal, the two most important factors that would make it an ideal capital for his newly acquired territories. It was on Fatah Bibi's tactical advice that Dost Mohammad laid the foundation for the fortification of the city of Bhopal. The fort was aptly named as Fatehgarh fort after her. Its ramparts can still be seen near the present Gandhi Medical College and VIP Road.

After Dost Mohammad's death, Bhopal attracted many rapacious marauders, vying to conquer it. Again it was the saintly Mamola Bai, who had the wisdom and foresight to extend warm hospitality to the debilitated army of General Goddard, realizing that the British could potentially play a crucial part in the history of the region.

Simultaneously, Mamola also cajoled and negotiated with the powerful Marathas and the Nizam of Hyderabad to prevent them from usurping her kingdom. After her, during the great siege of Bhopal in 1812–13, Qudsia Begum's perseverance saved the still embryonic Bhopal state from being gobbled up by the Scindias and the Bhonsles. Like her mother Qudsia, the second Begum, Sikander Jahan also shrewdly and presciently used raw nuances of statecraft to secure for herself and for Bhopal an everlasting support and gratitude of the British Crown. During the historic First War of independence in 1857, Sikander Begum sheltered a number of British families and missionaries in the Raisen fort. A period of peace and calm – which is always the rudiment for the arts and culture to flourish – followed. It was under the third Begum, Shah Jahan, that Bhopal became a throbbing center of poetry, music and the fine arts.

But an overwhelmingly maternal approach towards her subjects was that of the fourth Begum, Sultan Jahan. In her twenty-five-year reign, Sultan Jahan conceived and implemented many groundbreaking administrative reforms, which today are considered a mandatory part of any welfare state, but which were unheard of even in a constitutional monarchy like Great Britain at that time. It is no wonder then, that Sultan Jahan was so deeply respected and loved by her subjects that they referred to her as *'Sarkar Amma'*!

Bhopal owes an everlasting debt to the magnificent and unparalleled contribution of these outstanding women rulers who foresaw the future and acted with farsighted wisdom. In their pursuit of their beliefs and convictions, they often sacrificed their own womanly desires and yearnings for the greater cause and good of their subjects.

During their sterling reign, the Begums of Bhopal undertook many general reforms. However, the most conspicuous and tough to implement reforms were the ones related to women's welfare.

The Harbingers of Modern Health Care for Women

In Tolstoy's classic *War and Peace*, Princess Lise Bolkonsky demands that her baby be delivered only by a male midwife. It seems that was the latest fashion amongst aristocratic gentry in Europe of the mid-nineteenth century. Prince Andrei, Lise's husband, on the other hand, searched for meaning in life and despised his wife for her upper-class lifestyle and the

Nawab Sikandar Begum

hypocrisies associated with it. Lise, who valued fashion trends of the time more than customs and traditions of feudal Russia, sadly, died during childbirth in pursuit of those shallow values.

This example from representative literature of that time amply proves that women's health, even in the upper crust of the society in feudal Europe of medieval times, or even as recently as the nineteenth century, received little or no attention.

What, then, was happening differently in the Bhopal principality of those times, vis-a-vis women's health? With strict segregation of the sexes in those days, a demand for a male midwife would be nothing short of blasphemy. The enlightened and pragmatic Shah Jahan Begum realized the dire necessity of women related health reforms, and initiated the construction of a hospital specifically catering to women who observed the *purdah*. But she could not find qualified woman nurses to staff her ambitious project. It was Lady Lansdowne, wife of the then Viceroy of India, who not only helped Shah Jahan Begum fund the project, but also ensured that it was staffed with qualified female doctors and nurses.

The Lady Lansdowne Hospital for women was inaugurated in Bhopal on 24 May, 1892. Shah Jahan Begum chose this particular day as it happened to be Queen Victoria's birthday! This unique hospital, fully run and staffed by women, for women, was certainly no mean achievement for those ultra conservative times.

The continuity and modernisation of this project got further fillip when Sultan Jahan Begum took over in 1901, after Shah Jahan Begum's death. She soon realized that it was costing the state exchequer a small fortune to employ European nurses. In her autobiography, *An Account of My Life*, she has recounted:

> 'Owing to the backward state of female education and the absence of training institutions, Indian women seldom possess even a rudimentary knowledge of the duties of a nurse.'

Quick to act on her concerns, Sultan Jahan started the Lady Minto Nursing School in 1909, and later in 1912, the Lady Hardinge Infant Home – a prototype of the modern-day children's crèche.

With great foresight, Sultan Jahan attached the nursing school and the infant care home to the Lady Lansdowne Hospital. Sultan Jahan also made sure that her concerns for and thoughts on women's health issues found a forum and reached a much wider audience outside her areas of influence. She was the founding president of the All India Ladies Conference in 1914, where she is known to have animatedly debated on, among other things, raising the age of marriage for girls to ensure proper growth before they faced childbirth and motherhood.

Now known as the 'Sultania Zanana Hospital', the historic Lady Lansdowne Hospital has stood the test of time, and still continues to serve the interest of the women folk of Bhopal, particularly those from the deprived sections of the society.

Women's Education and Emancipation

The contribution of the Begums towards the education and emancipation of the women of Bhopal is invaluable, in particular, that of Sikandar Begum and her granddaughter, Sultan Jahan.

Inauguration of Lady Lansdowne Hospital for women now known as the Sultania Zanana Hospital

They fought the deep-rooted misogynistic feudal order, almost a century-and-a-half ago, to lay a strong foundation for the superstructure of education in Bhopal. Despite them being the sovereign rulers, both had to overcome many undercurrents of resistance which came in the way of their endeavour, particularly in the area of education for girls.

'*Iqra*', which is Arabic for 'read', is the first word revealed by Allah upon the Prophet in the holy *Quran*. Both Begums were very religious and drew inspiration from the Holy Book. But, for the womenfolk of their state, they sought to combine Muslim piousness with reformist zeal, and were able to successfully implement far-reaching educational reforms.

Sikandar Begum established many schools and encouraged erudite men from Jeddah, Yemen and Turkey to settle in Bhopal. She was apparently more inclined towards promoting Islamic studies, with only a peripheral influence of liberal ideas from the West.

Sensitive and respectful to the religious and social boundaries of her subjects, Sultan Jahan also established a

Sultan Jahan Begum

school exclusively for Hindu girls – the 'Birjisia Girls School', in 1907. A skill-based school was started for widows and other impoverished women, to teach them economically viable skills like embroidery, weaving and needlework, from which they could earn livelihood.

A more ambitious and highbrow elite school, only for girls from ruling families, was also initiated by Sultan Jahan. She named it 'Sikandaria Girls School', after her grandmother. Headed by an Englishwoman, Margaret Wheeler, it was a boarding school located within the residence of the Begum – 'Qasr-e-Sultani', now known to us as the Ahmedabad Palace. Her three granddaughters went to this school along with children of other Bhopal nobility. Earlier, too, Sultan Jahan had allowed her daughter-in-law, Maimoona Sultan, to be groomed by European governesses and teachers – something unheard of in those days.

Sultan Jahan's contribution to women's education, particularly with regard to the traditional Muslim society, is in no way lesser than that of Sir Syed Ahmad Khan's, who established the Mohammadan Anglo-Oriental College, in Aligarh in 1875, to encourage modern western education amongst the Muslim society. Begum Sultan Jahan holds the distinguished honour of being the first and the only woman Chancellor of the Mohammadan Anglo-Oriental College, which was to become the famous Aligarh Muslim University in 1920.

She was also Chairperson, Women's Educational Reform.

So, it is largely because of Sultan Jahan Begum's farsighted and concerted efforts in the field of education that today, Bhopal boasts of a cultured, thriving and essentially stable middle class, which in pre-independence India was restricted only to the big cities directly administered by the British, like Bombay, Calcutta and Madras.

Lady Lansdowne

Why Matriarchy Thrived and Survived in Bhopal for Over a Century.

No sociological, political or economic empirical research or analysis will perhaps be able to provide the reasons for the fascinating and trailblazing phenomenon of successful matriarchic succession in the princely state of Bhopal, over a period of more than a hundred years. This is particularly significant in the present times, when there is an emphatic global demand for women's equality and gender neutrality.

The era of the Begums of Bhopal continues to attract admiration and curiosity from both, the serious scholar of history, as well as the common layman interested in learning about the past. The Begums' gravitas, administrative and political acumen, their perseverance, their upright Victorian sense of morality under their overarching Quranic sagacity, and at times their cunning and manipulative capabilities, especially during adversity, can be listed as some of the attributes that must have played a major part in their becoming successful and popular rulers.

One of the most commendable and intriguing aspect of the Begums' rule was their triumph in subverting a draconian and completely unfair policy of the English – the infamous law called the 'Doctrine of Lapse', promulgated by Lord Dalhousie, the Viceroy of India from 1844 to 1848. Under this law, a princely state without a direct male descendant of the ruler, could automatically be annexed and placed under the direct control of the East India Company.

The East India Company continued aggressive expansion of its territory through such despotic and tyrannical acts in the name of the British Crown. This unjust law later also proved to be the kernel for the First War of Independence. It must have been extremely challenging for the Begums to keep the fledgling state of Bhopal afloat and thriving during such trying times. Shaharyar M. Khan, the grandson of the last Nawab of Bhopal, attributes three main reasons for the firm entrenchment and success of the Begums in his book, *The Begums of Bhopal.*

The first was their intrinsically feminine instinct as women, to hold on to and preserve what they owned, through negotiation, persuasion or compromise, much unlike men, who were more likely to get into fights because of their egos. Thus, Mamola Bai ceded territories and forts to the Nizam and the Peshwas in the long term interest of the Bhopal state, while at the same time welcoming General Goddard, who gave much needed strategic support to Bhopal. Sikandar Begum's help to the British during the mutiny of 1857 was more an act of clever diplomatic strategy than mere sycophancy.

Secondly, the Begums achieved public support and acceptance from their subjects due to their spotless personal integrity, humaneness, commitment to good governance and many more remarkable qualities that they possessed.

Thirdly, Bhopal and Central India, per se, have had a precedence and culture of dominant women rulers or advisors to their consorts. Beginning with Fatah Bibi, the wife of Dost Mohammad Khan, then Mamola Bai, Rani Kamlapati and many other women rulers of Bhopal can be said to have had the same influence on their husbands as perhaps Noor Jahan had on Jahangir.

The Rajgond history chronicles two mighty queens who descended from the family of the Ginnaurgarh rulers, Rani Feroz Kunwar and Rani Mardan Kunwar, who once ruled over the kingdom of Bari. Lore has it that at one point, they became so powerful that they would apply tilak on the foreheads of their courtiers with their toes! They had a seal which read 'Main Kundan Gondi, Rani Bari infizal'.

The women rulers' influence and power was largely due to their survival instinct against all odds, and astonishingly, because of the effect that the Pindari women had on the Pathan women. In his book, Shaharyar Khan says:

> 'The Pindara women claimed their rights in sharing the booty and became assertive, robust and politically conscious. This Amazonic tradition in the Pindara women probably rubbed off on to the Pathan settler women of Bhopal, making them unusually aggressive and dominant.'

It is a historical fact that the Central Indian region, more specifically the areas adjoining the Malwa Plateau, underwent the most violent transition and was the most vulnerable to instability, following Mughal Emperor Aurengzeb's death and the resultant loosening of the Mughal court's control on the territories that they ruled. The very foundations of public administration and civil society were threatened, which led to the unleashing of a Jurassic instinct for survival, particularly amongst the womenfolk.

These very qualities transformed normal women from mere nobility into powerful and astute rulers, who not only had an impact on the course of history of their time, but also left an indelible footprint for women of the future to emulate.

Death Be Not Proud...

The reign of the Begums of Bhopal ended when Sultan Jahan's son took the crown. However, their dynasty is memorable for their achievements as women, particularly Muslim women in Colonial India, and is an inspiration for the women of today as they continue to struggle for equality in a male-dominated world.

But how did each of the Begums die?

The first de facto Begum, Mamola Bai, who was reverentially also called 'Maaji Sahiba', ruled over and consolidated the Bhopal state for fifty years. She died gracefully at the age of eighty of natural causes, in 1795. Just before her death, she had negotiated a tough deal with the arch enemy of the Bhopal state – the Marathas.

The second Begum, Qudsia, also died at the age of eighty, in 1881. In a perhaps unparalleled historical event, erstwhile Bhopal saw all its four Begums alive, together. And Qudsia Begum lived to see three of her women successors take the throne. This is nothing short of a unique phenomenon in the history of dynasts.

Sikandar Jahan, the third Begum, was an avid traveller. After attending the grand durbar held at Agra in November 1866, she returned to Bhopal, taking a circuitous route so that she could see the countryside. After her return, she began complaining of a dull and sometimes piercing pain in her abdomen. Overlooking it as a digestive problem, Sikandar continued with her routine life. But the problem was much more serious. On

Shahjehan Begum

30 November 1868, writhing with pain in the Hawa Mahal Palace, she died of what may have been cancer. Sikandar died in her prime, at the age of fifty, with her mother Qudsia, and her successor, Shahjehan Begum at her bedside.

On a hot May afternoon in 1901, the official residence of Shahjehan, the fourth Begum – the Taj Mahal Palace bore a ghastly look. As Sultan Jahan, Shahjehan's estranged daughter, approached the palace to seek forgiveness from her mother whom she had not spoken to for the past thirteen years, she could hear the mournful howling of jackals drifting in from the Idgah hills... an ominous sign. As if this was not enough, the moment Sultan Jahan's buggy entered the ramparts of the palace, a falcon swooped down on a screeching sparrow, and grabbing the little bird in his claws of death, flew away. After ruling for thirty-three years, Shah Jahan Begum lay dying of cancer of the mouth.

Sultan Jahan later wrote poetically of her mother's death:

> '...whilst I looked on, a mighty whirlwind, with a sound like the roaring of oceans, swept over it, and the earth and sky were shattered....'

Twenty-nine years later, in 1930, Sultan Jahan's own death was also as tragic. At the age of seventy-two, Sultan was a happy and contented woman, who had recently won a tangled battle for succession for her 'little Hamid' – who would grow up to be the last Nawab of the erstwhile princely state of Bhopal –

Hamidullah Khan. Sultan Jahan had performed all her religious obligations as well.

At Qasr-e-Sultani, the courtyard, which had seen many historical decisions being sealed and signed, was now being converted into a makeshift operation theatre. The official surgeon of the state, Dr. Sohrabjee, under the supervision of the palace doctor, Dr. Johary, was busy sterilizing surgical equipment. Until then, only a handful of people knew that Sultan Jahan could be suffering from some form of cancer as she too had been complaining of severe stomach aches. Cancer, it seemed, ran in the genes of Bhopal royalty. Shahjehan Begum, Sikandar Begum, and Sultan Jahan' son, General Obaidullah, had all died of cancer.

The operation on Sultan Jahan was successful and everybody heaved a sigh of relief when the surgeon emerged and revealed that all that was wrong with the Begum were a few gall bladder stones. But alas, Sultan Jahan's old and frail body could not take the strain of the surgery and, sadly, she died within a few hours of it.

With her, also ended the one-of-its-kind and legendary rule of the five Begums of the princely state of Bhopal.

How the words below from John Donne's *Holy Sonnet* come alive:

> *'Death be not proud, though some have called thee, mighty and dreadful, for, thou art not so....'*

TWO

THE DAUGHTER WHO ABDICATED THE THRONE

When the British began their conquest of the subcontinent, many laws of the land, particularly those implemented by the Mughal rulers, were subsumed into their modern judicial process. However, the law of primogeniture, which stated that the first-born male child of a ruler stood to inherit the parent's throne and the entire estate, underwent some amendments. This was done ostensibly to protect the interest of the vassal states and their subjects. But it was, in effect, a ploy to place a pliant ruler on the throne, who would remain loyal to the overall interests of the British Crown. There are many instances in Colonial history where crowned or titular kings were dethroned and regents appointed in their place by the British.

A regent, from the Latin word 'regens' – 'that who reigns' – is a person selected to act as head of state (ruling or not) because the legitimate ruler is either a minor, is not present, or is debilitated. A monarch is one who heads a monarchy, a form of government in which a country or entity is usually ruled by an individual who normally rules for life, or until abdication.

In erstwhile Bhopal, the regency arrangement continued through the reign of all the ruling Begums. Mamola Bai was the

Sikandar Begum, Shahjehan Begum and the widow of Balthazar Bourbon

de facto regent and ruler to her two step-sons, Faiz Mohammad and Hayat Mohammad, for almost as many as fifty years. For eighteen years, Qudsia Begum exercised all executive powers as a regent to her daughter Sikandar, but could herself never become a full-fledged ruler by right.

On 27 July 1847, Qudsia's daughter Sikandar was proclaimed as the sole regent on behalf of Shahjehan, her nine-year-old minor daughter. Sikandar Begum eventually ruled for a total of twenty-one years, the first thirteen as regent and the last eight as the rightful ruler. This happened because Shahjehan Begum, who had been proclaimed a ruler by a British decree, volunteered to abdicate the throne in favour of her mother. This was indeed quite extraordinary and is perhaps the most unconventional occurrence in the history of succession in Colonial India, because the British had to seek Shahjehan Begum's permission to let her mother become the ruler.

Favoured by the British for her faithful support to them and her daring decision to host English families during the Sepoy Mutiny of 1857 so that they could be safe, Sikandar knew that she had earned deep admiration and goodwill of the British, both in Calcutta and in London. Queen Victoria had already ascended the British throne in 1837, and is said to have been particularly moved by Sikandar's loyal support.

Sir Richmond Shakespeare

Sikandar, an ambitious and calculative woman, petitioned the Governor General, Viscount Lord Canning, staking her claim to the throne. She argued that with all the authority already vested in her, she could not be denied her rightful title as the bona fide ruler. This put the British in an awkward position, because they had already declared Sikandar's then minor daughter, Shahjehan, to be the ruler when she attained the age of twenty-one, through a decree.

Sir Richmond Shakespeare, the political agent stationed in Indore, was dispatched to Bhopal to intervene and resolve this issue. To quote Shaharyar Khan:

> *'In one of the most poignant moments in Bhopal's history, Sir Richmond Shakespeare sought permission to speak privately to Shahjehan'.*

It was only after Shahjahen's confirmation that she was volunteering to step down without any pressure or coercion from anybody, that Sikandar was officially recognized as the ruler by the British government in December, 1859.

This also marked the end of the rule by proxy of the regents from the royal house of Bhopal. However, Sikandar could rule as the Nawab Begum only for another nine years, when she passed away in 1868, aged only fifty. After this, her daughter Shahjehan Begum was again enthroned as the Nawab Begum.

THREE

MAMOLA BAI - THE MATRIARCH EMPIRE-BUILDER

Not many know about a phenomenal woman, Mamola Bai, who even in those medieval, largely oppressive times, managed to change the course of history all by herself. Mamola Bai was the first wife of the second Nawab of Bhopal, Yar Mohammad Khan. After Yar Mohammad's death in 1742, Mamola, through incredible statecraft and extraordinary strategy, saved the nascent state of Bhopal from being usurped by feuding Pathan clans.

Even though childless herself, she acted as regent to her step-sons, Faiz and Hayat. Later, when Faiz started to show increasing signs of becoming a religious recluse, Mamola became the de facto ruler and potentate of the state, making policies and running day-to-day state affairs with great aplomb for a whopping fifty years, until her death in 1795.

Mamola Bai, reverentially referred to as 'Maaji Sahiba', had extraordinary foresight, typical only of a true empire-builder. She made sure that the fish ensign – the 'Mahi-Marateb' – was conferred upon her late husband, Yar Mohammad Khan by Asaf Jah, the Nizam of Hyderabad, who until then held the official *Sanad* (legal deed) of Bhopal. The Mahi-Marateb reinforced Mamola's claim to the Bhopal state, and remained the state's royal emblem until its eventual merger with the Union of India.

Mamola Bai was declared the second Rabia Basri (an Arab Muslim saint and mystic) by the Sufi Pir, Ghous Ahmed Shah Gailani. This declaration was formally recognized by the then Mughal emperor.

An Artist's Impression of Mamola Bai

Mamola's spiritual guru was Hazrat Shah, whose dargah is still seen today on the Takia tapu (island) in the Upper Lake in Bhopal. A story goes that once when Mamola took gravely ill and was in the throes of death, she was brought to Hazrat Shah. He is said to have pronounced: '*...lakh mar jaayen, lakh ka palanhaar na marey*' (a lakh people may die, but not the savior of a lakh people). Legend has it that after a few hours, while Mamola regained consciousness, Hazrat Shah himself lay dead!

Just like her predecessor, Rani Kamlapati, who gifted a portion of her kingdom to Dost Mohammad Khan, on which he was able to sow the seeds of the state, Mamola Bai, too, consolidated the fledgling state of Bhopal and laid a strong foundation for the triumphant and noteworthy rule of four consecutive generations of the famous Begums of Bhopal.

Mamola Bai's origin is still debated by historians, but two undeniable facts have emerged. One is that she was of noble Rajput descent, and the other is that she was given in marriage to Yar Mohammad Khan, as was customary in those days for the smaller subsidiary states to forge matrimonial alliances with bigger kingdoms.

An eighteenth century mosque – the 'Masjid Maaji Sahiba' – built by Mamola Bai, still stands opposite Gauhar Mahal, facing

Masjid Maaji Sahiba

the Upper Lake in Bhopal. Adjacent to this mosque is another spectacular small red mosque which is known as 'Lal Imli Wali Masjid' where Maaji Saheb is said have planted a red Imli (tamarind tree), that still bears fruit. This is a standing testimony to the continuity of the eras – both literally and metaphorically.

FOUR

THE BEGUMS' REVENGE ON MISOGYNISTS

Though Nawab Nazar Mohammad had signed a treaty with the British in 1818 that ensured protection to the Bhopal State against any external enemies, the internal threat of a palace coup because of the squabbles between the descendants of Dost Mohammad Khan always loomed large. Qudsia Begum, as regent, was struggling to save the throne for her only child Sikander Begum, who had been declared heir apparent to the throne once she came of age, by a decree of the British government.

Amidst this tumultuous political intrigue, Lancelot Wilkinson was appointed as the British Political Agent in Bhopal in 1830. This spelt a serious setback for and also an ominous threat to the continuity of the rule of the Begums. Wilkinson, who was known for his bigoted mindset, was vehemently opposed to any leadership or public role for women. His misogynistic and egotistic attitude was stoked by the fact that he now had the power to dislodge a woman regent and satisfy his ego and his regressive world view.

'The woman question' (*querelle des femmes*), which was until then the purview of only hardcore fundamentalists, was now going to be addressed by a supposedly liberal Englishman.

Immediately after he took over as the Political Agent, Wilkinson set about studying the Islamic law on inheritance and the English law on primogeniture, with a special emphasis on the infamous 'Doctrine of Lapse', proposed by Lord Dalhousie.

After sometime, he sensed favourable indications from Qudsia's rival coterie, headed by Amir Mohammad Khan who earlier had been denied the throne by his father, Wazir Mohammad Khan, in favor his younger son Nazar Mohammad. Amir, with the help of Wilkinson, hurriedly got his own son, Jahangir Khan married to Qudsia's daughter, Sikandar. Amir realised that since Sikandar was already the heir apparent, Jahangir would have to remain content with the status of King consort. Therefore, machinations to depose Qudsia, and subsequently sideline Sikandar and get Jahangir to the throne had to be planned with the help of Wilkinson.

Amir did not have to try very hard. Wilkinson had already dispatched a letter to British Secretary of State, Charles McNaughton, articulating his opinion as to why Jahangir Mohammad Khan should be handed over the reins of the Bhopal State, instead of Sikandar.

For the final settlement of the dispute, a minor battle ensued between the forces loyal to the Bhopal court under Qudsia Begum, and the disparate and unprofessional army of Jahangir Khan near the settlement of Ashta. Qudsia's army won hands down! But the cunning Wilkinson, as was his wont, again played dirty here; not only did he arrive in Bhopal with an armed contingent from Sehore, he also brandished a letter from Charles McNaughton which directed Qudsia to hand over the reins of power to Jahangir Mohammad Khan. Jahangir took over the throne in 1837 and ruled until his death in 1844.

The young Sikandar Begum, who had closely watched these developments and was not in a position to take sides, developed

Charles McNaughton

a deep dislike for Wilkinson, and decided to teach him a lesson to get even with him.

For this, Sikandar chose the occasion of a state banquet, where Wilkinson was to be the chief guest. He had, by now ensconced himself firmly in his seat of power. At the banquet, in an audacious move, very unlike the urbane English etiquette expected of an officer of his stature, he dared to come uncomfortably close to Sikandar. Then, toying with her diamond earring, he remarked *'Begum Saheb, what beautiful jewellery you are wearing!'* At this, almost at lightning speed, and in front of the aghast guests, officers and courtiers, the spirited Sikandar Begum planted a resounding slap across Wilkinson's face, and in a regal tone, said, *'Wilkinson Saheb, don't you know that it is an insult for a Muslim woman to be touched by a stranger?'*

The second instance when the Begums had to face a misogynistic situation was during the reign of Shahjehan Begum. The villain this time was Sir Lepel Griffin, the Resident Commissioner based in Indore. Lancelot Wilkinson had been the Political Agent in Bhopal for eleven years, and was offered the Secretary-ship to the British government as the Resident Commissioner at Lucknow at salary of Rs.3,000 per month. Even though his pay at Sehore was lower, at Rs.2,000 a month, he chose to continue there in order to fulfill his desire to overthrow the rule of the Begums.

A sketch from The Illustrated London News of Shahjehan Begum at a ceremony

Unlike Wilkinson though, Griffin may not have been a misogynist in the true sense of the word. If at all he was one, he successfully veiled his comments and arguments with great diplomacy, often putting the onus for his behaviour on British laws. He was smart enough and ambitious enough to 'manage' the affairs of the State with tact, rather than letting his personal bias overshadow his decisions. But Shahjehan Begum definitely perceived him as misogynist, and this time around, the Begum herself was to be partially blamed for the atmosphere of mistrust and palace gossip which surrounded her tenure as the Nawab Begum.

Shahjehan Begum's long-time paramour, Siddiq Hasan, who was a Wahabi fundamentalist, encouraged the artistically inclined, liberal poet and musician Shahjehan to go under the veil. This was the time when the British were at loggerhead with the Ottoman Turks in a different part of the world, fighting for global supremacy.

Sir Lepel Griffin, the British resident at Indore and Major Thompson, the political agent, deviously counselled the widowed Shahjehan Begum to remarry, this time to Siddiq Hasan, so that she could take over as the Nawab. To quote Shaharyar Khan:

> 'In an example of the most devious chicanery, the British resident and political Agent artfully suggested to the Begum that she should re-marry, as Islam encouraged widows to marry again.'

In a strange and unsavoury twist, Siddiq Hasan went a step ahead and spread rumors of Shahjehan being pregnant with his child. This move of Siddiq's alarmed the British and the marriage had to be fast-tracked to avoid any embarrassment to the royal couple.

But the resident commissioner soon realised that they had made a terrible mistake, when he began to receive secret information on the activities of Siddiq Hasan, which bordered on being almost seditious. Apart from this, the local Barrukat Pathans were dead against the non-Pathan Siddiq Hasan who they considered to be an outsider. To his dismay, Griffin received a barrage of requests from no less than Nawab Shahjehan herself to confer Siddiq with the title of Nawab, and bestow on him the customary seventeen-gun salute recipient status. By the time Griffin could compile the reports against Siddiq, the Viceroy's office had already approved the conferment of both the honours to Siddiq, as a matter of routine protocol.

Griffin then set his target on Shahjehan. He began to talk her into coming out of the veil. Even the then Viceroy, Lord Lansdowne, conveyed his disapproval of the veil to the Begum, with whom he had interacted when she did not practice the purdah. The Viceroy is on record to have said that, '*...young for her age, (she was) was not disagreeable to look at.*' Shahjehan

Colonel Lancelot Wilkinson

Begum not only refused to give up the veil, but also charged Griffin with interfering in her religious beliefs, which was against the policy of his government.

By now, Griffin had compiled enough reports to nail Siddiq and indirectly pin-down Shahjehan. He wrote to the Viceroy:

'...whether English officers and gentlemen and the direct representative of His Excellency, the Viceroy, be required to transact business with a man whom they know to be a traitor to Her Majesty the Queen-Empress.'

Eventually, on the basis of Lord Griffin's report, the British Government divested Siddiq Hasan of all the honours, including the seventeen-gun salute, the honorary gifts, and the title of Nawab that had been granted to him.

Shahjehan Begum was utterly humiliated as this was announced at a public durbar by Griffin. What the Begum did thereafter was unprecedented effrontery to the British and a symbolic rebellion against the Queen-Empress. For this impudence, Shahjehan Begum could well have had her gun-salute status lowered, or her various decorations withdrawn, particularly the prestigious 'Star of India', which she had received only a couple of years earlier. Even worse, she could have been dethroned.

After Griffin's announcement at the durbar, there was pin-drop silence, except for the unintended clinking of the

Sir Lepel Griffin (sitting on the left in a white jacket)

scabbards of the courtiers. The Begum stood up suddenly, and thundered, *'Griffin's worth is less than the dirt off my shoes...,'* and stormed out of the durbar in a rage, leaving behind red-faced British officers.

It is to the credit of the India Office and the benevolent outlook of Queen Victoria that all of Shahjehan's purported misdemeanours were condoned, on the one condition that Siddiq Hasan was banished from Bhopal.

FIVE

THE BEGUMS' DREAM – THE ADVENT OF RAILWAYS IN BHOPAL

From the time Qudsia, the first Begum Nawab of Bhopal, came to know of the first railway train that ran from Bombay to Thane in 1853, she began dreaming of gifting a rail connection to her beloved principality and linking it to the national railway grid. In the three decades after railways first started in India, Khandwa to the west of Bhopal, and Agra to its north, remained the last terminuses of the Great Indian Peninsular Railway – within enticing reach, yet not close enough for Bhopal. The state, as a result, languished in terms of development and quick access. During the prolonged devastating famine in Central India in the 1860s and 70s particularly, the absence of a faster mode of transport made it difficult for relief to reach the suffering masses in time.

Qudsia Begum was particularly pained to see the havoc this great famine had unleashed. By then, she had abdicated the throne in favour of her daughter, Sikandar in 1837, as per an earlier arrangement with the British East India Company. She, therefore, could not do much officially to influence the right people. But the feisty person that she was, she kept up the demand and petitioned the British in her personal capacity to facilitate the laying of a railway line to Bhopal.

Sir Henry Daly

Both the Begums, Qudsia and Sikandar, continued their efforts to get the British to start a land survey for laying the railway line. She also pressed her granddaughter, Shahjehan Begum, to urge the Resident Commissioner, Sir Henry Daly (who, incidentally, was the founder of Daly College in Indore). But Shahjehan Begum had some reservations about the funding for the project. While she agreed to contribute funds from the state treasury, she also wanted a share in the profits. Here, the dowager Qudsia Begum intervened again and promised to contribute a sum of twenty lakh rupees out of her personal savings from her own private 'jagir'.

This benevolent and charitable act of Qudsia's becomes particularly significant in the light of the fact that the Maharaja of Rewa and the Raja of Sarguja, the neighbouring feudatories had already refused permission for a railway line to pass through their territory. They were apprehensive, as they believed that the railway would contaminate the religious and political sentiment of their subjects... thereby showing their narrow-mindedness and utter disregard for a modern approach to administration.

Finally, on 27 December 1877, by an agreement between the British and Shahjehan Begum, the construction of a railway line from Bhopal to Itarsi commenced. And on 18 November 1882, the first steam-powered locomotive chugged into Bhopal, with the inauguration of Bhopal railway station!

By 1897, the track had been further extended to Agra. But alas, both the Begums who were instrumental in connecting Bhopal to the rest of India were not able to see their dream

The Bhopal Railway Station during the British Raj

come true. Sikandar Begum had died in 1868, and Qudsia Begum in 1881.

Shashi Tharoor in his book, *An Era of Darkness,* argues that '*in its very conception and construction, the Indian Railways was a big British colonial scam*' and was '*a splendid racket for everyone, apart from the Indian taxpayer.*' Quoting the Governor General Lord Hardinge that the railways would be beneficial '*to the commerce, government and military control of the country*' he tries to vindicate that the British did not bring the railways for the benefit of the natives and had always had a larger plan in mind towards Empire building and economic exploitation in India. Tharoor may be right in his analysis; however, this was not the case with the Bhopal State.

Thus the very idea of a railway communication in the Bhopal State started as a step towards uplifting the destitution and bringing hope and succour to the masses unlike what

Shashi Tharoor has argued. But in retrospect, Tharoor stand vindicated because the encouragement and partial funding with the technical support that the Raj Government provided was not as philanthropic as the Begums would have liked it to be.

There are strong possibilities that the Viceregal office shrewdly ensured quick deployment of troops and war materials to contain the ever boiling cauldron of rebellion in the restive regions of Central India. This also considering the unexpected blitzkrieg of the First War of Independence that almost doomed the East India Company's rule just a decade before. It was only after this that a permanent British force, partially paid by the Bhopal State, was kept in Sehore to be deployed at short notice. The Shylock like negotiations which the British Political Agents held with the Princes also goes to prove the Empire's approach towards their subjects. It was in fact the Military and logistics that determined their agenda under the cloak of social and economic development.

SIX

DEMOCRACY IN A KINGDOM?

Democracy as we know it, is the rule of the masses. Ever since the old Latin dictum *Vox Populi, Vox Dei* meaning *'the voice of the people is the voice of God'*, entered the political lexicon – democracy has become the most acceptable, humane and justifiable mode of polity. During the course of its development, it has sustained the onslaught of manipulations and subjugation, but has emerged more refined and strong as the ideal form of government mankind has attempted to evolve for itself.

India, can proudly count itself amongst handful of ancient civilisations, along with the Hellenistic and Ptolemaic kingdoms of the past, to have had a notable record of republican and democratic governance. Kalinga (ancient Orissa) is one of the oldest known democracies in the World. It had a monarchical parliamentary democracy system, and was a republic.

During the Mauryan era, at the time of Ashoka – the great, social and trade associations had a quasi-democratic mechanism according to which they conducted their daily business affairs. Particularly noteworthy is the 'Sreni' or 'Guild' system, which became so efficient and effective as an association of traders, merchants and artisans, that it could influence and manipulate royal decrees, and was powerful enough to put pressure on the authority of even the kings.

Nowhere thereafter do we come across any semblance of a more democratic institution in history, until India attained freedom from the Raj – except in the erstwhile state of Bhopal. This was again, a harbinger of the times to come. The rulers of Bhopal, a vassal state of the British Dominion, even in a stifling, colonial environment, dared to undertake bold, democratic reforms.

During the rule of Sikander Begum in the latter half of the nineteenth century, a 'Majlis-e-Shoora' was introduced as a form of monarchical parliament, which was a nominated body. It consisted of eminent professionals, nobles who represented different regions, religious scholars and experienced administrators. Known to promote revolutionary ideas and concepts which concerned the emancipation of her subjects, Sikander Begum possibly tried to base this institution on the lines of the House of Lords in England. The Majlis-e-Shoora enacted laws and had a major say in policy making. The members had complete freedom of speech and passed laws through modern parliamentary procedures. It was here that the major decision to change the official court language from Farsi to Urdu was taken in 1858. The council not only brought transparency to difficult judicial jargon, but also gave the common man a chance to understand complex court rulings and orders.

Later, Sikander Begum's granddaughter, Sultan Jahan, gave another powerful boost to democratic reforms in the state by introducing the 'Majlis-e-Mashwara', an advisory body which also served as a legislative council. She brought further pioneering grass-root level improvement by having municipal elections.

Hamidullah Khan, Sultan Jahan's successor, proved to be even more liberal than the Begums. He enjoyed organising debates and discussions on the latest domestic and international political developments of the time, which was the sign of an open, receptive mind. His views on the Khilafat movement, and the shabby treatment by the British office in Calcutta of the descendants of Nawab Wajid Ali Shah at the Metia Burz, were well-known.

He openly celebrated the victory of Turkey, ostensibly an enemy state, in the battle to regain control over Smyrna (Izmir). He encouraged demagogues within his own territory, and despite many secret reports by the British government about the activities of Gandhian freedom fighters in his land, he invited the freedom fighters to congregate and confer in his domain. It is therefore, important to understand the substantial contribution of the erstwhile rulers of Bhopal towards strengthening decentralisation of power in its most modern sense. They could have easily destabilised their own dynastic seat of power in doing so, and could have even overwhelmed the British to take action against them.

Without any doubt, the Begums of Bhopal could foresee the writing on the wall!

SEVEN

THE DESTINY OF KINGS

> *'Not all the water in the rough rude sea / Can wash the balm off from an anointed king;*
> *The breath of worldly men cannot depose / The deputy elected by the Lord'*

Who is a king? Is he divinely anointed and invulnerable as a direct deputy of God, or is he merely a human being like any other? The above lines by the incomparable Shakespeare (*Richard II: Act III, Scene ii*) make you think about this conundrum.

In the annals of Indian history, there is a very interesting incident about Sher Shah Suri, a private infantry foot-soldier in the first Mughal emperor, Babur's army. After Babur defeated Ibramim Lodhi in the first battle of Panipat in 1526, a huge celebratory feast was organized in the Mughal camp. Babur was enjoying the revelry along with his son Humayun, when he noticed a young soldier slicing pieces of meat off a barbequed lamb with his dagger. Babur's innately sharp leadership instinct kicked in and he immediately cautioned Humayun about this particular soldier. The soldier was Sher Shah Suri, who, within just eight years after Babur's death in 1530, wrested the Mughal throne from Humayun and became the ruler of Hindustan.

Nawab Ghous Mohammad Khan

Interestingly, in the royal house of Bhopal too, destiny has played an important role in many of its outstanding members attaining the pinnacle of kingship, though not in the running to be kings by order of succession.

Mamola Bai, through circumstances created by the untimely death of her husband, the second Nawab, Yar Mohammad Khan, ruled Bhopal as a regent for fifty long years.

It was destiny that intervened again to put a more deserving claimant on the throne, who did not otherwise stand a chance. It was during the siege of Bhopal in 1812–13, when the fledgling, inept and weak Nawab Ghous Mohammad Khan had all but lost the kingdom of Bhopal to the Marathas. It was the charismatic Wazir Mohammad Khan, great grandson of Dost Mohammad, who had earlier been evicted from Bhopal after a palace coup, returned and put his might and intellect behind the Nawab's forces, winning the day for the kingdom, and the throne for himself.

Wazir ruled for a little over three years. Again, as per the law of primogeniture, Wazir's first-born son should have been the one to take over. But Wazir Mohammad kept his older son Amir Mohammad from being crowned heir apparent because of his waywardness and decadent lifestyle. Thus, Wazir's younger son, Nazar Mohammad was made the seventh Nawab, but he too died an unnatural death when he was accidentally shot by his nephew.

Nasrullah Khan

The kingdom thus once again veered towards anarchy. That was when a French nobleman from the royal house of Bourbon-Balthazar Salvador de Bourbon, who along with the loyal and highly respected Sardar Bakshi Bahadur Mohammad Khan, paved the way for the smooth takeover of reins by the second Begum of Bhopal, Qudsia, who ruled as a regent for her daughter Sikandar, from 1819 to 1837. But because of the misogynist British political agent, Lancelot Wilkinson stationed in Bhopal then, Qudsia had to hand over the reins to her son-in-law, Jahangir Mohammad Khan, who in turn tried to kill his wife – the nominated heir to the throne, Sikandar Begum. Miraculously, Sikandar survived and became the third Begum and tenth Nawab of Bhopal in 1844.

Destiny though continued to play her game – Sikandar, unfortunately died at the age of just fifty. Her daughter, Shahjehan became the fourth Begum in 1868. Shahjehan had only one daughter, Sultan Jahan from her first husband – Sardar Baqi Mohammad Khan. Interestingly, Shahjehan Begum disliked her daughter immensely for certain reasons and even though Sultan Jahan was the declared heir apparent, Shahjehan left no stone unturned to stop her daughter from ascending the throne. She even desperately tried to have a child with her second husband, Siddiq Hasan Khan, but failed to. Sultan Jahan took over as the twelfth Nawab and fifth Begum in 1901, when Shahjehan died of cancer of the mouth.

But the most spectacular hand was yet to be dealt by destiny – even though Sultan Jahan Begum had three sons, it was the youngest, Hamidullah Khan, who would become the thirteenth and the last Nawab of Bhopal, when his two older brothers, Nasrullah and General Obaidullah died of diabetes and cancer, respectively. Both the older brothers had sons, who laid claim to throne, but eventually, it was destiny that had its way.

EIGHT

SHAHJEHAN BEGUM'S 'JUSTICE IN A DAY'

When the charismatic Martin Luther King Jr. thundered these prophetic words, *'Injustice anywhere is a threat to justice everywhere,'* and *'No, no, we are not satisfied, and we will not be satisfied until justice rolls down like waters and righteousness like a mighty,'* the World absorbed these pearls of wisdom with spellbound reverence!

However, a hundred years before him, in the Bhopal principality, the eleventh ruler, Nawab Shahjehan Begum, often admonished her courtiers and royal officials with such lines, whenever she found her subjects being mistreated. She was particularly interested in the implementation of a modern judicial system, and had a jail constructed on the Arera hills (which until a few years ago functioned as the Bhopal Central Jail), based on the British Jail Manual.

She initiated several prison reforms, probably the first such farsighted measures, much before the declaration of the inviolable human rights charter by the United Nations. She started the concept of reform centres instead of punishment centres, in which she embarked upon training the prisoners to be good citizens by imparting vocational skill development so that they could take up livelihood outside. She was also the first to demarcate the roles of the army and the police by establishing a civil police official called 'Shahar Kotwal', for general law and order, and security. Particularly, women were much safer and would perform their outdoor errands under the protective watch of the police force.

Even though the principality followed the modern system of justice with customary appellate authorities, whenever distressed citizens approached her directly with the complaints of her own estate official, the Begum came down heavily on the erring official, accepting the version of the complainant as final. Her 'justice in a day' edicts were awash with tears of gratitude of her subjects. Many such incidents have been mentioned in the book *Talaash-e-Bhopal,* which has been documented by Khalid Mohammad Khan in his seminal book *Beete Din Bhopal Ke,* that vindicate Shahjehan Begum as the most benevolent and empathetic ruler of her time.

One such decision which may appear to have been taken in a huff, but was not, pertains to a widow of the Patel of village Thoona-Pachavan in Sehore. The land in this village was very fertile and was owned mostly by the Patel. After the Patel's death, many revenue officers started eying the property. Over the years, some family members of the revenue minister Imtiaz Ali forcefully started encroaching the land and buildings belonging to the widow, almost reducing her and her two small children to penury. Having left with no option, the widow approached the Begum Nawab, through a woman who was in charge of the palace sanitation. When the Begum heard her grievance, she ordered the erring official to be arrested forthwith, and the immediate restoration of all the usurped property to the widow.

Almost like Martin Luther King Jr., Shahjehan Begum announced she would not have food until she got confirmation of compliance of her instructions. As the adage goes 'Justice denied is justice delayed', these judicial reforms showed that Shahjehan Begum was certainly far more prudent and efficient, particularly in the light of the fact that in the present day, more than four crore cases are still pending resolution with the District Courts in our country.

NINE

A TEMPESTUOUS MOTHER-DAUGHTER RELATIONSHIP

> Elizabeth: Madam, you are not well.
>
> Queen Mary: They say this cancer will make you queen, but they are wrong. Look there, it is your death warrant. All I need do is sign it.
>
> Elizabeth: Mary, if you sign that paper you will be murdering your own sister. When I am queen, I promise... to act as my conscience dictates.
>
> Queen Mary: Well do not think to be queen at all!

Thus went the conversation between Mary – the Queen of England and Ireland, the heir-apparent and her half-sister Elizabeth, in the 1998 film, 'Elizabeth', directed by Shekhar Kapoor.

Since time immemorial, royal families have fought internally over their right to rule and their regal claim over their subjects. Our own great epics *The Mahabharata* and *The Ramayana* too, are essentially about the war of succession between blood relatives.

It is said that the great Ashoka had murdered ninety-nine of his blood-brothers to ascend to the throne of Pataliputra. Jayachandra's treason with Prithviraj Chouhan, Shakti Singh's disloyalty towards Maharana Pratap, Aurangzeb's imprisonment of his father Shahjehan, and the murder of his older brother and the rightful claimant to the Mughal throne, Dara Shikoh – history's '*many cunning passages, contrived corridors,*' are chock-a-block with such instances.

However, during the Raj era, hostilities between claimants to the throne did not remain that gruesome. Instead, they became more cumbersome and time consuming as legal procedures started to come into play, with petitions flying back and forth, and more significantly, the diktats of the India Office in London and the Viceroy's court in Calcutta.

But rarely do we hear of a hate-story between a mother and a daughter as intense as the one witnessed in the Bhopal royalty – the abject animosity between Shahjehan Begum and her daughter Sultan Jahan – one, the reigning monarch and the other, the heir apparent. The distasteful public display of mutual hatred and ignoble power-play between the mother and daughter had managed to divide the Bhopal society at the time.

Chronicles point to various reasons for the discord, but the most specific reason boiled down to Siddiq Hasan Khan, a rank outsider, who Shahjehan Begum had married. Shahjehan Begum did not conform to the strictly puritanical, almost Victorian code of conduct that was followed by the two preceding Begums, Qudsia and Sikandar. A rebel of sorts, she married Siddiq Hasan Khan, who was a non-Afghan of questionable descent.

Siddiq soon started to interfere in the affairs of the State, and the undercurrent of the tension got ignited when, at a public Darbar, he started a smear campaign that underplayed the achievements of Sikandar Begum's reign. The British resident commissioner had already warned the Viceroy's office about the seditious activities of Siddiq Hasan. Sultan Jahan was supported in her denouncement of Siddiq Hasan by the loyal houses of the Baqi-Khels and the Jalalabadis.

There is probably a true incident that became royal gossip and which old Bhopalis often narrate with disdain: once Siddiq Hasan was taking his postprandial stroll on his terrace, which had a clear view of the side of the palace where Sultan Jahan lived. It was a coincidence that Sultan Jahan also came out of her quarters along with her chambermaids, at the same time. She is reported to have chastised Siddiq Hasan for breaking into her privacy. Siddiq is said to have gone and complained to Nawab Shahjehan Begum about this. This apparently enraged Shahjehan so much that she, at that hour of the night itself, immediately called her khemedars and asked them to prepare a tentage accommodation in and around the present location of the Tajmahal Place. She left the palace and stayed in the tentage until the time some under construction portions of the Tajmahal Place were not fully built. Later a throbbing city, Shahjehanabad, was established around the same place.

Shahjehan made a resolve to punish Sultan Jahan. When the royal family travelled to Calcutta to attend the royal Durbar of 1881, Shahjehan publicly humiliated Sultan Jahan and her fiancé Ahmed Ali Khan at the Calcutta railway station by refusing to allow them to board the royal convoy to the Durbar. They had to hire a buggy to reach the venue. Further, she stopped all financial grants to Sultan Jahan, including even the revenue from Sultan Jahan's own private jagir, and also divested her of the title of 'Princess'. The tensions got further aggravated when Sultan Jahan refused to allow her daughter Bilqis Jahan to move to the Tajmahal Palace to be with her

A Rare photograph of Sultan Jahan with her mother Shahjehan Begum

grandmother. Later, when Bilqis died, Shahjehan blamed her death on Sultan Jahan.

Bizarrely, another sore point between the mother and daughter was the number of children that they had. While Shahjehan hadn't been able to conceive even a single child with Siddiq Hasan, Sultan Jahan had given birth to five children, including the first male heir to the throne of Bhopal after generations.

Sultan Jahan writes in her autobiography, *Gauhar-e-Iqbal (An Account of My Life)*, that when she visited her mother one last time on her death bed, in a voice filled with sorrow and anger, Shahjehan said to her, *'Leave me alone. You can come after I am dead.'* However, Sultan Jahan later tearfully confided in her granddaughter Abida Sultan that her mother's last words to her had been much harsher. In front of the seven-year-old Hamidullah Khan, who would grow up to be the last Nawab of

Yar Mohammad Khan, son of Dost Mohammad Khan

Bhopal, the dying Shahjehan had lifted her head, and addressing her attendant, had said, '*Tell this woman to leave me in peace. I am dying... it will be her turn soon.*'

Shahjehan Begum died of cancer in 1901.

TEN

NIGHT OF THE LONG KNIVES

O sleep, O gentle sleep, Nature's soft nurse,
how have I frightened thee...
Uneasy lies the head that wears a crown.

This soliloquy in Shakspeare's *Henry IV* offers the most striking and apt description of the state of mind of kings and statesmen over the ages. During colonial times, the natural line of succession for the kings and the jagirdars was the logical, straightforward law of primogeniture through biological bloodline, unlike today's complex equations of power structure.

In spite of this, the position of the king was fraught with assassination attempts, lowering of statutory pomp and ceremonies, and in some cases, even forced abdication. Ironically, this was because of the very same law which ensured and decreed the heir apparent and regents. Palace intrigue invariably revolved around the groups, grooves and Godfathers. This always lent a surcharged and emotive ambience among the palace officials, courtiers, cronies, and the vast congregation of cousins and direct descendants of the royal bloodline.

In the initial, violent history of the state of Bhopal while it was still evolving and being consolidated, no other act can be deemed as dastardly and heinous as the murderous attack on

Jahangir Mohammad Khan, the Ninth Nawab

Sikandar Begum, the heir apparent to the throne, by her own husband, Jahangir Mohammad Khan, the ninth Nawab.

In the complex arrangement of power sharing and appeasement of the rival claimant, Amir Mohammad Khan, the oldest son of Nawab Wazir Mohammad Khan, was overlooked by the British and his younger brother Nazar Mohammad Khan was crowned as Nawab. After Nazar was killed by an accidental pistol shot by his nephew Fauzdar, Begum Qudsia became the de facto sovereign to rule Bhopal.

Amir Mohammad, though, had not forgotten the humiliation he had suffered at the hands of the British. Through clever machinations and by invoking old Pathan tribal loyalty, he ensured that his son Jahangir got married to Qudsia's only daughter and heir apparent, Sikandar. With the help of Lancelot Wilkinson, the misogynistic British political agent stationed in Bhopal, Amir further ensured that Qudsia abdicated the throne, and as per arrangement, managed to get Jahangir crowned as the ninth Nawab.

Still not satisfied, and fearing counter manoeuvres by Qudsia and her loyalists, Amir hatched a conspiracy to assassinate Sikandar. He convinced Jahangir to kill Sikandar, promising him a cast-iron alibi to vouch that he was somewhere far away and not present in the palace at the time of the murder.

On a hot and humid night in 1838, when a dreamy-eyed,

newly-wed Sikandar stepped out of her bedroom into the courtyard, enveloped by the heady fragrances of *raat ki raani* and *mogra,* she noticed the silhouette of a man with a naked sword in his hand, extinguishing, one by one, the oil lamps that lit the courtyard. Allegorically, the scene eerily played out the powerfully dark lines in *Othello*: '...*Put out the light and then put out the light.*' Sikandar recognised the man as her husband Jahangir. But as there was no escape, she hastily hid herself behind a pile of thick bed cushions moments before Jahangir, his brain suffused with drugs and alcohol, struck her with the sword. Miraculously, Sikandar survived with only superficial wounds.

The news of the assassination attempt spread like wild fire and further discredited Amir and Jahangir's stature. However, the magnanimous Sikandar pardoned her husband, much against the rallying cry for revenge from the loyalists of Qudsia. But, poetic justice prevailed and within six years, the decadent and profligate Jahangir died of liver cirrhosis at the young age of 29, thus paving the way for the next generation of women rulers to rule the kingdom of Bhopal for another ninety years.

ELEVEN

A ROYAL MÉNAGE À TROIS

Trust the French to come up with such mischievously alluring terms as *ménage à trois*. History is replete with examples of this, with even a biblical reference to it in *The Book of Genesis* which mentions Lamech (a descendant of Cain) in a *ménage à trois* relationship with Adah and Zillah. There have been allusions that Queen Catherine Parr of England and Ireland, the widow of Henry VIII, along with her fourth husband, Thomas Seymour shared a *ménage* with the future queen, Elizabeth I. Our own epic, the *Mahabharata* goes a step further, with Draupadi's depiction of a dutiful wife to five brothers. A form of polyamory, *ménage à trois* has been a subject of intense psychoanalysis over the years and a favourite of the parallel and, of late, even the mainstream cinema. Most notable are *Vicky Cristina Barcelona* made by the legendary Woody Allen in 2003 and the 1962 French film *Jules et Jim* made by the iconic François Truffaut.

It is common knowledge that the rule of the Begums was the golden era for the Bhopal State on all parameters of governance. The Begums were known for their strict Victorian righteousness, and were pious and devout. It is, therefore, an interesting surprise that in the Bhopal royal house, there existed a *ménage à trois* about 150 years ago!

Siddiq Hasan Khan, was a perfume-seller and an Islamic

Siddiq Hasan Khan

scholar, who would often lecture in the local mosques after Friday prayers. The Maulvis took note of him and recommended him for a clerical assignment in the royal household. Siddiq was married and had three children.

Following the assignment, he soon started giving lessons on

the Arabic language and Quranic texts to the heir apparent – the third Begum Nawab Shahjehan Begum – who had recently lost her husband. Soon, a full-fledged love affair blossomed between the two. Shaharyar Khan writes in his book, *The Begums of Bhopal*, *'...leaving Shahjehan a distinctly merry widow when she succeeded Sikandar Begum in 1868.'*

Shahjehan, quite unlike the earlier two Begums and also her own daughter, was an elegant *femme fatale* with an unrestrained ardour. Things moved quickly thereafter, and Siddiq confessed the affair to his wife, Zakia, who then insisted on meeting Shahjehan. The three started to live together with ostensible consensus. The situation was apparently amicable to the extent that whenever there was a tiff between Siddiq and Shahjehan, Zakia would use her closeness to Shahjehan to sort out the issues between them.

But eventually, predictable human traits of jealousy and rancour prevailed, and the *ménage à trois* fell apart. The royal *ménage* seems to have been based largely on survival instinct, at least from Zakia's perspective, as she probably only wanted a life free of poverty for herself and her children.

The story of the rise of Siddiq Hasan Khan from a perfume seller from Kannauj in the then United Province, to being the consort of the Nawab Begum of Bhopal is overwhelmingly beyond belief, but then, did the Bard not say '*...Love is blind, and lovers cannot see the pretty follies that themselves commit.*'

TWELVE

POSTAL SERVICE IN THE ERSTWHILE BHOPAL STATE

Since times immemorial, the greatest desire of humankind has been to communicate. The purpose could be personal, religious, or administrative. From the primitive hunter-gatherers, who had their drum-beaters, smoke signals, cave paintings and symbols in the ancient times; the pigeons and 'Harkaras' (*Dak* runners) of the medieval times, to the advent of the modern postal service started by the British, and finally, to the present-day revolution created by real-time communication devices like the cellular phone, electronic mail (Email), instant messenger services like WhatsApp, etc., communication has not only been the focal area of development, but the methods and means of communication have also come a long way.

The pigeon as a medium of communication occupies an important place in the subconscious of Indians. The famous mythical parrot, 'Hiraman', in the epic poem 'Padmavat' by Jayasi is still considered to be a competent communicator of messages and tales! Similarly, at least in all uniformed services in the subcontinent, the 'DR' – short-form of the '*Dak* runner', and later, the 'despatch runner' is still a commonly used term. Even though postal services under the early Rajput kings and Muslim rulers, starting with Qutb-ud-Din Aibak to Shershah

A sketch of a 'Harkara' (Dak Runner)

Suri and then under the great Moghuls, had improved vastly and became swifter and more reliable, their technology and *modus operandi* remained old-fashioned, however.

It was the English administrators of the East India Company who brought the modern postal service to India. This was based on the model postal system introduced in England by the social reformer, Rowland Hill. By all accounts, their purpose of introducing this in India was certainly not as an administrative reform, but only as a means of restraint. The first Indian Post Office was established in 1837, and the first adhesive stamp, the *Scinde Dawk*, (Sindh Dak) was introduced in 1852 by Sir Bartle Frere, the British East India Company's administrator for the province of Sindh.

Modern and reformist princely states like Travancore, Baroda and Mysore soon started their own postal services. The

The First General Post Office in Bhopal

Imperial Posts dominated the Raj era, but several independent postal systems of various Indian princely states that printed their own postage stamps also existed. The British ensured that only their postage stamps were used for sending interstate mails, and the Princely States' stamps were kept limited within their own boundaries. Later, they categorised these states into Feudatory States and Convention States, the latter having a postal convention (or agreement) with the Post Office of India to provide postal services.

The Bhopal state under Sikandar Jahan Begum tried to emulate certain aspects of the Imperial Postal Service of the British Raj for government-to-government communication with the prevalent system of medieval Royal insignia and seals. Sikandar did lay the foundation of the first General Post Office in 1862. This GPO catered to the limited territorial postal service within her State. But her effort to bring in public postal service was stalled by her untimely death in 1868.

Bhopal Government Postage Stamp of One Anna Six Pies

Stamp issued during Shahjehan Begum's reign, in 1876

When it came to daring and bold reforms among the Begum Nawabs – Shahjehan was a notch above others. It was during her reign that the very first postage stamps of the Bhopal state were issued. Initially these stamps lacked quality and aesthetic appeal. Just a glance at these earlier stamps was enough to convince anyone that they were printed hastily on an archaic printing-press and on a limited budget. These were half and quarter *anna* stamps printed in 1876 and 1878, which had *HH Nawab Shahjehan Begum* printed in an octagonal frame.

However, from the late 1890s until 1949, Bhopal State printed some extraordinary stamps which are now philatelists'

Bhopal State Postage Service Stamp of One Anna, issued in 1908

Bhopal State Postage Service Stamp of One Anna, issued in 1940

treasures. One such stamp was the triangular stamp of Bhopal. This was issued by the regional postal service of Bhopal during the British Raj in 1937. This was printed with an error, which in philatelists' vocabulary, is termed as a 'Service' overprint. This stamp was reissued in 1939, in green colour.

THIRTEEN

SARKAR AMMA'S FREUDIAN SLIP OR A ROYAL FAUX PAS?

The English sense of humour invariably revolves around the play of words and intonations. Thus, the in the early twentieth-century, the Oxbridge elite often narrated anecdotes of the unintentional mixing of sounds of words by Rev. William A. Spooner (1844–1930) warden of New College, Oxford, who was renowned for such hilarious slips. They came up with the word 'Spoonerism' which soon found its way into the Oxford English dictionary. It means 'a verbal error in which a speaker accidentally transposes the initial sounds or letters of two or more words, often to humorous effect, as in the sentences – you have hissed (missed) the mystery (history) lectures, or, you can leave Oxford by the town drain instead of down train; a well-boiled icicle for well-oiled bicycle; a blushing crow for a crushing blow; hush my brat for brush my hat etc. Later on the famous English TV serial in the late Seventies 'Mind your Language' immortalized such gaffes! Thereafter, a more serious psychoanalytical term 'Freudian Slip', for such unintentional muttering evolved.

But what was the reason behind Her Highness Begum Sultan Jahan's (Sarkar Amma) hilarious English, which sometimes landed her in precariously embarrassing situations?

Abida Sultan, daughter of the last Nawab Hamidullah, she writes in her memoir that:

> 'Not having studied English beyond the first two pages of the English primer, Sarkar Amma used to boast that it had been enough for her to master the language.'

But often, this used to end in hilarious situations. She invariably pronounced 'conspiracy' as 'kon-pyracie'. She hardly had to hold any informal conversations with the Britishers in Bhopal, as these most often involved the formal, official jargon used in the everyday grind of administration. But when abroad, for example during her long stay in London in 1925, she used to spend long hours with the English and other European royalty, particularly their consorts and ladies-in-waiting, who were sent by Her Majesty, the Queen to give her company. After a few days, most of them had become familiar with her smattering of English. Not able to pronounce some of the tongue-twisting names, she would come up with her own terms of endearment. Like, she used to refer to one Countess Tomascovitch of Russian descent as 'Countess Tomato'!

However, this one event, although hilarious, could have spelt disaster for Her Highness had it not been for the quick course correction by her daughter-in law. The then Viceroy of India, Lord Reading's wife called on the Begum during her visit to London. The Begum knew that Lord Reading was earlier the Chief Justice and had a

Rev. William Archibald Spooner

decorated legal career. After the initial exchange of pleasantries, suddenly, surrounded as always by royal English ladies, Sarkar Amma casually remarked, 'I know Lord Reading is a great liar.' There was pin-drop silence in the room and Lady Reading stood there, shell-shocked. The day was saved by Maimoona Sultan, Sarkar Amma's daughter-in-law, who sheepishly explained that Sarkar Amma actually meant to say that Lord Reading was a 'great lawyer'!

It may not have been a classic spoonerism, but was it a royal faux pas, a Freudian slip or simply a case of the ubiquitous Bhopali 'bakr', which Sarkar Amma could not overcome?

FOURTEEN

SPY VS SPY: SHAHJEHAN BEGUM OUTMANOEUVRES ENEMIES OF HER CONSORT!

It was a cold foggy day in 1885 at the Bhopal railway station. As the guard was about to signal the driver to move the train, a nervous 'Harkara' (courier), his face covered with a cloth, arrived from the palace with some urgent mail to be deposited in the royal mail wagon. Though not amused by the delay, the English guard, after checking the royal seals on the packages, safely lodged them in the royal mail wagon.

As the train rolled out of Bhopal city, the English guard craned his neck out of the window to enjoy some cool breeze – and was utterly shocked and horrified to see thick black smoke and balls of fire billowing out of the royal mail wagon. After managing to stop the train and inspecting damage, he realised that strangely, except for the royal mail wagon, which had burned down to ashes, no other part of the train had been touched by the flames!

In running a government, espionage is one of the most effective weapons that is used to maintain power. The so-called second oldest profession in the world already has a celebrated Indian text in *Chanakya Niti*, Kautilya's acclaimed treatise on statecraft. It is said to have been studied by no less than the legendary Niccolò Machiavelli.

In those days, tensions were rife in Bhopal regarding the impending arrest and deportation of the prince consort, Siddiq Hasan Khan, in the ongoing enquiry being conducted by Sir Lepel Griffin. Nawab Shahjehan Begum had left no stone unturned to counter the allegations against her consort, who was being tried for the grave offence of sedition. His Wahhabi activities and anti-British writings were being cited as evidence. But only Shahjehan Begum knew of some really foolproof incriminating documents that were soon going to be placed before the enquiry commission as hardcore evidence that could finally nail Siddiq Hasan. With the help of her *bureau d'espionage,* Shahjehan managed to smuggle the original documents from the Viceroy's secretariat and locked them up in a safe that was hidden under her bed. The keys to the safe were always hooked to her *kamarband*!

Siddiq Hasan was the *bête noire* of the older Bhopal royals, who detested his Shia origins and non-Afghan lineage. They wanted him out of the palace at any cost. Sir Griffin had completed all preparations to hand out the final sentence to him. Since the decision involved the Royal household, he had briefed the Viceroy, Lord Dufferin, and had personally requested for reinforcements for his own safety.

In a sudden twist in the tale, just a few days before the final hearing, the safe under Shahjehan Begum's bed was found open and the all-important documents hidden in it were found missing. Who stole the documents and how they were then destroyed in a brilliant counter-coup by setting the royal mail wagon on fire remains a mystery to date, but it is certainly thought to be a masterstroke of Shahjehan Begum's *bureau d'espionage*.

The daughter and heir apparent of the last Nawab, Abida Sultan, while mentioning the incident in her memoir, writes:

> '...no clue was ever found as to how the safe had been opened, or by whom? Neither was the mystery of the counter-coup – the mail wagon catching fire ever solved.'

FIFTEEN

STATE POLICE FORCE OF THE BEGUMS OF BHOPAL

The Police in colonial India was an important arm of the Raj, mainly created to 'suppress' and to 'contain' minor law and order situations. During overwhelming law and order disruptions, the Army would be invariably deployed almost immediately. However, when the British administration sensed that the entrenchment of the British Empire in India was complete, they introduced some semblance of civilian policing in the otherwise predominantly militarised policing. Thus, the modern police system which European countries evolved for themselves in the early nineteenth century was never actually implemented in their colonies.

This meant that the procedures and rules of the London Metropolitan Police were very different from the acts and rules of the Calcutta police under the British. The Imperial Police comprised of the Superior Police Services, which was officered exclusively by the British, and the Subordinate Police Service, largely recruited from amongst the natives. The famous English novelist George Orwell served in the Indian Imperial Police. The civilian police force therefore, continued to be somewhat of an oxymoronic concept and,

> '...the semi-military constabularies were converted into a form resembling the, "essentials of the British pattern" ... but still retaining certain continuing supplementary functions of a military character.'
>
> Excerpt from: *Policing the Empire/Policing the Metropole: Some Thoughts on Models and Types*, by Clive Emsley.

The force was headed by an Inspector General who was a serving Brigadier on deputation from the Army. In Uttar Pradesh, in common jargon a Superintendent of Police is still referred to as 'Kaptaan Saheb' because, for a very long time during the British Raj, the SP used to be a serving Captain from the British Army. The princely states and the principalities under the British Crown followed the colonial policing model almost in toto.

If we explore the origins of the police in the erstwhile Bhopal state, the earliest mention of the civilian police force having some similarity of the modern-day police, can be traced to Chottey Khan, who was the adopted son of Mamola Bai or Maaji Saheba, the first de facto woman ruler of Bhopal. She appointed Chhotey Khan as her Chief Minister in November 1780. He turned out to be a tough administrator who gave the Bhopal State its first police force, complete with an intelligence department. He even introduced the Mughal system of appointing 'Shahar Kotwals' and posted police officers in rural districts. But the 'Thana' system was not yet incorporated and the police continued to be a part of the judicial system.

This system of policing continued to function almost as it was for another seven decades in erstwhile Bhopal, without any significant changes. It was Sikandar Begum who infused some elements of the British police model. It however, continued to remain a subordinate arm of the judicial department.

It was only in 1912 that Sikandar Begum's granddaughter,

Famous English Novelist George Orwell served in the Indian Imperial Police Force (standing third from left)

the progressive reformer Sultan Jahan Begum, who finally established a separate police department. She delinked it from the *Nasir-ul-Muham* after perceiving that under the efficient leadership of its chief, Munshi Israr Hasan Khan, the police had metamorphosed into a disciplined force from an 'undisciplined bevy', capable of managing their own affairs. The credit for this should also go to Khan Bahadur Mohammad Sarwar Khan, who was a senior police officer serving the British in the Central Province. He infused important elements of modern policing like scientific crime detection and investigation techniques into the force.

It is incredible that about a hundred and ten years ago, Sultan Jahan instituted a merit-based recruitment procedure for the police force. Standard regulations regarding the physical traits like height and weight minimum age, basic qualification and medical tests were implemented. New, functional uniforms and the weapons were issued. The salary of a constable was Rs.8 and that of a sub-inspector, Rs.50. The strength of the police force was increased to 2,650, and included a corps of boys who, interestingly, were the harbingers of what we call the Home Guards today.

A note by Lord Minto, the then Viceroy, during a visit to Bhopal lauds the professionalism of the Bhopal Police. It says:

> '...the Bhopal police are superior to those of any other State. Indeed, some of their officers and sepoys are as smart and capable as any that could be found amongst the Government police throughout India.'
>
> (From: *An Account of My Life,* by Sultan Jahan Begum)

This, then, is the fascinating account of the Begums' police force – from Shahar Kotwals and *Nasir-ul-Mahams,* to precursors of the modern-day police force that we have now. Yet again, the Begums of Bhopal proved their acumen and ability to create and nurture systems that not only consolidated their principality, but elements of which also got passed down to posterity and continue to be utilised by us even today.

SIXTEEN

BRITISH SENSE OF HISTORY: HOW SIKANDAR BEGUM WAS HONOURED FOR HER LOYALTY

Innumerable scholars and authors have put forth valid, and invalid, arguments on the economic exploitation of India and Indians by the British during the Raj era. What most of them have not taken into account are some of the more thoughtful and sensitive gestures of the British that have sought to honour their loyalists in the most profound ways.

The erstwhile colonial rulers were adept at nuanced understanding of history, and the traditional and cultural value systems of the land they ruled. The kings, princes and merchants who helped the British in precarious situations, for example during the First War of Independence of 1857, were bestowed with bounties from the empire, often exhibiting great magnanimity, even at the cost of their policies on statecraft.

In the process of consolidating the scattered pieces of territories he had conquered, Dost Mohammad Khan, the founder of the Bhopal royal house, lost his most cherished possession, the Berasia *pargana*, to the adjacent kingdom of Dhār because of a bloody realignment of power centers in Central India. The acquisition of this piece of land, which he had leased in 1709 from an absentee Mughal noble from Delhi, was Dost's first, after his tumultuous arrival from the rugged terrain of Tirah in Afghanistan.

His descendants who became successive Nawabs could only perform the role of reluctant and disinterested negotiators in preserving the moth-eaten territories of Bhopal. It was not until the reign of Mamola Bai, and later, Qudsia and Sikandar, that the Bhopal State emerged in the shape that it retained until India gained Independence in 1947.

Lord Canning, Governor-General of India (1856–1862)

The Berasia *pargana* was eventually ceded to the British by the Raja of Dhār, although it continued to be a touchy subject for the descendants of Dost Mohammad. They rightly had a sentimental attachment to this particular jagir, because it had set in motion the expansion and subsequent consolidation of the State of Bhopal.

It was left to Sikandar Begum to wrest her claim on this ancestral property. Sikandar was arguably the most iconic of the woman rulers of Bhopal. She was intelligent and shrewd, and successfully expanded the territory of Bhopal not through war and annexation, but by the way of persuasive petitions and hefty grants of *sanads* and legal estate papers. She gave her wholehearted support to the British forces during the First War of Independence in 1857. She is said to have even warned her mother Qudsia to desist from funding the rebels clandestinely.

The British government under Governor-General, Lord Canning, in a special Darbar held in Jubalpore (Jabalpur) in

1861 to honour Sikandar Begum, not only accepted her claim to be elevated to the status of a Ruler from a Regent, but in a most insightful decision, handed back the *pargana* of Berasia to her.

Lord Canning's generous gesture was not only meant to restore the rights of the great-great-great granddaughter of Dost Mohammad Khan, the original owner of the land. It also displayed his erudite and wise understanding of the hearts and minds of the people he governed, because to the Bhopal royals, Berasia was not just another piece of land, but a symbol of continuity and a sense of belonging which, in more ways than one, connected them to the culture, mores and value systems of the sacred land which they chose to call their motherland, and nurtured it with their sweat and blood!

SEVENTEEN

BRITISH STATESMEN WHO HELPED CONSOLIDATE THE BHOPAL STATE

It is rather easy to overlook the good and constructive work done by foreign rulers, particularly the British, when analyzing the history of their period. The 240 years of uninterrupted rule of the Orakzai branch of Pathans in Bhopal would not have been possible without the support and manoeuvrings, which often required the bending of rules or offering out-of-the-box solutions, by some of the British statesmen. In the history of the Bhopal State, British officials whose career-graph got unwittingly intertwined with the Bhopal royals, went on to play a prominent role in upholding the Empire's grip globally. Their intriguing karma connection with the Bhopal royalty not only gave them recognition, but also brought them under direct control of the India Office in London, very often resulting in them being handpicked for highly coveted appointments.

Their acts further displayed the inherent ethos of loyalty and service to the Crown, which were the hallmark of British statesmen and officials, in consonance with their motto: *Auspicio Regis et Senatus Anglia,* i.e. 'By the Command of the King and Parliament of England.' This fervour encompassed all aspects of their official dealings.

In the early eighteenth century, when Bhopal was on the verge of being gobbled up by the neighbouring Maratha states, and was facing a serious crisis of succession and leadership, it was as if divine intervention secured the future of the nascent Bhopal State. Mamola Bai, the then ruler of Bhopal grabbed this opportunity with both hands, and thus paved the way for lasting English support, which continued till the merger of the Bhopal State with the Union of India in 1949.

In November 1778, a unit of the army under the command of British General Thomas Goddard was reduced to foraging, after getting lost in the unforgiving jungles of Central India, infested with mosquitos, tigers, the marauding Pindaris and pursuit from the combined armies of the Marathas and the Rajputs. Goddard was under orders to defeat the Marathas, but having severed his links with the supply-chain, was retreating after inflicting heavy casualties in the Marathas strongholds of Poona and Surat, when he and his troops lost their way in dense and dangerous jungles.

When Goddard and his men eventually managed to reach the outskirts of Bhopal, the farsighted dowager Mamola Bai was quick to foresee the growing power of the British and their modern army. She extended unconditional hospitality to General Goddard and his troops. They were put up at the Raisen fort and were stocked-up with rations and other logistical support. Mamola also ensured that traditional courtesies and ceremonies that were generally reserved for visiting heads of state, were accorded to Goddard. In turn, General Goddard was profusely appreciative of Mamola Bai's kind gestures in his Memorandum of Dispatches (MODs) to his seniors. More importantly, Goddard also recognised an effective future course of diplomacy and the need to cultivate this Muslim State into a bulwark against the Marathas – their arch enemy in Central India.

Similarly, in 1818, the seventh Nawab, Nazar Mohammad Khan raised Rupees 51 lakh as aid and provided arms and ammunition to General Adams during the famously successful British crackdown on the menace of the Pindaris. This profound magnanimity by a not-so-rich State like Bhopal was taken note of, and reciprocated by the British in full measure by formally handing back to Bhopal five *parganas* earlier ceded to the Marathas, as well as the forts of Hoshangabad and Islam Nagar (the latter having been paid as a tribute by the decadent Nawab Ghous Mohammad to the Scindias).

The British also hastened the signing of the treaty in 1818 with the Bhopal State, that was adumbrated for the first time by Mamola Bai, and which finally secured the borders of the Bhopal State from any infringement by its rival states. Subsequently, with this treaty, Nazar secured what Dost Mohammad, his forebear a hundred years before him had envisioned.

But the fatal 'accident'/ 'assassination' of Nazar Mohammad, once again put the Bhopal State in turmoil. It was the presence of mind and farsightedness of another Englishman, Major Henley, the British political agent based in Sehore, who halted the juggernaut of misfortunes Bhopal State could have been thrown in the path of. Major Henley's report of the 'accidental shot', ostensibly fired by Nazar's eight-year-old nephew, Fauzdar, was a collection of words and derivatives which glossed over any conspiracy theory about the 'murder' of the Nawab. Had Henley been forthright and truthful in his report, a chain-reaction of the legendary Pathan vindictive trait within the family would have plunged the Bhopal royalty into an abyss leading to a catastrophic end.

Again, during the reign of Qudsia, Jahangir Mohammad's illegitimate son, Dastgir Mohammad Khan, was propped up by some prominent Bhopal royals, notably Amir Mohammad Khan and Assad, the Diwan of Bhopal. The resident commissioner

Lord Birkenhead, the Secretary of State for India (1924–1928)

at Indore, R.C. Hamilton, not only rejected the elevation of Dastgir, but also dispatched Major J.D. Cunnigham to arrest Amir and Assad, who were now trying to seize power by force. Major Cunnigham is credited with preserving the rule of the subsequent Begums by ensuring the regent-ship of Qudsia for the sake of Sikandar, the future Begum of Bhopal.

The maximum credit of upholding the implicit trust of the British must go to Sikandar Begum, who like Mamola Bai, went out of her way to protect British soldiers and their families in the Hoshangabad fort safely, during the highly turbulent years of the First War of Independence. Queen Victoria recognised Sikandar's devotion to the British Empire and conferred upon her the title of 'Ruler' which elevated her stature from being just a titular head of state.

The role of Sir Lepel Griffin, resident commissioner during the reign of Shahjehan Begum, was similar to that of Major Henley. Griffin, against Shahjehan's wishes, sent adverse reports about Siddiq Hasan Khan, her consort, who had usurped the title of Nawab by subverting Shahjehan Begum's liberal view on Islam. Sir Griffin upheld the law of primogeniture and the sanctity of the royal lineage in the true manner of the English tradition. As Barbara D. Metcalf says in her book:

> 'Shah Jahan Begum, however, did not want to be saved – even if Griffin was convinced that Siddiq was nothing more than a rank deceiver who had duped a hapless woman, maybe even by using sorcery, to keep her in control.'

Griffin himself had on many occasions mentioned that:

> '...I have seen most of the princesses of Europe, and [no other face is so] lighted by high intelligence and wisdom.'

Had Griffin not ensured the ouster of Siddiq Hassan, Bhopal probably would have been engulfed in an ideology of a malevolent Wahabi Islam which was totally alien to the 'Barru-Kat' Pathans, whose blood and sweat nurtured the evolution of the Bhopal State.

Lastly, the interesting twist to the famous succession case that Lord Birkenhead, the Secretary of State for India, gave in favour of Sultan Jahan speaks volumes about the cherished relations that the Bhopal royals had with the English nobility. Lord Birkenhead, with his vast knowledge of history and succession laws, reportedly recommended to the then Viceroy, Lord Reading, to consider the Islamic law of succession against the prevailing law of primogeniture. With his learned advice, Brikenhead gave Bhopal the erudite and liberal Nawab Hamidullah, as against the epileptic and atavistic Habibullah Khan, son of the oldest son of Sultan Jahan, Nasrullah Khan.

Having analysed the contribution of these Englishmen in nurturing the roots of the Bhopal State, it must also be surmised that the quid pro quo factor was more important than extending a hand of support to Muslim nobility, particularly when Europe was in the midst of a bloody war with the Ottoman Turks.

EIGHTEEN

THE CURIOUS CASE OF ROYAL HISTRIONICS

Noblesse oblige is an interesting French expression which means: privilege entails responsibility. In simple words, it is the idea that someone with power and influence should use their social position to help other people. But there have been occasions in history when the royalty and at times, the nobility, have found themselves in irreversibly awkward social situations.

The Duke of Cambridge, Prince William, once candidly mentioned during a media interaction that often there occur comical moments when meeting the Queen gets a bit too overwhelming for some people:

> 'A lot of people get very excited and nervous around her and I've seen some very comical moments,' he said. 'I've seen people literally faint in front of her. And it's quite a startling moment as to what to do – when you [see someone] faint in front of the Queen.'

Interestingly, Prince William's great-great-grandfather, King George–V, faced a similar situation, and with no less a person than the Nawab Begum Sultan Jahan of Bhopal, when the Nawab Begum fainted while meeting the King Emperor!

Nawab Begum Sultan Jahan In London

The high profile visit of Begum Sultan Jahan to London in 1925 was ostensibly to pay her obeisance to the British royalty, and to greet the Duke and Duchess of York on the birth of their daughter Elizabeth.

However, the most important factor which necessitated the Begum's visit was the battle of succession that her only surviving son, Hamidullah, was facing back home. It was a complex case in which the law of primogeniture as followed by the British government of the time was pitted against the Muslim law of inheritance. In this, Habibullah, who was the eldest son of Nawab Nasrullah Khan, and the grandson of Begum Sultan Jahan, was being projected as a rightful claimant of the throne after her.

But, after the death of her two older sons Nasrullah and Obaidullah, the Begum had groomed her youngest son Hamidullah to be her heir. There was also the palace politics

King George-V and Queen Mary.

between the Jalalabadis and the Baqi Khels pathan nobility that was affecting this pursuit of hers. She had already lost her case in the court of the Viceroy of India, and also in the last court of appeal – the British Cabinet in London.

The unrelenting Begum then decided to call upon the highest office of the Empire, and requested an audience with the King Emperor George–V. She was already approaching seventy and was now quite frail. When she met the King and Queen, she pleaded her case in an indirect, roundabout manner. The King was highly compassionate and listened with great concern and interest to the appeal of this *burqa*-clad ruler from India. However, he explained to her his inability to help her because, he being a constitutional monarch, did not have any discretionary powers to impress his decisions upon the British Cabinet.

In a last ditch effort, the Begum even removed her *naqab* and displayed her grey hair and wrinkles, much to the King Emperor's discomfiture, all the while reminding him of Queen Victoria's benevolence to the women rulers of the Bhopal State and their sustained allegiance to the British Crown. The King tried to convince her again, but she gently countered him by reminding him that Queen Victoria had also been

Coronation of the last Nawab of Bhopal Hamidulla Khan

a constitutional monarch. She even lapsed into a short, incoherent monologue – really a motley assortment of words and expressions from all the languages she could speak – and started crying!

The persistence and the stress from the realisation that the King Emperor was her last resort, took a toll on the septuagenarian Begum, and while muttering the inane monologue, she fainted! Though there are no records to prove the intervention of the King Emperor in any way, what is definitely on record is the fact that the British Cabinet eventually reversed the decision of the Viceroy of India, and upheld the appeal of Nawab Begum Sultan Jahan, to let her youngest son Hamidullah succeed after her.

NINETEEN

THE DISHONOURABLE REGICIDE OF NAZAR MOHAMMAD KHAN, THE SEVENTH NAWAB

In Shakespeare's *Macbeth*, *'Fair is foul, and foul is fair,'* is a leitmotif that finds resonance throughout the play. Shakespeare made sure he projected the act of killing King Duncan by Macbeth as a dishonourable regicide – the deliberate killing of a ruling monarch or an heir apparent, or any other reigning sovereign. Monarchs, kings and their immediate family who are bestowed with the Royal status, brings with it grandeur, privilege and power – but also danger, particularly the risk of assassination by those craving that power, as well as anarchists who want to create disorder in the society. Arguably, the most (in)famous regicide would be the assassination of the Archduke Franz Ferdinand – heir to the Austro-Hungarian Empire – in June 1914. It was this assassination that triggered the First World War, thereby changing the course of history.

In India, as is earlier mentioned elsewhere in this book, Ashok – the Great, murdered ninety-nine brothers of his to usurp the throne of Magadh. In 396 C.E. in China, Emperor Xiaowu of the Jin Dynasty was murdered by his concubine, Lady Zhang. Similarly, in the Roman Empire, Brutus's killing of

The Islamnagar Fort where Nazar Mohammad Khan was murdered

Julius Caesar and innumerable other examples of assassinations over the centuries, of kings, queens, princes and princesses the world over, have made the act of regicide an inalienable part of attaining power and entitlement.

The erstwhile State of Bhopal, too, was witness to one such gruesome political assassination. This was the horrific killing of the Seventh Nawab of Bhopal – Nazar Mohammad Khan.

This murder is unparalleled in its ruthlessness, inventiveness of its modus operandi, and is a masterclass in the art of creating an unimpeachable alibi.

Nawab Nazar Mohammad, who had been ruling for three and a half years, was basking in the glory of the successfully concluding a recently ratified treaty with the British that not only recognized him as the *de jure* Nawab, but also ensured him of the full support of the British, in the event of an attack by the hostile neighboring Maratha kingdoms of Nagpur and Gwalior.

Nawab Nazar Mohammad Khan

This was seen as a major accomplishment in 1819, as a result of which the royal house of Bhopal had firmly ensconced itself in the polity of the British Empire. After facing a succession crisis, in which his father Wazir Mohammad Khan, the saviour of Bhopal, chose him over his elder brother, the profligate Amir Mohammad Khan, it seemed Nazar's battles were over at last. Little did anyone realize that his enemies were plotting a heinous crime that would shake the entire feudal family fabric of Bhopal.

On 11 November 1819, Nazar was reclining on a cot with his eighteen-month-old daughter Sikandar and a few cousins on the ramparts of his ancestral fort in Islamnagar, contentedly soaking up the warmth of the mild winter sun and enjoying the prattle of his infant daughter. The serenity and stupor of the languid afternoon were suddenly shattered by the sharp crackle of a pistol shot. Apart from the shrill crying and kicking of little Sikandar, who had fallen to the ground from his lap, everybody else was frozen at the sight of the Nawab lying motionless in a pool of blood oozing out from his left temple.

When Qudsia rushed out of her room upon hearing the shot, she immediately noticed her eight-year-old younger brother, Fauzdar Mohammad Khan, holding the smoking pistol still pointed in the direction of her husband, Nawab Nazar Mohammad! This pistol had, ironically, been gifted to Nazar by General Adams as a token of appreciation of his loyalty.

It eventually transpired that Nawab Ghous Mohammad, who had been deposed by the overwhelming public outcry in favour of Nawab Wazir Mohammad during the great siege of Bhopal, had meticulously planned Nazar's murder to look like it was an accident at the hands of a child playfully fiddling with a pistol.

Preliminary investigation by the family confirmed that the round was fired by taking a deliberate and pointed aim at Nazar Mohammad's temple. In those days, it was not unusual for boys of royal families, particularly among the Rajputs and the Pathans, to learn how to use weapons and firearms at an early age.

The British government, sensing trouble amidst the growing demand for revenge and rift between powerful families of Bhopal, decided to play down the situation, and asked its political agent, Major Henley to prepare a report on the incident. Major Henley camped in Islamnagar and prepared a slim report, in which he tried to prove that the fatal shot fired by Fauzdar Mohammad was indeed an accident resulting from a curious child fiddling with a firearm. Henley's report is testimony to the shrewd and manipulative manoeuvres the British very often resorted to.

The only far-reaching positive fallout of this incident was that Qudsia Begum became the Regent on 14 November 1819, thus paving the way for the smooth and successful historic reign of three successive Begums after her.

TWENTY

THE MAGNANIMITY OF THE NAWABS

When the Nawab of Oudh, Asif-ud-Daula came to know that owing to his legendary generosity, the people had coined a ditty in his honour: 'Jis ko na de Maula, usko de Asif-ud-Daula'.

He is also said to have coined another one in the same meter: *'Jis ko de de Maula, usko kya de Asif-ud-Daula'.*

The magnanimity and the altruistic side of erstwhile rulers of princely states in pre-independence India were never publicly announced. They were largely passed down the generations of the beneficiaries, mostly as family tales. More often than not, it was the rulers themselves who discouraged publicity and hoopla, and preferred to cover their benevolent acts with the predictability of routine affairs.

The Nawabs of Bhopal, too, performed their share of acts of kindness and charity, with humility and subtlety. Four prominent instances that stand out, and are still talked about by some members of the Nawabs' descendants.

Nawab Moez Mohammad Khan was the eldest son of the fifth Nawab, Ghous Mohammad Khan. Even though Moez was not able to wrest the *de jure* powers of the head of state, he still lead a highly decadent and hedonistic life. He met the expenses of his extravagance with the income from his personal *jagir*. He was very fond of exotic and expensive things, and traders from all over would flock to him to display their wares and entice him into buying them. Moez did not spend just on himself. Whenever he was happy after a shopping spree, he was known to throw lavish parties for the traders who he patronised. He was also sensitive enough to realise that his minions and servants would normally never be able to savour royal *haute cuisine*, and so he would organise lavish banquets for them as well.

But, as was bound to happen with such reckless squandering, some of his staff devised a method to extricate substantial amounts of money from Moez whenever they were in need of it. They thought that the Nawab would never part with any money unless there was a dramatic reason for it. They would therefore, cook up outlandish stories, like telling him that the gold coins which were lying in the treasury, were being eaten by termites and needed to be put out in the sun immediately! Though the Nawab obviously understood their hidden agenda, he allowed them to bring out the gold coins and pretend to dry them in the sun. During the course of sifting gold coins, he would deliberately toss away a handful here and a fistful there, which the servants would then gleefully pounce upon.

The ninth Nawab, Jahangir Mohammad Khan, was a good friend of the ruler of Panna, a neighbouring state. He was once invited to stay at the palace of the Maharaja of Panna, and was accorded a grand reception. As was customary, while leaving for home, the Nawab wanted to tip the orderlies and other staff of the Maharaja who had served him so well. But the Maharaja had already instructed his staff not to accept any gifts from the Nawab. Sensing this, the Nawab resorted to a trick, and before he left, he put enough gold coins and precious stones under the pillow on his bed in the guest quarters, and also flung some under the bed. He presumed that the house-keeping staff and other attendants would find the booty and keep it, thus serving his purpose.

But the Nawab was outsmarted by the honesty and integrity of the Maharaja's staff. To his surprise, when he was bidding goodbye to the Maharaja, he was told that the servants had found gold coins and gems in his room which he had probably forgotten to pack. The Nawab's repartee, however, disarmed the Maharaja. The Nawab refused to take them back saying they now no longer belonged to him, and by a divine gesture, were meant for those who had found them.

It was not just in terms of money and treasures, but also through of kindly gestures towards their subjects, that truly benevolent rulers left a lasting impression, which became a part of local folklore with the passage of time.

There is a story often narrated by some old residents of a *mohalla* called *chhavni valaytiyan itwaara*. Most houses located in this *mohalla* belonged to the 'khuddar' (loosely meaning self-respecting) *Barru-Kat* Pathans. All the houses had low boundary walls built of mud tiles. Once, a member of the royal family happened to be passing through this *mohalla*, riding an elephant. Because of the height of the elephant, he could easily see into the courtyards of the houses from the *houdah*. When the Pathans saw this, they blocked the cavalcade and conveyed to the royal riding the elephant that he could not pass through this *mohalla* as his entourage was intruding upon the privacy of their womenfolk. This, at a time when a person could be put to death merely on the assumption of disrespect to the royalty in any way. To his credit, the Nawab, too, promptly ordered his retinue to change course immediately.

The fourth such incident is about Begum Sikandar Jahan, who wanted to build a palace for herself. For this she chose a site which already had a hut along with the traditional Hindu *tulsi chaura*. Both belonged to a poor brahmin. Sikandar ordered her officials to rehabilitate the brahmin in a place of his choice and adequately compensate him. But the brahmin refused to move, citing the puja that he and his forebears had been performing at the *tulsi chaura* for hundreds of years. Sikandar, showing utmost respect for the sentiments of the brahmin, asked her architects to design the palace, keeping the hut and the *chaura* intact!

Many such tales and legends are passed on through palace staff and other denizens, though more often than not replete with bombastic details, nevertheless manage to bring to the fore a different, more human face of royalty.

TWENTY-ONE

THE CURIOUS CASE OF THE ROYAL DRESSING GOWN

The colonial English press always mocked the strange dressing sense and apparel of visiting dignitaries from British protectorates and colonies, if they did not fit in their social protocol (which they very often did not). Through uncharitable headlines and the use of colourful phrases, they would belittle the visitors in a bid to entertain their readers. Churchill's disparaging remark – the 'half-naked fakir' – for Mahatma Gandhi infamously became a pet phrase with London newspapers of the time.

That said, even the stiff upper-lipped English were in awe of the pageantry and regalia surrounding, in particular, the Indian royalty. Indian royals would try to fit in by trying to speak and behave more like the English than the English themselves! The refined Oxbridge accent, impeccably stitched Savile Row suits, scented Balkan Sobranie cigarettes smoked through gem-studded, gold cigarette holders and Louis Vuitton travel accessories, all formed an essential part of the Indian royals' trappings, which were on display specially during their trips to Europe.

But there were exceptions, of course. The feisty Sultan Jahan Begum of Bhopal never believed in such ostentation, not even while calling on the King Emperor himself. She always appeared in public in a *burqa*. Her frugality and ignorance about what may be termed as 'worldly trappings' could, however, sometimes land her in situations that could be taken as breach of protocol.

During a visit to London in the winter of 1925, her advancing age and London's severe winters kept her huddled in her bedroom. Sultan Jahan was an avid shopper. Exclusive luxury stores like Harrods, Selfridges and Gerrard lined up at her doorstep to display their merchandise, and she would shop from the cozy comfort and privacy of her bedroom. On one such occasion, much to her delight, she found some gowns in one of the displays. She thought these to be formal gowns that she could replace her *burqas* with, to successfully counter the English winter. No ordinary coat could cover her up to her ankles as the *burqa* did. So she ordered for a few of those gowns to be bought for herself.

Even her attendants were unaware of her intentions, and assumed that the new dressing gowns were meant to keep Her Highness warm inside the house. But the Nawab Begum was so fascinated with the comfortable robes that one fine day, adorning a tiara and dressed in one of her new dressing gowns, she landed up at the Buckingham Palace for a highly formal visit to King George and Queen Mary.

Her suave heir apparent and youngest son, Hamidullah Khan, who himself was extremely conscious of protocol, came to know of this debacle only when London newspapers splashed photographs of the incident on their front pages with mischievous headlines like – 'Her Highness, Nawab Sultan Jahan Begum, G.C.S.O., G.C.I.E., G.B.E., Ruler of Bhopal State, at Buckingham Palace in a Mauve Dressing Gown'. Hamidullah was dumbfounded at this, and had to approach some English royals who he was close to, in order to mitigate this blunder lest it was perceived as cocking a snook at the Crown, and be declared a serious breach of protocol on Begum Sultan Jahan's part.

Hamidullah was, after all, aware of the severity with which some of his fellow royals had been treated when they inadvertently landed themselves in some unintentional and trivial breach of protocol, which the London Office on the recommendation of the Viceroy, had construed to be a *lese-majesty*. Some had had their titles downgraded, while others had make do with a reduced number of gun salutes, to mention a few repercussions. However, it was because of his friendship with the Prince of Wales and other English aristocrats, that Hamidullah could manage to keep his simple but worldly-wise mother off the list of protocol breaching Indian royalty.

TWENTY-TWO

MUSIC AND DANCE AND SULTAN JAHAN BEGUM

Queen Elizabeth II apparently has a favourite song that she likes dancing to. It is the famous ABBA pop number, 'Dancing Queen'! Reportedly, a few years ago, after a palace banquet, the Queen took to the dance-floor saying, 'I always try to dance when this song comes on, because I am the Queen, and I like to dance!'

Tidbits, gossip, speculation, news items or practically any scrap of information on royal families and royal happenings have always been eagerly lapped up by the public. In olden times, too, the lives of kings and princes would be observed in great detail and then gossip and conjecture was spread around by palace maids and servants, the 'hazzams' (barbers and masseurs), or royal hangers-on.

The last Begum Nawab, Sultan Jahan, is largely perceived to have had a 'stiff upper-lip' – a dour demeanour that usually did not betray any human foibles or emotion, at least in public. She frowned upon frivolous gestures and actions in public. However, some hilarious instances involving her have been mentioned by her granddaughter Abida Sultan, in which the ageing 'grey tigress' started taking lessons in music and on one occasion, even performed a traditional Afghan dance! To quote Abida Sultan:

> 'Occasionally ...Sarkar Amma would work herself up into one of her frivolous moods, snatching away the drum from one of her retainers, and would bang away to the accompaniment of her own tremulous cracked voice, painfully out of tune and out of time!'

During one of her vacations in Ooty, she even tried to play the mandolin, despite being completely tone deaf. Then, once again, at the age of sixty-seven during her visit to London in connection with the famous succession case in 1925, completely out of the blue, she started to learn to play the harp, and also sang duets with her new-found friends amongst the titled nobility of London. Amongst them was one Countess Tomascovitch, who was perhaps as tone deaf as the Begum. Together, the two ladies would sing in their shrill voices, making such strange sounds that her granddaughter Abida Sultan, who was accompanying her to London, has written:

> 'When we first heard the weird sounds emanating from Sarkar Amma's sacrosanct bedroom, we mistook them for her cats and cockatoos!'

Another instance, perhaps the only one that reveals the human angle of the Begum's personality was during the *nashra* ceremony of her granddaughter. Upset over the arrogance shown by the more refined royal gentry of Bhopal, like the family of her in-laws – the Jalalabadis – she, in the presence of many of her women subjects, broke into an impromptu local Afghan folkdance, the *luddi*, which is generally performed by males and has some not so lady-like movements!

Such stories that offer glimpses of the human side of royalty also substantiate the torment and heavy personal cost that they pay for being born to the manor.

TWENTY-THREE

THE SAGA OF SARKAR AMMA'S 'ACHĀR'

In the raging ideological debate on the indigenousness of sub-continental people, we tend to forget how, for ages, India has seamlessly tamed, nurtured, assimilated and evolved a unique and unparalleled civilisation and culture through the innumerable tribes and races which were either indigenous or had migrated from different corners of the World, and made this land their home. The celebrated social theorist and political psychologist, Ashis Nandy, calls India a melting pot, in which all ingredients assimilate together to enhance the flavour of and add their own unique qualities to the mixture, as against a salad bowl in which each ingredient retains its individual flavour and texture.

The rulers as well as the Afghan nobility of Bhopal passionately imbibed the local culture. Sultan Jahan Begum, fondly called 'Sarkar Amma', loved a very rustic kind of 'achār', which became the reason for a rib-tickling piece of juicy gossip in the British press!

During the succession row in 1925, the Begum, along with the heir apparent had to petition the King Emperor in person. For this, she had to travel by ship to England. Bhopal being a 19-gun-salute state, the Nawab was to be welcomed ceremonially at the port of Dover. On the day of her arrival, a massive crowd including the King Emperors' representatives and the press had gathered to receive the 'exotic' woman ruler of an Indian State, who still went around in a *burqa*.

When the Begum alighted from the ship with her uniformed and dazzling retinue and walked amidst the boom of the gun-salute and the band playing the Bhopal State anthem, she suddenly stopped and demanded that her achār should go along with her in the same car. A steward was dispatched at the double to fetch the crate of the achār from the ship. The hapless fellow, not knowing the contents of the crate, lugged it upside down on his head, with the heavily spiced and rather unpleasant smelling oil spewing down his face and uniform. Horrified and visibly shaken, he was unable to bear the preposterously un-English pungent aroma of the mustard oil in the achār, and seeing his spotless white uniform turn terribly greasy and tawny, he disgustedly tossed the entire crate into the sea, right in front of the cheering crowd and furiously clicking cameras.

In her autobiography, *Memoirs of a Rebel Princess*, Abida Sultan, has a full chapter dedicated to this hilarious idiosyncrasy of her grandmother:

> 'Sarkar Amma, perhaps for the only time in her life, was rendered speechless. The shock of her precious achar being kicked into the sea in front of the ceremonial welcome party proved too much for her! But my poor father [Nawab Hamidullah Khan], whose elaborate preparations had ended in a fiasco, witnessed by the British Representatives, press and public, took the longest to be consoled.'

TWENTY-FOUR

VISIT OF THE SECRETARY OF STATE FOR INDIA

The frenzied preparations and the hustle and bustle of the retinue of nattily dressed concierges, liveried doormen, valets in embroidered 'chanvars', lackeys buttoned-up in ceremonial attire, the unobtrusive movement of the rather stiff and dour-faced English butlers, the discernible nervousness of the Begum dressed in her best *burqa* with a glittering tiara, giving the last minute instructions, the children who were preparing to blow a cloud of sneezing powder into unsuspecting visitors, this entire hullabaloo confirmed that someone very eminent was about to visit 29, Portman Square – the temporary residence of Nawab Sultan Jahan Begum of Bhopal, in London.

Ever since the time Captain William Hawkins visited the Mughal court of Emperor Jehangir in 1608, followed by Sir Thomas Roe in 1615, who was successful in obtaining two *farmans* from the Mughals, confirming free-trade which was made exempt from inland toll, the Britishers had been in awe of the grandeur, splendour and ostentatiousness of the Timurid courts and darbars. With the subsequent expansion of the East India Company, the English *nouveau riche,* referred to as 'Company Bahadurs', started emulating the lifestyles of the Mughals and the Indian royals. These are the very people that

William Dalrymple calls *The White Mughals,* in his eponymous and celebrated novel.

Gradually, recognising the fixation of Indians with pomp and regalia, the Raj officials started to exploit this to create awe and fear of authority, and sometimes to pamper their own egos as well. They began to overhype their official visits and inspections to principalities ruled by Indian rulers with ceremonial mega-*Darbars,* that came to be called the 'Chota Muaayana' and 'Bada Muaayana', terms that are still popular in the mofussil districts of India. Back home in England though, they would continue to behave and conduct themselves as commoners.

The interesting incident that was about to occur, would enlighten Begum Sultan Jahan of the fact that even senior ministers and much decorated officials of the Raj could lead austere lives. The distinguished guest who was to visit her at her London residence and for whom the extensive preparations were being made was no less a person than the Secretary of State for India, Frederick Edwin Smith, 1st Earl of Birkenhead, GCSI, PC, KC.

Lord Birkenhead was also obliging the Begum with this return visit for a highly protocol driven and sensitive dialogue on a 'vital state matter' relating to the tenuous succession case going on at that time. This visit was particularly important for the Begum, as she considered Lord Birkenhead as the last straw she could cling on to, in the hope of swinging a favourable decision for Nawab Hamidullah Khan to succeed her.

With all the frills in place, the Begum walked up to the door to receive her guest at the appointed time, wondering whether he would arrive in a Bentley or a Rolls Royce, with an escort car to boot. Suddenly, she heard Baddock, her butler, arguing with someone in a loud voice. When she peered through the door, she was aghast to see Lord Birkenhead standing there in a shabby suit holding an umbrella, being shown the gate by Baddock, who she heard saying, '*Sir, you will have to wait, as we are awaiting Lord Birkenhead's limousine.*' To this, the visitor patiently replied, '*I am Lord Birkenhead and I came by bus.*'

Even Sultan Jahan Begum, who was known for her frugal and spartan lifestyle, could never have imagined that a representative of the Queen who was placed above the Viceroy in the hierarchy of appeal, would arrive for an official visit on a bus!

TWENTY-FIVE

WAHEED MIAN

There are very few instances of a male member of a royal house committing suicide. There are recorded instances, though, of royals taking such an extreme recourse, after the family-line had been thrown out of power. Only rarely do we come across a prince from an old and established dynasty which is in power, who has taken his own life. The one that at once comes to mind is Prince Alfred of Edinburgh, who was a grandson of Queen Victoria. Alfred is rumoured to have shot himself to death in 1899, reportedly because he was suffering from a venereal disease which causes mental instability as well.

Unfortunately, in 1924, the illustrious royal house of Bhopal also had to face this heart-rending calamity. Begum Sultan Jahan's second son, General Obaidullah suffered from a mercurial and extremely volatile temper, which would flare up unexpectedly and often for no logical reason. His uncontrollable rage would then manifest itself in merciless physical abuse, including whipping, towards his children. Obaidullah was particularly harsh on his oldest son, Waheed Mian, during these angry outbursts, and would target him even for small, innocuous things.

In time, Waheed secretly married a girl from an aristocratic family, Sheher Bano, who had become pregnant during their courtship. The gossip surrounding the hush-hush marriage of his son was too much for General Obaidullah to take. He unleashed a volley of ruthless physical abuse on the couple. Sheher Bano suffered a nervous breakdown and subsequently died within months of the marriage. Waheed Mian continued to tolerate the onslaught from his father. But after some time, his spirit, too, appears to have given way due to the continuous savagery, and he decided to take the extreme step of killing himself.

Let us hear an account of this tragic scene from a member of the royal family, who does not wish to be named:

> 'The Deccan sun was sinking as Waheed trudged up the hollow wooden stairs, his footsteps beating to a quiet echo. On entering the room, he turned right and made his way straight to where he knew it was kept: the third drawer of the teak chest in the far corner. Waheed tugged the brass handle and, without pausing, reached at the back, quickly drawing the pistol from its leather case. Turning the service revolver over and over, he stood admiring, once more, the poise and symmetry of its smooth body. He listened to the nearby call of the *muezzin* as the room slowly filled with darkness. The house was stirring for Magribh, they would soon be striding to the family's mosque 200 yards away. Waheed caught the strong scent of *itar* in the room and flinched; his father had used it that morning. Pushing open the chamber with his left hand, Waheed checked for bullets, then placed the revolver gently at the end of his thick, gracefully curved right brow. He squeezed his eyes tight. Waheed was crying, but there were no tears; parts of his body were still numb from the beating that morning. There would be no more defeat, no more humiliation. The cold tip of the Webley-Scott tightly pressed on his youthful skin, Waheed tensed his forefinger upon the trigger.

We were forbidden to climb those steps. The doors were locked and cobwebs hung from every corner of the wooden staircase which lead to that room. The stairs were dusty and hardly saw any sunlight. A musty smell came from the termite-eaten wood; the derelict house was eerie. Creatures that inhabited it hooted and howled in the darkness, bats sinisterly flew in and out, and if you could cross the passage in which the staircase stood on the way to grandmother's side without wetting yourself, the other kids would applaud.

After playtime, all the kids of the house often gathered under the madhukamini tree with its bitter-sweet scented white flowers. It stood tall next to the passage that led to the stairs. We children would speculate on why everyone was so secretive, what it was that stopped the adults from telling us about the abandoned part of the house. Nothing was ever explained to us.

Julie would say, 'There is a *djinn,* there who kills children.'

'No,' Omar, the most scared one of us all, would reply, 'there is a *bhoot* in there who can enter you and take over your body and soul.'

After school, we would often sit with my nanny and other servants during their afternoon break in the sun, as they combed each other's hair and chewed *paan*. We loved listening to their stories about the people who had lived in that old, decrepit house. They told us how no one in the family wanted to speak of Waheed, who had been a handsome and intelligent young man. They never mentioned Waheed's father by name, as they believed it would invoke his spirit, which they insisted was still in the house, raging on and fuming, a palpable presence which still petrified the living.'

TWENTY-SIX

WHEN MAHARAJA OF GWALIOR HAD TO PAY A BRIBE!

The emergence of the popular princely kingdoms, as we know them today, were fraught with bloody intrigues, treachery and unholy alliances. But, at times, they showed great diplomatic finesse in handling officials of the Raj in Calcutta. The confusion, prolonged political implosions, and the frequent forming and breaking of alliances between various contenders, and ultimately, the disintegration and gradual demise of the Moghul Empire, finally saw some stability after the First War of Independence in 1857 – cautiously and sagaciously administered by the direct rule of Queen Victoria through the India Office in London.

The history of the princely State of Bhopal is also dotted with treason and intrigue. The traditional enemies of Bhopal were the Scindias of Gwalior and the Bhonsles of Nagpur. During the reign of Hayat Mohammad Khan, after Maaji Mamola Bai's death in 1795, his cousin Amir Khan conspired and colluded with Daulat Rao Scindia, raided the treasury and looted one-and-a-half lakh rupees from it. Earlier, Daulat Rao, as one of the Generals of the Peshwas, had nearly decimated the Bhopal forces.

Similarly, Ghous Mohammad Khan, the fifth Nawab, bargained away the hard-earned territories of his ancestors to the Scindias to sustain his decadent and lavish lifestyle. So much so, that at one time, the Scindias became so audacious that they formally petitioned the British to claim the State of Bhopal as their tributary! It was only the strong resistance and astute statesmanship of Wazir Mohammad Khan, which saved the day for Bhopal. Later, Wazir also emerged as the knight-in-shining-armour because of his legendary and skillful resistance during the historic siege of Bhopal by the combined forces of the Bhonsles and the Scindias in 1813.

By early twentieth century, things started to appear quite hunky-dory. An intriguing reason for it was that by now, the princes had started assessing each other in healthy competition as far as aspects like the number of ceremonial gun-salutes earned, polo and cricket matches won, the protocol of seating arrangements during the grand *Durbars* and investitures, the number of decorations and medals pinned to their chests went.

However, in many respects, it was during the almost twenty-five-year long reign of Sultan Jahan Begum (1901–1926), endearingly called 'Sarkar Amma', that Bhopal witnessed the adoption and implementation of farsighted and far-reaching public development policies which earned her accolades from the British and aroused the curiosity of the other princely states.

It was her large-scale revenue related reforms that caught the attention of the Maharaja of Gwalior, Madho Rao Scindia (1876–1925), who decided to get a first-hand account of the Begum's sagacity. In order to get an unbiased insight, he disguised himself as a rustic peasant, and arrived on a train at the Bhopal railway station; hiring a *tonga* he arrived at *Qasr-e-Sultani*, the official residence of Sarkar Amma (*Memoirs of a Rebel Princess,* by Abida Sultan). The affairs of the royal household and access to the Begum were handled by Anwar Bua, the personal maid of Sarkar Amma.

When the Maharaja rang the doorbell, Anwar Bua appeared,

Maharaja Sir Madho Rao Scindia of Gwalior

and started berating the 'rustic peasant' for disturbing her evening prayers. But the 'rustic peasant' had done his homework well. He had heard that Anwar Bua appreciated receiving tips for her services on the sly. So, he discreetly slipped a couple of rupee coins into her palm, and was promptly ushered into the 'kutchehery' of Sarkar Amma.

When the old Begum saw the peasant, she immediately noticed that something was amiss. She perhaps saw that that the peasant was not exactly dressed as a peasant generally would, or that his accent seemed too polished for a peasant. She promptly subjected him to a volley of questions and pinned him down with her detailed knowledge of the *parganas,* the villages and names of the village headmen, thus unmasking the identity of the 'rustic peasant' in no time!

TWENTY-SEVEN

WHEN THE PRINCE OF WALES WENT MISSING!

In the February of 1922, Edward, the Prince of Wales (who later went on to become King Edward VIII, and then the Duke of Windsor) visited Bhopal. It was after a long time that a member of the House of Windsor and for the first time an heir apparent to the British Crown was visiting Bhopal. Therefore, a spectacular welcome was expected to be accorded to him. Not since the time of Nawab Shahjehan Begum had such an ostentatious and extravagant event been organised, that too, by Nawab Sultan Jahan Begum, who was known to be extremely frugal and stringent about how money from the State exchequer was spent. However, this time, given the occasion, she had decided to loosen her purse strings.

The royal guest was pleased with the grand arrangements and the hospitality accorded to him. He was more than delighted to accept the offer for a 'shikar' expedition once his official engagements were over, without which his visit to India would probably have been a lackluster one.

The shikar was arranged in Kachnaria, near Sanchi, which was a known tiger habitat. It had been discreetly stage-managed so as to ensure that the Prince of Wales would definitely be able to shoot a tiger or two. But as luck would have it, the

The Prince of Wales and H.H. Sultan Jahan

royal guest could not even sight a tiger, let alone shoot one. It was thought to be all the more disturbing for the Prince of Wales, as in the past, his cousin Dickie Mountbatten (later the last Viceroy of India-Lord Mountbatten) had been much luckier and had shot not one, but two tigers!

Since there had been a clarion call by Mahatma Gandhi to boycott the Prince's visit, the Prince had been provided an extra inner cordon of security, apart from his normal security cover. This additional security cover was supervised by none other than the head of the Royal Bhopal Force, Colonel Obaidullah and his two brothers – the heir apparent Naseerullah, and Hamidullah. The security apparatus was kept subtle and unobtrusive, and highly hierarchical in order to maintain the Prince's privacy, given that he was the Crown Prince of the World's most powerful empire at that time.

But Colonel Obaidullah was not one to leave anything to

chance. Discreetly, he would himself make the customary rounds of vigil around the Prince's encampment at about midnight. One night, he noticed that the flap of the Prince's tent was ajar, and he thought that the slightly tipsy and tired Prince must have left it open to let in some fresh air. However, he decided to peep inside, just to be sure. To his utter shock and dismay, he discovered that the Prince was missing from his tent!

There was more consternation when investigation revealed, that the Prince's bed had not been slept in that night. It was immediately presumed that he had been kidnapped. In the confusion and commotion that ensued, a close aide of Colonel Obaidullah who was directly responsible for the Prince's security, threatened to commit suicide, while others went into advanced stages of a nervous breakdown! There was no sign of the Prince until breakfast the next morning, and then suddenly, he surfaced as miraculously as he had disappeared.

It was later discovered that the Prince was so discomfited at not being able to even sight a tiger during the shikar, that he assumed that it was due to the overwhelming presence of a large number of shikaris for his safety in his entourage, that the tigers had not dared to venture anywhere near the kill zones that had been earmarked for the Prince. He therefore decided to slip out of the camp on his own, and loitered around unprotected in the jungle the whole night. But alas, tigers still eluded him!

Later, to keep his *amour propre* intact, the Prince was declared, through a royal pronouncement and media flash, to have hunted not just three tigers, but other game as well! Thus, Reuters in its media advisory of 7 February 1922, reported:

> 'The Prince of Wales returned to Bhopal from Kachnaria this afternoon. The Royal party of seven guns bagged three tigers, one panther, eleven sambhars, one cheetah and two neelgais.'

TWENTY-EIGHT

THE PRICE OF A BEGUM'S HAND

Most of the famous royal dynasties of Medieval India have left their footprints in nearly all spheres of life. More often than not, the royal houses that succeeded them, subconsciously and sometimes deliberately, imbibed and practiced the cultural mores, way of living and other traits that they inherited from the dynasties preceding them. For example, the Mughal emperors inherited the lavish lifestyle, urban outlook and distinctiveness of Ghiyas-ud-din Balban, the last major Sultan of the Delhi Sultanate, who had in turn borrowed these aspects from the Persian courts.

Thereafter, in nearly all cities or urban settlements in Medieval India, traces of the Mughal ethos were noticeable. In fact, in some instances, the legacy is still surviving. One such remnant of Mughal heritage is the 'Meena bazaar'.

It was started by Humayun, the second Mughal Emperor, in Agra and was held during the first five days of *Navroz* (the New Year), a period referred to as *kuhs ruz* (roughly meaning fun-filled days). The Meena bazaar was a market exclusively for ladies of the royal household, ladies from other noble families and women from the harem of the emperor. These women set up their own stalls and traded in goods like fabric, dress-material, jewellery, hand-crafted artefacts, toiletries, food-stuff and other sundry knick-knacks of interest to women-folk. The only males who had access to these 'females only' fairs were the emperor himself and high ranking princes.

During his reign, Shahjehan, the fifth Mughal Emperor, elevated the concept and adapted it into an elite marketplace called *Bazaar-i-Musaqaf* (literally meaning a market with a roof), to showcase the astonishing wealth and refined taste of his empire. This was Asia's first covered market, and still exists as Meena bazaar in the precincts of the Red Fort in Agra.

Needless to say, Meena bazaars cropped up in nearly all prosperous cities of the Mughal era, like Lucknow, Lahore, Murshidabad, Dhaka and Hyderabad – as markets for the upper crust. Goods, often consisting of the expensive *shatoot* and *pashmina* shawls, saffron, finely designed handicrafts etc. were sold at rather high prices. Notably, earnings were distributed amongst the not-so-rich women as *Zakat,* an Islamic act of piety.

In erstwhile Bhopal, although many aspects of the old Mughal courts were brought into fashion and were practiced, particularly by Shahjehan Begum, a Meena baazar, re-christened as 'Pari bazaar', was established only in 1904 by Sultan Jahan Begum. She wanted the women of Bhopal, irrespective of the class and creed, to set up stalls and trade in a gamut of goods and items so that they could augment their household income. The goods sold here were predominantly articles used by the women. Women from noble families often visited this market to make purchases and also to appreciate the products on sale and encourage the practice, Sultan Jahan Begum herself being a regular visitor to this bazaar.

Pari Bazaar also became a meeting place for the older generation of ladies to share gossip and the latest scandalous news, and for younger girls to exchange information on their latest romantic liaisons!

Indira Iyengar, in her book – *The Bourbons and Begums*

of Bhopal recounts an interesting story about the repartee of a woman bangle-seller, which goes thus:

> On one of her routine visits to Pari bazaar, Sultan Jahan Begum stopped at a stall which had some very attractive bangles on display. It was a big moment for the overjoyed stall-owner who, in her enthusiasm of being honoured by the visit of Her Highness herself, fully covered the Begum's hands with beautiful bangles. Sultan Jahan, in all her humility, appreciated the woman's gesture and enquired about the price of the bangles. To this, the woman quoted an exorbitant amount. Not amused, the Begum asked her as to why she was being overcharged. The witty repartee of the woman was, 'I am not asking this price for the bangles, but for the price of hands that wear these bangles.'

The origin of the Meena bazaars during the Mughal era was patronising and patriarchal, because of the *purda* system and the practice of strict segregation of the sexes. But in the case of Nawab Sultanjahan of Bhopal, emancipation and empowerment of women were the paramount reasons for her to establish her own *Pari bazaar – the Market of Fairies*!

Bhopal continues to honour this tradition through endeavours almost similar in essence and motive, like the annual 'Potters Bazaar' and various other handicraft 'haats' in Gauhar Mahal. These are no longer 'only for women' markets, though the clientele is primarily women, as are the sellers who take out time out from their domestic and professional schedules to display and sell their own creations.

TWENTY-NINE

THE ROYAL RETRIBUTION

The general ambience and atmosphere of the princely states during the Raj era, particularly in the early nineteenth century after the First War of Independence of 1857, was pretty much laid back and languid. The administration revolved around the routine tax collection with symbolic welfare schemes. The British resident commissioner invariably ran the show. Historians generally aver that it suited the British to encourage the Princes to lead a decadent lifestyle filled with musical soirees, shikars etc. to keep them from planning or staging a coup of any sort against the Raj. The Princes patronised many musicians, singers, artists, instrumentalists, who in turn, developed their specific genres which now form an important part of the cultural legacy of the subcontinent.

Bhopal certainly was not a run-of-the-mill princely State. The Begums ensured that the *hoi polloi* were kept happy. They stayed away from all symbols of princely decadence. Shahjehan Begum however was different; she gave a new meaning to this so called symbol of decadence. She herself was an accomplished musician and knew the nuances of the *aaroh* and *avroh* of the ragas and was a known connoisseur and patron of Hindustani Classical music. Her Court was adorned with renowned classical singers like Ustad Mohammad Khan, Kathak dancers like the famous Kalka Binda and instrumentalists like the great tabla player, Kishan Maharaj, who would perform regularly at her court.

Once, a famous classical singer from Bombay (who could perhaps have been Gauhar Jaan or Zohrabai), who was known to keep audiences waiting and sometimes also refused invitations to perform from kings and princes, conveyed her desire to perform in Bhopal. She had heard about the grand musical evenings organised by Shahjehan Begum and other Bhopali aristocrats, and the liberal land grants and precious gems they gave artists as 'nazrana'. But no one in Bhopal would invite her because of the exorbitant fee she charged. Stung by the snub, the singer started a smear campaign against the Bhopal royals, and was heard taunting their stinginess. When Shahjehan Begum heard of this, she decided to invite the singer to perform in her court.

The evening was extraordinarily alluring, with an eclectic gathering of exalted aristocracy of Bhopal, court musicians and English sahibs and memsahibs anxiously waiting for the arrival of Shahjehan Begum. Soon, the petite Begum emerged and ensconced herself on her *gaddi.*

Writes Shaharyar Khan in his seminal book *The Begums of Bhopal*:

> 'The singer along with her troupe rose and paid her the customary obeisance. No sooner than she started to sing the *alaap,* Shahjehan Begum put both her hands on her ears shrieked, *'I have never heard such a besura (out of tune) voice – please spare me this torture, pay this woman double her fees but I cannot spoil my evening with the murder of these beautiful ragas'.*

Shahjehan Begum, thus, paid back the snooty singer in her own coin. The singer was publicly humiliated for commenting derisively on the Bhopali culture and aristocrats who were known patrons of art and artists. The modus operandi of this royal retribution is conspicuous for the finesse with which it was executed, and remains a memorable oral tradition, still passed on by Ustads and Gurus to their respective Shagirds and Shishyas.

SECTION FOUR

Feudalism and Modernity

ONE

THE NAWAB OF BHOPAL AND THE INDEPENDENCE MOVEMENT

Bhopal was at centre-stage during the tumultuous political scenario of the forties, right from the Quit India movement of 1942, until its eventual merger with the Union of India in 1949. The modern, erudite and liberal Nawab Hamidullah Khan – the last Nawab of Bhopal – was respected equally by both, the nationalists struggling for Independence, and the British government. He had a close rapport with Pt. Jawaharlal Nehru, as well as Lord Louis Mountbatten.

A complex personality, Hamidullah Khan could be, at the same time, a regressive feudal royalist with modern political views, or a shrewd and ambitious game-changer. He loved his people without a doubt, but was unappreciative of any ideologically different political movement brewing in his state. An example of this was when leaders of a merger movement – the Praja Mandal movement – had posters with anti-British slogans printed, urging the Nawab of Bhopal to join the Quit India movement, he reacted with hostility and had all the top leaders of the movement arrested. This caused in widespread public unrest, and eventually culminated in the merger of the Princely State of Bhopal with the Madhya Bharat state of the Union of India on 30 April 1949.

N.B. Bonarjee, First Chief Commissioner of Bhopal

Hamidullah was on very good terms with deposed as well as constitutional monarchs of Europe, the Indian Sub-continent, Turkey, Saudi Arabia, Afghanistan and Iran. His genuine affection for Bhopal was amply clear by the fact that from the time he took over as the Nawab in 1926, he began to usher in a series of reforms, which incontrovertibly propelled Bhopal on the road to become a modern State.

Although he even invited Mahatma Gandhi to visit Bhopal in September 1929, and was largely perceived as a son of the soil and a patriot, Hamidullah was lured by Mohammad Ali Jinnah's invitation to merge Bhopal with the proposed state of Pakistan. Jinnah reportedly offered him a lucrative, hard-to-turn-down proposal – that he would be made the premier of the newly formed Pakistan, once he accepted the merger and after Jinnah announced his retirement from politics in June 1947.

Torn between his personal ambition, his attachment to his family and to the land of his forefathers, Hamidullah went into an anguished state of confusion and indecisiveness. He also seemed to have a genuine desire to maintain sovereignty with the other princely states as he had been elected as the Chancellor of the Chamber of Princes twice, first in 1932 and again in 1944.

His troubled mental state, when he had to finally decide

Princess Abida Sultan

on the of merger of Bhopal has been vividly captured by his eldest daughter, Abida Sultan, in her autobiography:

> 'On being ushered to his room, I found him sitting alone, sweating heavily. He then pulled out his revolver and pointing it straight at me, ordered me to sit down. "I am leaving soon for Pakistan," he said, "I want you to take over the affairs of the State. I shall probably be appointed Governor-General. Jinnah has asked me to come over."'

Abida's reply was equally candid:

> 'I am unarmed. As for the State, it is for you to decide what you want to do with it. I shall not be a party to its merger in the Indian Union and for people to say that a woman could not prevent the handover of a State that our forebears had won through blood and sacrifice.'

Huzun of an Heir Apparent

The Princely State of Bhopal was taken over by the government of the Union of India on 1 June 1949. The archaic system of feudalism that had existed in its myriad forms – monarchy, taluqdari, jagirdari, zamindari etc. – and in spite of all its inherent fault lines and shortcomings, had thrived for hundreds of years. It may have been an inadequate system of governance, but some of the best and most enduring artistic, cultural and architectural motifs and practices emerged from feudalism, with active and absolute patronage of the rulers.

For the erstwhile ruling elite and their kith and kin, the loss of feudal estates would have been interlaced with a sense of welcoming and anticipation for something new and different, along with an agonising sense of loss.

It's not a coincidence that when a behemoth of an empire falls, many segments of the society which have thrived on the system are left asunder, and an overwhelming sense of the loss and dejection prevails, which results in clinging to the remnants of the past. It is something close to nostalgia, or as Orhan Pamuk describes it through the Turkish word, 'huzun', in *'Istanbul: Memories of a City'.*

When Louis XVI was going to be guillotined in France, a last chance was given to him by the erstwhile royalists who included Talleyrand and others. They asked him to publicly announce that he was no longer the king of France but was the king of the French. Louis XVI had refused to do this.

The sensitivity to understand such complex and devastating emotion is rare. A poignant incident on the day of the merger, 1 June 1949, negates the belief that bureaucrats often lack empathy. The Bhopal State was declared a 'Part C' State after the merger, and was to be governed by a Chief Commissioner appointed by the President of India.

The Nawab of Bhopal arriving to meet Mr V. P. Menon on the merger of Bhopal with the Union of India

N.B. Bonarjee, ICS, was appointed the Chief Commissioner for Bhopal. Extremely well-disposed towards the Bhopal Royal family, particularly Begum Maimoona Sultan and her heir apparent Abida Sultan, Bonarjee was well aware of the agony the royals were undergoing during the process of handing over the reins of power to a democratic government. As head of the government of Bhopal, he was to organise a joint ceremony to celebrate the merger, where the flag of erstwhile royal Bhopal State was to be lowered, and the national flag of India was to be hoisted in its place. Protocol demanded that Nawab Hamidullah Khan be present on the occasion. But since Hamidullah was not available, Bonarjee decided to invite Princess Abida Sultan for the ceremony.

But the feisty Princess wrote back, *'Mr Bonarjee, you are going to lower Bhopal's flag after 250 years of rule by my family. I will not come and nor will any other member of the ruling family.'* Although this was almost blatant effrontery to the head of government, Bonarjee's reply to the princess was steeped in humility and respect; he wrote back saying, *'Princess, I understand your sentiments. I should have known before inviting you. We shall meet later.'*

As Faiz Ahmad Faiz has said:

'Azmat-e-rafta ke nishāñ pesh-e-manzar meñ
kisī sāya-e-dīvār se liptā huā saaya koī
dūsre sāye kī mauhūm sī ummīd liye.'

(Vestiges of past glory
have begun to look hazy against the skyline
and there, in front of the eye,
a shadow embraces the shadow of a wall,
cherishing the faint hope for another shadow).

TWO

'GANDHIGIRI' IN BHOPAL

Principalities during the colonial era, including Bhopal, despite being sovereign states in their own right, tended to directly or indirectly pledge their allegiance to the British Crown. The rulers of these principalities had to maintain a delicate balance between their patronage to the British on the one hand, and channelising the fast evolving nationalist sentiments of their subjects, and for at least some of them, their own reverence for Mahatma Gandhi and his crusade for independence, on the other.

Nawab Hamidullah Khan was himself a closeted admirer of the Mahatma. His sophomore days at the Aligarh Muslim University had moulded him into a liberal and modern democrat. In 1932, the Bhopal Royal family accompanied Gandhi to London, and got to know him personally when they spent time with him on board the ocean-liner, 'Kaiser-e-Hind'.

The behind the scenes manoeuvrings of Begum Nawab Sultan Jahan and Hamidullah Khan in support of the *Khilafat* movement (1919–1921) as a pan-Islamic movement, brought both of them closer to the Mahatma. This also had its precedence in the gifting of the holy strand of hair to Begum Sultan Jahan by the last Ottoman Emperor. Mahatma Gandhi supported the *Khilafat* movement not because he wanted the decadent *Khalifat* to continue owing to his uncompromising

Gandhi at the Bhopal Railway Station

secular *weltanschauung*, but because he wanted to stop the European powers from declaring war on an Asian country.

It was not surprising therefore, that immediately after Hamidullah was sworn-in as the thirteenth Nawab, he invited Mahatma Gandhi to Bhopal. The Mahatma arrived in Bhopal on 11 September 1929, on a three-day visit. Thus, 'Gandhigiri' in Bhopal was definitely not a mass movement in the initial years, but was to trickle down gradually into the subconscious of the denizens of the State.

Furthermore, in essence, Gandhigiri was already being practiced by the Begum Nawab Sultan Jahan, and this was noticed and acknowledged by Gandhiji himself. When Gandhiji met Sultan Jahan after she had abdicated in favour of Hamidullah, she greeted him in her palace seated on a mattress laid out on the floor, and attired in her usual choice of fabric – cotton. Intrigued, Gandhiji is said to have asked Sarojini Naidu, who was a good friend of the Begum's: *'Is this how she lives always... with such simplicity and humility, and such affection for her subjects? Or is this just a put-on for me?'*

Rahat Manzil, where Mahatma Gandhi stayed during his Bhopal visit

During Gandhi's short stop-over at the Bhopal railway station in 1933, the Nawab spared no efforts to keep the visit a secret. But Gandhi made sure that the news of his arrival spread via his trusted emissaries who, in politically correct terms, were called the 'prabhat pheriwalas'! It is only because of political patronage that they received in the early stages of their political careers, that renowned Gandhians like Shankar Dayal Sharma and Ramcharan Rai etc. cut their political teeth.

The places that the Mahatma went to during his visit to Bhopal also earned their place in history. A special prayer meeting was held in the atrium of the 'Rahat Manzil', adjacent to the Ahmadabad Palace where Gandhi stayed, and all the members of the Bhopal royal family participated in it. 'Benazir Maidan' became a historical ground after Gandhi addressed a huge public gathering there. 'Modh Ki Bagiya', where the local Gujrati Samaj honoured Gandhi, also gained a mention in history.

THREE

THE LAST *QIṢĀṢ* IN BHOPAL

Q*iṣāṣ* is Arabic for 'retaliation in kind', or simply, 'revenge'. It is a system of retributive punishment that the Islamic Sharia law allows to the victim or his kin, against a convicted perpetrator of murder or intentional bodily injury. In the case of murder, *qisās* gives the victim or his kin the right to take the life of the killer, if the latter is convicted and the court approves. Those entitled to *qisās*, also have the option of receiving monetary compensation (*Diyya*), in exchange for granting pardon to the perpetrator.

Although in this day and age, it appears to be an extremely brutal and primitive form of jurisprudence, Immanuel Kant, the renowned German philosopher who is considered to be the harbinger of modern philosophical theory, justified it. He states that the act that the person has performed 'is to be regarded as perpetrated on himself'. This he refers to as the 'principle of retaliation'. So, in its application a thief would have had his hands chopped off and the murderer would be guillotined etc. Thus, the metaphysical inference of Kant's justification of retributivism, vis à vis the mode of punishment, lies in the ethics of retaliation and is induced by the ethics of equality.

The Bhopal Princely State being a predominantly Muslim state, too had *qisās* as a form of punishment for its Muslim subjects. The punishment, which was most often a public execution, was conducted at an open ground, which is currently known as the Lal parade ground. The 'Lal' (the colour red) in its name apparently comes from the blood of the convicts who were executed there under *qisās*. A public announcement of the date and time of a *qisās* execution was made eight days in advance, so that those who wished to witness it could do so.

Because of the truly multi-religious culture of Bhopal, many rich and influential Hindu merchants, who could not bear the sheer brutality of public executions, would often offer to pay retribution money to the victim's kin, thereby buying a pardon for the convict.

In the year 1937, Miss Brown, the Anglo-Indian principal of Sultania School in Bhopal, decided to organise a cleanliness drive in the school. In the process, some old books, documents and files that were thought to be redundant were thrown away as trash. Inadvertently, a few pages from the Holy Quran got mixed up with the waste paper and got discarded with it. Someone happened to discover this, and reported it to the religious clergy. This led to massive indignation in the Muslim community, who took it as humiliation and grave disrespect of their Holy Book. The Nawab, realising the gravity and volatility of the situation, immediately ordered an enquiry into the incident. If found guilty, Miss Brown, a Christian herself, could go on trial for blasphemy – a very serious offence, indeed.

The Bhopal State being an ally and protectorate of the British, the Nawab was advised in private by the British Political Agent stationed there to go soft on the prosecution of Miss Brown. It was made clear to him that a conviction of any kind meted out to a European living under the patronage of the British Crown, would not go down well with the Viceroy's office.

Thus, Miss Brown was absolved of all charges against her at the enquiry stage itself. However, in order to appease the sentiments of his Muslim subjects, the Nawab implored his people to grant forgiveness to Miss Brown. The public appeared to let the matter rest there, but for one person – who went by the name of Banne Khan. He decided to stalk Miss Brown with the intention of killing her. One day, as she was strolling near the Motia talaab, he stabbed Miss Brown with a knife, fatally wounding her. Banne Khan was tried and convicted for murder in 1938, under the *qiṣāṣ* law.

As Nawab Hamidullah Khan was away on one of his political soirees as Chancellor of the Chamber of Princes, his daughter and heir, Abida Sultan, held fort in Bhopal during this time. The Qazi confirmed the death sentence given to Banne, and as per law, the decision on the mercy petition rested on Princess Abida. There were mass demonstrations in favour of Banne Khan, asking for his death sentence to be commuted, and even demanding the invocation of royal pardon. But the death sentence to Banne Khan was upheld by the Princess and he was publically put to death.

After this, however, sensing the extensive damage the situation had caused to the religious sentiments of the people, the British prevailed upon the Nawab to abolish this gruesome system once and for all. Thus, Banne Khan's public execution in 1938 was the last *qiṣāṣ* execution to take place in Bhopal. Incidentally, the last public execution in the United States of America was in Owensboro, Kentucky, in 1936. It was of a black man who was found guilty of the rape and murder of a wealthy white widow.

The fact remains that an enlightened kingdom like the Bhopal State with its model welfare schemes never ever tried to do away with such an anachronistic and inhuman law. The Nawab, even though ostensibly modern and omnipotent, was none the less under the sway of the Qazis and the Maulvis. The British also seemed to have looked the other way when it came to their interference in religious matters. Only when it came to their own race did they prevail upon the Nawab to end this practice.

Clearly for the natives, justice was always opaque, like the character of Dr. Aziz in E.M. Forster's celebrated novel, *A Passage to India*.

FOUR

THE BATTLE FOR BHOPAL AS CAPITAL

In Manzoor Ahtesham's celebrated and award-winning novel, *Sookha Bargad,* which is set in the Bhopal of the fifties and sixties, one of the protagonists laments, *'...yah socho ki yah shahar agar rajdhaani na bana hota to yahan kya hota?'* This angst actually echoed the sentiments of most of the residents of Bhopal in the early fifties. Those were post World War-II days, when the aftereffects of famine were aggravated by widespread unemployment and therefore, discontent and disillusionment.

After its merger with the Union of India in 1949, an independent Bhopal State continued to exist, first as a 'Part-C' State, administered by a Chief Commissioner, and later from 1952 to 1956, as a federal state, with Shankar Dayal Sharma as its first and last Chief Minister. This period also witnessed many peoples' movements for regional and linguistic identity and representation. Pt. Nehru could clearly read the writing on the wall, and took the bold decision of carving out federal states on the basis of the predominant language spoken in the particular region, even though this decision was fraught with deeply divisive undercurrents. Thus, the State Reorganisation Commission (SRC) was formed in 1956, and based on its recommendations, four regions – parts of Central Province and Berar, Madhya Bharat, Vindhya Pradesh and Bhopal State were merged together to form the state of Madhya Pradesh.

Pt. Ravi Shankar Shukla, the first Chief Minister of Madhya Pradesh

The real battle began when powerful regional satraps, like the Maharaja of Gwalior, the Holkars of Indore, Nawab Hamidullah Khan of Bhopal and political heavyweights from Jabalpore (now, Jabalpur), started serious lobbying for their respective cities to be declared as the capital city of Madhya Pradesh. Nehru left it to Pt. Ravishankar Shukla, who later became the first Chief Minister of Madhya Pradesh, to decide on the capital. After numerous debates, altercations, and claims and counter-claims, which, no doubt, must have left many bruised egos, Shukla finally decided on Bhopal to be the capital. This happened just in the nick of time, as Jabalpore was almost selected because of its importance to the British, the presence of a High Court and large military establishments there. Indore, too had its fair share of claims: it was the largest city in the state, thriving with enterprise and business. Gwalior's claim was its historicity and its proximity to New Delhi.

How did Bhopal, then, prevail over the strong competition to win the coveted honour? There are several reasons that can be attributed to this – most importantly, Pt. Nehru's hints to the ad hoc cabinet – he was a friend of Nawab Hamidullah Khan. The other important factors that clinched the deal for Bhopal were its geographical centrality and it being on the main railway line. Further, the scope of all-round incremental development, the presence of a perennial source of water

Ravishankar Shukla being sworn-in as the First Chief Minister of Madhya Pradesh

supply, a moderate climate etc. Last but not least, Bhopal had a long tradition of seamless amalgamation of diverse elements in its culture, making it the proverbial 'melting pot', which in turn, symbolised the true spirit of the newly-built nation of India – 'Unity in Diversity'!

FIVE

THE FAÇADE OF SOVEREIGNTY

It is a widely believed misconception that during the Raj, rulers of the princely states of the sub-continent enjoyed the status of sovereign rulers, wielding supreme and unchallenged power. The actual fact was that both, the Viceregal office in Calcutta and the India Office in London, interfered not just in the matters of the state and statesmanship, but even in the personal lives of the satraps to an extent which, in today's day and age, would be deemed scandalous and greatly invasive to personal privacy. Most of these provincial states and their gun-salute brandishing feudal lords started to emerge as individual entities after the First War of Independence in 1857. They not only consolidated their territories in a ratio that was directly proportionate to their support to the British administration, but also amassed great wealth through sycophantic deference to the officials of the Raj.

How the British dealt with any transgressions by these vassals is a lesson in quid pro quo diplomacy. The Bhopal State witnessed serious threats from the all-encompassing and all-powerful grip of the Raj twice, when the office of the Viceroy had to contemplate repealing of the status and curtailing of the powers of the then ruler or their close kin.

The first incident concerns the Nawab Begum Shahjehan's consort Siddiq Hassan Khan, who was a non-Pathan and a Muslim scholar, and is credited with the founding of the *Ahl-*

e-Hadith movement. Soon after he joined the services of the royal house of Bhopal, he started wielding powers that could be thought of as equivalent to those of a prime minister's. His wife, the dowager Shahjehan Begum, was unaware that secretly, Hassan was promoting Wahabism, which propagated an austere form of Islam that insists on a literal interpretation of the laws laid down by the Quran. This was obviously an anathema to the British administration, which feared that this could instigate a pan-Islamic movement against them.

An enquiry under the Resident Commissioner, Sir Lepel Griffin, recommended the withdrawal of all titles bestowed upon Siddiq, and arresting him on charges of sedition. The Political Agent, Edward Thompson through his network of informants further confirmed that Siddiq Hassan had misappropriated many of the powers of the Nawab Begum.

The second incident involved the last Nawab, Hamidullah Khan, whose proximity to Pt. Nehru and Mahatma Gandhi and his Left of Centre leanings during his student days at the Aligarh Muslim University alarmed the British government. The authorities opened a dossier on him and monitored his movements and activities closely. To prove their unstinted and loyal support, Bhopal royalty also had to bear the inglorious responsibility of hosting the banishment of Maharaja of Rewa, Gulab Singh, who shared a nineteen-gun salute status with the Bhopal ruler.

Abida Sultan, the daughter of Nawab Hamidullah Khan, vindicates this and similar other embarrassments. She writes:

> 'This event underlined the vassal status of the princely states that, though superficially independent under seemingly omnipotent rulers were, in fact, under the paramount rule of the British government.'

SIX

THE KOH-I-NOOR CONNECTION

The book, *Koh-i-Noor: The Story of the World's Most Infamous Diamond*, by William Dalrymple and Anita Anand, traces the origin of the iconic diamond from mythology up to the time it ended up with its present owner, Queen Elizabeth II of England. It recounts that the most dramatic and intricate sequence of events in the succession of the diamond was, perhaps, when it was passed on by Shah Shuja, the ruler of Afghanistan, to Maharaja Ranjit Singh, the founder of the Sikh Empire. Shah Shuja had inherited the diamond from his grandfather, Ahmad Shah Abdali, the founder of the Afghan Empire.

It, however, does not mention successors of Shah Shuja. Hypothetically then, in the quirky and unforeseen '*...cunning passages, contrived corridors and... whispering ambitions ... of history*', as TS Elliot puts it, the descendants of Shah Shuja might still have been the owners of the coveted stone, at least for some period of time, before it went into the hands of Ranjit Singh. Thus comes the Bhopal connection of the Koh-i-Noor.

Sultan Jahan Begum, when it came to finding a match for her youngest son, Hamidullah Khan, was apparently eager to wriggle out of the boundaries of the fast fossilising royalty of Bhopal. She did not want Hamidullah, who was being groomed in most modern ways of life, to marry into the conventional

Ahmed Shah Abdali

Shah Shujah Durrani

and orthodox families of the Baqi-Khels and the Jalalabadis. The reason was, predominantly, her fear of the growing control of the Jalalabadis and the Baqi Khels, who could checkmate her own power through palace intrigue. She, therefore, dispatched a loyal adviser, Qandhari Khan, who was also well-versed with the Pashto language, to Kohat and Peshawar in Afghanistan to search for a suitable bride for Hamidullah from amongst the descendants of the erstwhile Afghan royalty.

The search ended when Qandhari Khan gatecrashed into the house of an Afghan widow, after spotting a five-year-old girl frolicking in water in the courtyard of that house. The little girl was Shahzadi Maimoona Sultan, a direct descendant of Ahmad Shah Abdali, and the grand-niece of Shah Shuja. Maimoona later went on to become the consort of Hamidullah Khan when she was married to him at the age of thirteen. She became the Begum of Bhopal in 1926 with the coronation of Hamidullah Khan as the Nawab of Bhopal. Maimoona was also imparted modern, Western education along with her husband, and is believed to have led the most sophisticated and refined lifestyle amongst all the royals of her time, writes Shaharyar Khan, her grandson:

> '...playing Dvorak and Chopin on the piano, her garden parties for British memsahebs, her smoking scented Balkan Sobranie cigarettes in long cigarette-holders, her speaking in French...'

SEVEN

THE BUZZ OF THE BEE ATTACK

After polo and cricket, perhaps the most popular sport amongst the royalty of vassal states during the Raj era was 'Shikār'. It would be an understatement to call shikār just a sport or a pastime as far as the Bhopal royalty were concerned, because for them shikār was a way of life, more than anything else!

Bhopal, located on the cusp of a tropical region and semi-arid terrain, is endowed with thick forests as well as savannah-like grassland. As far as wildlife was concerned, a rich and diverse variety of all kinds of animals existed here, providing every kind of game – big and small – including the one that was most prized of them all – the tiger. Successive rulers of Bhopal are known to have obliged not only the British, but also the kings and princes from neighbouring states, by hosting elaborate shikār jaunts for them.

A bizarre and rather embarrassing incident occurred in the late thirties during the reign of Nawab Hamidulah Khan, during one such shikār outing organised for Jām Sahib, the Maharajah of Nawanagar during one of his visits to Bhopal. The Jām Sahib was prone to attracting bees, as some people are because of particular pheromones that they secrete.

The hosts were well-aware of the possibility of a bee attack during the shikār, given the profusion of beehives in the area.

The Maharaja of Patiala and Jam Ṣahib, the Maharaja of Nawanagar

A massive bee clean-up operation was undertaken to snuff out the beehives by specialist teams. Jām Saheb himself was provided with bee-proof gear. With elaborate arrangements in place, including a 'Machān' (an aerial perch, usually erected in a tree, from where approaching game can be easily spotted from a distance), and a 'Hānka' (a group of drum-beaters to confuse and trap the targeted game), the tiger hunt began.

But, as it turned out in a quirky twist, the excited Jām Sahib, waiting in anticipation to shoot his precious game, himself became the hunted – the Maharaja's camp was attacked by a big swarm of angry, vicious bees!

Extremely sensitive to aromas, bees are easily attracted to particular pheromones that some humans secrete. It was as if this particular swarm of bees did not think much of the royal pheromones to which they were being treated, and decided to buzz in for a direct hit on Jām Saheb's entourage. Though the terrified Maharaja only suffered a few mild stings himself, as he was immediately bundled into a waiting Rolls Royce car and driven away to safety.

It is believed that Nawab Hamidulah, having himself survived several such bee attacks over the years, was determined to go ahead with the game hunt in spite of the freak incident. He offered to take the Jām Sahib to another area some thirty miles away, that had an abundance of tigers.

But the 'once stung', the Maharaja is said to have politely declined the offer, and to have beaten a rather hasty retreat instead!

EIGHT

THE RUSSIAN REVOLUTION AND PEOPLE'S MOVEMENTS IN BHOPAL

The Russian Revolution of 1917 changed the face of political mass movements across the World. In the protracted 'Great Game' between the English Empire and the Russian Empire, only the goalpost changed from the Russian Empire to the newly created USSR. Extreme anxiety and insecurity gripped the mandarins of the Empire, as London itself was on uncertain grounds over its stand on the Leftist movement. The Labour Party, the largest political party in Britain, is ideologically aligned 'Left of Centre'. It was going strong at the time and had formed its first government under Ramsay Macdonald in 1924, within just six years of the Russian Revolution.

However, the complacent Nawabs and Rajas of the sub-continental kingdoms and principalities, were comfortably ensconced in the protective cocoon offered by the British Empire, and had little reason to want to shed this cozy cover. They did not realise the impending crisis of public discontent and eventual rebellion. They had to be shaken out of their stupor by the British government officials of that time and their dedicated teams of informers and spies.

Jaan Nisar Akhtar

In erstwhile Bhopal however, the impact of this looming crisis was not sudden, because of three main reasons. Firstly, the Bhopal State was landlocked with almost impregnable forests surrounding most of its boundaries. This formed an effective deterrent to any mass movement of the people. Secondly, barring the comparatively small urban population, the majority of inhabitants were tribal, or small farmers. And thirdly and significantly, under the long and continuous reign of four generations of the Begum Nawabs, many large-scale programmes for social and people's emancipation, especially women's welfare, in addition to other people-oriented development schemes including those for improving basic infrastructure and amenities, had already been successfully and effectively implemented.

However, during the reign of Nawab Hamidullah Khan, who himself was of a liberal bent of mind since his Aligarh University days, many educated and intellectual young men and women flocked to Bhopal. This movement had the tacit encouragement of the Nawab, who placed many of these people in important positions in administration and the academia. By doing this, he probably wanted to project himself to be like the Turkish demagogue, Kemal Ataturk who, it is believed, was his ideal.

Two major famines and large scale urban migration in the 1930s had resulted in the first signs of social discontentment emerging – the first came from the textile-mill workers' agitation in 1932. Only a year earlier, some neo-liberals and progressive intellectuals from Bhopal had formed the 'Mazdoor Sabha', with five office-bearers.

Mazdoor Sabha, born in Bhopal, was to become the rudiment of the formal political entity, the Communist Party, which would become a recognised and respected political party later, and would play a significant role in the political firmament of United India.

But, it became apparent soon enough that the textile workers were not a united, cohesive front that could muster the expected impact. The factions within it also started inciting large-scale strikes (lock-outs) and demonstrations, without having a definite ideology or even effective leadership of their own. The random strikes (refusal to work as a form of protest) they organised were mostly based on subversive propaganda.

Nawab Hamidullah Khan would certainly have been aware of these developments, but probably chose not to act on them, considering them to be a sort of catharsis for the growing ilk of armchair intellectuals.

The actual, bona fide communist movement took root in Bhopal only in 1945, when pioneers of the movement, the renowned Urdu poet and writer Jaan Nisar Akhtar, (father of Javed Akhtar, the celebrated author, poet and lyricist), and his wife Safia joined Hamidia College in Bhopal as professors.

Jaan Nisar was a house-hold name as far as Urdu literature was concerned. With his deep and zealous commitment to the cause of the leftist movement, he established a new organisation called the 'Anjuman-e-Tarakkipasand Mussanfeen', with the original founders of the Mazdoor Sabha, which was eventually merged with the new organisation.

Akhtar gave the communist movement a much-needed political dimension. He began tapping into the ongoing agrarian unrest, in order to identify people's issues that he could take up and work on from a grass-roots perspective. For doing this effectively, he invoked the age-old and uniquely Indian 'oral tradition' concept. This would help him ferret out information and properly understand the basic cause(s) of issues affecting the masses, from the bottom upwards. Akhtar also played a vital role in the movement for the merger of princely states with the proposed Union of India, along with the Praja Mandal.

Nawab Hamidullah, too, had by now realised that he could no longer afford to turn a deliberate blind eye to matters simmering below the surface. The unrest and discontentment of the general public was fast approaching its boiling-point, and was ready to erupt into full-fledged, forceful people's movements against the British administration and the Nawab's rule. He ordered brutal crackdowns on the members and leaders of Anjuman-e-Tarakkipasand Musanfeen and Praja Mandal.

The Communist movement, thus, had an all-encompassing influence even in feudal Bhopal, and later went on to impact other similar grassroot people's movements in India.

NINE

THE NAWAB'S INCOGNITO GUEST

Rare are the occasions when the ideological divide between great men is lessened by a shared passion. There are many instances on record of heads of state, kings and princes, who have let their hair down when they are out of the ever scrutinising gaze of the paparazzi and more importantly, away from their own core-group of hangers on.

Chiklod, a sleepy locality about forty-five kms. outside Bhopal, was a favourite retreat of the Bhopal royals. Its surrounding forests of Khajuri and Ratibad swarmed with big game, even until as recently as the late 70s. Initially, the place had a modest 'shikārgah' with temporary tents and a small settlement to house the staff that served the guests visiting for the Royal shikār expeditions.

Nawab Hamidullah Khan, a 'Nausherwan' (a title given to those shikārees who had killed a minimum of nine tigers) himself, constructed a lavish retreat – a palace which also served as his summer retreat – but which also celebrated his passion for game hunting in a unique way. Apart from the stuffed-game trophies adorning the walls, the most striking feature of Chiklod Kothi was an entire staircase made out of antlers of the sambhar deer.

The Chiklod Kothi attracted likeminded visitors. Marshal

Marshal Josip Broz Tito, former President of Yugoslavia

Tito, President of Yugoslavia, visited India towards the end of 1954. Tito was one of the three statesmen of the time, who, along with Jawaharlal Nehru of India, and Gamal Abdel Nasser of Egypt, founded the revolutionary policy of Non-Alignment against the prevailing hyphenated US-USSR block diplomacy.

Tito chose to celebrate a quiet New Year's eve at Chiklod. It was Nehru himself, mesmerised by the sylvan surroundings of the Chiklod Kothi during his earlier visits to Bhopal, is said to have recommended the place to Tito. Nehru also requested his college-mate and friend Nawab Hamidullah Khan to host Tito. Interestingly, the Nawab was just a common citizen at the time, though Chiklod and the surrounding area was his private 'jageer'.

The Nawab was pleasantly surprised that like himself, Tito was himself a passionate game hunter. Though Tito's visit was ostensibly to enjoy a quite getaway, he had heard of the great tiger hunts that the Bhopal Nawab was known to organise. He requested the Nawab if he too could have the honour of going on a tiger hunt. Eventually, Tito could not bag a tiger, and had to be content with the delight of spotting several tigers from a distance.

Writing on the Shikār culture of the Bhopal royals, Harihar Swarup , a senior columnist with the Tribune recalls:

> 'A few years after the new state of Madhya Pradesh was formed in the late fifties, Marshal Tito visited Chiklod on a hunting expedition and was guest of the Nawab. He could spot few tigers but could not bag any one of them.'

Thus the great Communist leader was probably the only proletariat to have joined the great feudals, the Maharajas of Bikaner, Jaipur and Nepal to grace the Chiklod Kothi.

TEN

WHEN THE *AWAM* PRAYED FOR THE NAWAB

In Satyajit Ray's celebrated 1983 film, *Ghare Baire,* a particular trait of the character of the zamindar, Nikhil, is almost lost on the audience because of the predominant central theme of the film, which is women's emancipation. This curious trait of Nikhil's is his refusal to join the *Swadeshi* movement that was all the rage in the period that the film is set in. He is deeply ambivalent about the effectiveness of the movement as a means towards achieving freedom. He points out that it would require his subjects, who were primarily poor peasants, to buy comparatively expensive Indian-made goods, which they clearly couldn't afford. It would also drive small merchants out of business.

The film is based on Tagore's eponymous novel, which was probably the first written account of the sensitivity and sensibility shown by a ruler towards his people. In an atmosphere charged by the overpowering narrative of 'exploitation', this was the leitmotif of most of the literary work that emerged during that period, including works by literary giants like Premchand and Fakirmohan Senapati.

But the princely states like Travancore, Mysore, Baroda and Bhopal defied all conventional stereotypes of the master-

The Fokker C-2A Aircraft

servant relationship between the ruler and the ruled. In Bhopal particularly, with the all-encompassing legacy of love, compassion and succour that the Begum Nawabs left behind – the classes and the masses enjoyed a rapport that is not seen commonly even in modern day democracies.

An interesting anecdote pertaining to a near fatal air-accident confirms that such a bond did exist. The incident has been documented by Khalid Mohammad Khan in his book, *Dastaan-e-Bhopal.*

Nawab Hamidullah Khan was an avid aviator, and owned the most modern flying-machines available those days. His favorite was a Fokker C-2A aircraft, which he had purchased in England. Incidentally, it was Hamidullah who initiated the construction of the Bairagarh airport near Bhopal under the supervision of the well-known civil engineer of the time, Mirza Fahim Beg. The incident occurred when Hamidullah was returning from his Chiklod retreat in his newly acquired Fokker C-2A, which was being piloted by an experienced pilot. But as it approached the runway, the aircraft's landing gear developed a snag and got stuck. The fact that the aircraft had a limited amount of fuel left further aggravated the situation. As the word spread, people started moving towards the airport in droves, and a full-fledged, impromptu community prayer was held. The *Shahar Qazi* even advised the royal family to offer *Sadaqah* (voluntary charity).

The general ambience became all the more despondent when the pilot informed the ground control through a radio that he had gone through all possible emergency procedures, but couldn't get the landing gear to deploy. Then, suddenly, as the aircraft was making its last circle over the airport on an almost empty fuel-tank, the fault in the snag in the landing gear got resolved miraculously. A loud cheer from the thousands of spectators went out when the wheels of the plane safely touched down on the runway.

This spectacle of genuine affection and devotion affirms the symbiotic affinity between the masses and their leaders.

ELEVEN

HOLI IN THE ERSTWHILE BHOPAL STATE

Holi, the quintessential Indian festival, is closely connected with the weather-pattern of the subcontinent, and is truly the epitome of the amalgamation of different faiths, cultures and schools of thought. Holi, like all Vedic festivals, is replete with multilayered symbolism that has accumulated since ancient times, through to the present age of modernism.

Thus, somewhere, it is supposed to channelise lustful energies into love in its myriad forms. In its Shaivite and Vaishnavite derivatives, it is said to destroy lustful distractions and offer protection to the *Bhakt.*

In the psychoanalytical terms, it would be the equivalent of the sublimation or catharsis of sexual energies. But above all, this festival of colours is also the primordial or the *aadi* intonations of the onset of spring and the Puranic version of the cupid, Kamdeva, with his cane-sugar bow and flower-tipped arrows and darts, thus powerfully symbolising life in all its hues and vibrancy.

The Mughals ardently loved Holi and participated in it whole-heartedly, perpetuating the *Ganga-Jamuni tehzeeb* in its celebration. Much before the Mughals, the Sufi poet Amir

Khusrau composed a *Hori geet, 'Khaaja ghar aaye...,'* and later Bhakti era poets like Bulleshah, with his immortal lines, *'Hori kheluungii, kah Bismillah...,'* also demonstrated the universality of the festival.

Not much is known about the earlier Begums of Bhopal encouraging the festival of Holi. However, they did maintain a passive admiration and tolerance towards its celebration. This may have been partly due to their adherence to Islamic austerity and puritanism. With eighty-five percent of their subjects being Hindus, the founders of the Bhopal State may have had political reasons for maintaining this passive tolerance towards its celebration.

Actual royal patronage to the festival came later, when the vivacious Shahjehan Begum, who borrowed and replicated the art and culture from Moghul courts, started hosting Holi celebrations in the courtyard of her residence at the Taj Mahal Palace with colours mixed with *Kewra, Zafran* and flowers. The attendance in these soirees, though, was strictly limited to only the royal and aristocratic families of Bhopal. The invitees were gifted silver and gold *pichkaaris*. Begum Shahjehan was also a serious poet and even penned a song on Holi. *'Aaj piya sang khele hori, sab sakhiyan milke chalori...'.*

However, it was only the people's Nawab, Hamidullah Khan, who started playing Holi with the masses, and observing other Hindu festivals with his subjects. He held special durbars on Holi, where the *awam* (public) and the courtiers could come and pay obeisance and offer *nazrana* (gifts) to the royals. He also distributed sweets in schools and applied *tilak* to students.

People loved him so much that once, the villagers of Sehore invited him to play Holi with them in the traditional style. The Nawab accepted the invitation, but could arrive only a day after the actual festival. Nonetheless, he played Holi with the villagers with abandon. The reverence towards the Nawab is still reciprocated in Sehore and its adjoining areas where even today, Holi is celebrated a day after the actual festival.

Hamidullah perhaps realised that the plebian and the rustic element in the revelry was the only occasion he could enjoy unhindered proximity to his subjects, and vice versa. The move may have begun as a political and populist measure, but very soon the Nawab found himself fully immersed in the contagious and impartial merrymaking. That was and still is, the potential of the syncretic, all-embracing culture of Bhopal.

TWELVE

THE TROCADERO TART

In the grey, gloomy London of the late nineteen twenties, reeling under severe economic onslaught of the Great Depression and the intervening unstable and insecure period between the First and Second World Wars, dreams were the only ray of hope for the teeming masses. Consisting of industrial labourers, lower-ranking staff employed by private businesses and the ubiquitous unemployed, these were the people who bore the brunt of the catastrophic times more than any other class.

Marjorie Parkinson, a nineteen-year-old waitress did not just dream, she fantasised of better times. Like most of the lower middle class Londoners, she was awestruck by the legends of the mysterious and immensely rich orient she had heard, and dreamt of a heartbroken prince who would somehow find solace in her charms. As luck would have it, her impossible dream came true one fine day, when she saw in her restaurant, the 'Trocadero', a handsome Indian man curiously ogling the women. She hovered around him and was thrilled to realise that he too seemed to be reciprocating her advances. Finally, she could not contain herself, and struck a conversation with him. She was very pleased to learn that he indeed was a prince from India, as the flamboyant man bragged to her about his affluence and lineage. To her great surprise, the glib young man

Marjorie Parkinson

proposed marriage to her within hours of their first meeting.

The young man was in fact one of the scions of the Bhopal royalty, albeit a considerably minor one. He resided in the outhouse of the palace, and for all intents and purposes, was a parasite and a royal hanger on.

Partly blinded by her infatuation for him and partly because she saw in him her only chance of escaping the drudgery of life in London at the time, the seemingly gullible Marjorie willingly accepted the proposal and they got married post-haste. She of course had no means of knowing the truth about him, even if she had wanted to.

When the new couple arrived in Bhopal, the ladies in the court and the nobility treated Marjorie with great contempt, not only because she was a *firaangi* (white-skinned person), but also because the so-called prince was already married! But soon, Marjorie – the 'Trocadero tart', as she was derisively referred to by the ladies of the royal household, took a grip of her situation, and proceeded to shake the conservative society of Bhopal to its core.

She quickly dumped her two-timing oriental prince and started eyeing bigger catches. She was now a bona fide invitee to all major royal pastimes, like the midnight shikār jaunts, dance parties and similar other debauchery. She is said to have turned herself into a highly sought-after harlot with her refined manners and obvious charms. Her income increased in direct proportion to the increase in the number of rich and powerful men seeking her company. As the great Bard put it in his play *Anthony and Cleopatra*, Act II; Scene II:

> 'The appetites they feed, but she makes hungry
> Where most she satisfies, for vilest things
> Become themselves in her...'

Like Cleopatra, Marjorie too became a power centre, and trounced anyone and anything that came in the way of her enjoying a luxurious and decadent life. When she came to know that royal ladies and wives of the men who patronised her had ganged-up against her, with the active backing of the British gentry stationed in Bhopal, she is said to have shrewdly offered herself as a masseuse to them, and in some cases, to even have encouraged them into same-sex relationships, thus obviating any direct and effective resistance.

Marjorie – the Trocadero tart, returned to her native London sometime in 1946, with the riches she had amassed and the stories that she had created, after flitting about fearlessly on the moral horizons of Bhopal for around twenty years. She undoubtedly managed to leave a colourful, scintillating and licentious mark on the otherwise dour, purportedly unblemished and the largely perceived as chaste society of Bhopal!

SECTION FIVE

A Janus-Faced City – The Past in the Present

ONE

ANNUS HORRIBILIS – LEST WE FORGET

The agony and terror of that deadly intervening night between 2 and 3 December 1984, have been crystallised in my memory forever, and no subsequent night was the same as before, for many, many years to come.

The country was still in turmoil after the assassination of Indira Gandhi and the bloody riots that ensued. I distinctly remember myself as a teenager, dog-earing the latest literary sensations in the market – M.J. Akbar's debut book, *India – The Siege Within*, and Gabriel Garcia Marquez's, *One Hundred Years of Solitude* – and dozing-off, dreaming of someday becoming a decision-maker, running important affairs of the government, in our house in Professors' Colony.

Late that night, I suddenly woke up with a burning sensation in my eyes and a corrosive sensation inside my nose, all along its mucous lining. Some muffled but urgent voices on the street outside had now started to build-up to a crescendo. I heard heavy banging on our backdoor and heard someone shouting something. I saw my father opening the door. Alakhnandan, the famous theatre director and our neighbour, stood there half-drunk, screaming in a slurred voice, '*Vijaymohan ji, bhagiye ...parmanu yudh chid gaya hai...*' (Run, Vijaymohan ji, ...a nuclear war has broken out...).

'Shaheen', a memorial created by the renowned painter J. Swaminathan, and Robin David

As the heartrending events of that gruesome, merciless night unfolded, the World's worst ever man-made industrial disaster began to take shape. It was a gut-wrenching sight outside, a sea of people – men, women and children, the old and the young – running, walking, crawling, staggering, falling, all clamouring to somehow get to the New Market area, to get away from where the killer gas was concentrated. Some people had managed to enter our house, literally begging for some water. Some of them even rushed into our washroom and poured buckets full of cold water on their heads, in a futile attempt to somehow find relief from the excruciating agony they were in.

I, along with my brother, left the house and started walking towards 74 Bungalows. My father refused to go along with us, as the condition of his friend, the ailing Dr. Kedarnath Singh, a famous Hindi poet, who was staying as a Writer-in-Residence in the Nirala Shrijan Peeth, had worsened. The roads were choc-a-block, teeming with people writhing in agony. In desperation,

The memorial 'Mother and Child' sculpture by sculptor Ruth Waterman

many had crawled into storm-water drains, gasping for breath and groaning in abject pain.

My family was amongst the few lucky ones who escaped the deadly methyl isocyanate (MIC) gas leakage disaster that killed thousands of people that night. Deaths, in dwindling numbers, continued in the coming months and years, in the aftermath of the tragedy. My family too had to undergo many months of eye treatment and suffered side-effects because of the exposure.

The aftermath of the disaster saw artists, social activists and good Samaritans from Bhopal spearheading a campaign to try and ensure that such a tragedy did not re-occur anywhere in the World. Many international organisations too pitched in with financial and legal aid, towards fighting for the claims of the survivors.

Warren Anderson, Chairman and CEO of the Union Carbide Corporation at the time of the Bhopal Gas Disaster

Two important landmark structures emerged out of this dark period, which bear testimony to the irreparable damage – emotional, mental, physical and material, that the people of Bhopal had suffered.

The first structure is the memorial 'Mother and Child', a sculpture by the Dutch sculptor Ruth Waterman, installed just outside the Union Carbide plant, the primary culprit of the disaster. It carries the thought provoking message, 'No Hiroshima... No Bhopal... We Want to Live'. Ruth conceived this theme after staying with the survivors for many days, and crafted the piece with their participation. Her own traumatic experience of the Holocaust during World War-II, in which she had lost her parents, too contributed in a significant way in conceptualisation of the design of the sculpture. She had become so deeply dejected by the memories of time she had spent with the survivors in Bhopal immediately after the disaster, that she is said to have told her son from her deathbed that she wanted to spend her last days with the 'Midnight's Children' of Bhopal.

The second monument stands tall at the iconic Iqbal Maidan. It is named 'Shaheen', alluding to an eagle, and was created by the renowned painter Jagdish Swaminathan, and

Robin David. It quotes several *shers* (couplets) written on Shaheen by legendary Urdu poet, Allama Mohammad Iqbal. I remember vividly the animated discussions on this, in our house between J. Swaminathan, Robin David and my father.

Those were the days when Communism was on the wane and would completely collapse in its strongholds within the next few years, paving way for popular Socialism to take root. This was while the United States of America was fast becoming the epitome of Capitalist liberalism. Most of the old-guard in India, including artists, intellectuals and thinkers, harboured a strong dislike towards large business conglomerates and corporations, particularly those that were American. As far as the Bhopal tragedy was concerned, for them, Warren Andersen, the then CEO of the Union Carbide Corporation, was the archetypal villain in this sordid saga.

For the second monument, it was decided that the central theme would be to create an edifice which would not only testify against capitalist greed and exploitation, but would also evoke the poetic genius of Allama Iqbal. The sculpture does convey the preying ruthlessness of the eagle but somehow, I find it to be closer to the poetic muse and ideology of the international crusader Faiz Ahmed Faiz than Iqbal.

Iqbal has showered praise on Shaheen – the eagle, through his famous lines below:

> *'Parindon ki dunya ka Dearvesh hoon mein, ki Shaheen banata nahin ashiyana.'*
>
> ('I am the Dervish of the realm of the birds – the eagle does not build nests')
>
> *'Nahin tera nasheman Kasr-e-Saltani ke gumbad par*
> *Tu Shaheen hai-basera kar, paharon ki chattanon mai*
>
> (Your abode is not the dome of the Emperor's palace,

for you are an eagle, you should be living on the rocks of great mountains).

But Faiz in his nazm, *'Chopin ka naghma bajta hai,'* likens Shaheen to exploitation:

'Ek kunj ko sakhiyan chhod gayeen, aakash ki neeli rahon mein
Woh yaad mein tanha roti thi, liptae apni bahon mein
ek Shaheen us par jhapta hai.
"Chopin" ka naghma bajta hai...
Gham ne sanche mein dhaala hai , ek baap ke patthar chehre ko
Murda bete ke mathe ko, ek maa ne ro kar chuma hai...
"Chopin" ka naghma bajta hai.'

('A bower has been deserted by the maidens, left in the blanket of blue sky...
They cry alone in its memory, wrapped
in its arms... An eagle pounces on it;
"Chopin's" symphony plays on...
Sadness has sculpted a father's face to stone, a
mother cries and kisses the forehead of her dead son,
"Chopin's" symphony plays on...')

TWO

BAIRAGARH: THE INVISIBLE CITY

In the 1962 classic, *'Sahib Bibi Aur Ghulam'* the two diametrically opposite yet complimentary characters of 'Choti Bahu' played by legendary Meena Kumari and Waheeda Rahman as 'Jaba' carried a subtle message of the anachronistic, old feudal order in decay against the brash, fresh and ambitious new order. This is an apt analogy for Bhopal and its suburb of Bairagarh. Where 'Choti Bahu' carried an oppressive ambience to fulfill her desires, the bubbly 'Jaba' rears to go ahead without any hang-ups of the past.

Bairagarh has always been an engine to drive and sustain its big brother – Bhopal. Even though often spoken about condescendingly by the residents of Bhopal city. It has been a wholesale market for a very long time now, propelled by the dynamism of the Sindhi community, whose exceptional selling skills are well-known. Bairagarh is unfailingly the first to introduce the latest in consumables, electronic goods, jewellery, and garments to Bhopalis.

Most of us are aware of the fact that Bairagarh originated as a settlement for refugees from Sindh. However, not many know that the British revived it by building barracks to hold Italian prisoners of war there. These barracks housed as many as twenty thousand POWs at one time, who with their sheer *joie de vivre* captured the hearts and mind of Bhopalis. Many of the

POWs were extremely talented – some of them were serious painters who produced masterful paintings. Some others, who had been former professional orchestra artists, formed a band and performed at royal parties. Fazal Tabish, the well-known author and poet from Bhopal, mentions in his book, *Voh Aadmi* about a *'kauaa pakad gora'*, a reference to an Italian POW, who would entertain people by standing stark naked and absolutely still like a statue, so that crows would perch on him, and he would catch them!

Later, the same barracks and dormitories were thrown open to the Muslims of Gwalior, who had survived the riots there. During the partition, the migrant community of the Sindhis and Multanis were given land and vacant buildings in Bairagarh, and these communities have since contributed greatly to Bairagarh's exponential growth. It is said that during partition, when entire country was polarised on religious lines, the Muslims of Bhopal laid-out their 'safaas' (turbans), which is an age old custom of demonstrating insistence, on the streets to stop their Hindu friends and neighbours from leaving the predominantly Muslim state.

Over a period of time, with the Indian Army setting up its Electronics and Mechanical Engineers (EME) Centre, and the Bhopal Airport coming up there in the mid-60s, Bairagarh gained in stature and prominence. And it has never looked back since.

THREE

BHEL – THE PRICELESS JEWEL OF BHOPAL

Few Public Sector entities can boast of an everlasting impact on a 200-year-old city as BHEL Bhopal does. Bharat Heavy Electricals Ltd. has positively impacted the lives of millions of Bhopalis and also non-Bhopalis, ever since its inception almost seven decades ago. It came into existence on 7 November 1955, through an agreement between the Government of India and Associated Electrical Industries (AEI) of the UK, for the establishment of a factory for the manufacture of heavy electrical equipment in Bhopal.

The plan to bring such an ambitious project to Bhopal was the result of many farsighted and practical deliberations between the parties concerned, as the erstwhile states were exerting all kinds of political pressure on the nascent Government of India to locate the venture in their state. The States Reorganisation Committee (SRC) had not yet submitted its report to the government.

It is noteworthy that even before Bhopal was formally declared as the capital of Madhya Pradesh, the decision of setting up BHEL in Bhopal had already been taken. It was certainly a deliberate political plan, since the farsighted leaders of the then Central Province, like Shankar Dayal Sharma, had a strong say in

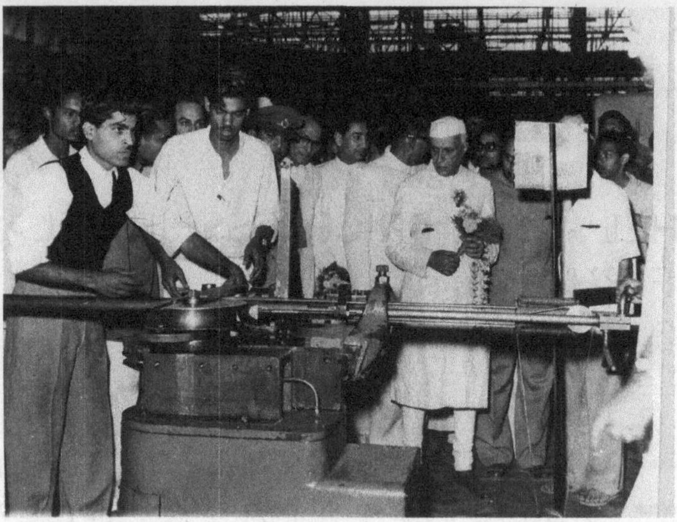

The Prime Minister of India Pt. Jawaharlal Nehru during the inaguration BHEL, Bhopal

policy decisions. Another factor which could have played an important role in this decision was the friendship between Nehru and Nawab Hamidullah Khan. The Nawab was always eager to institute modern concepts of development in Bhopal.

The establishment of the large factory and the subsequent development of a township around it for housing those who were employed in it and their families, which boasted of modern amenities, altered the urban landscape of Bhopal for the better.

At that time this placid and rather humdrum feudal city of Bhopal, with its sedentary lifestyle and easy pace was trying to extricate itself from the melancholia of its bygone days, and was trying to adjust its goalposts to align them, with those of the new independent and modern order of governance. It was gifted with the throbbing-with-life facility of BHEL, with its attendant ancillary of a world-class industrial township.

The dream of a city – a phantasmagoria with the amalgamation of the past and the present came about exultingly

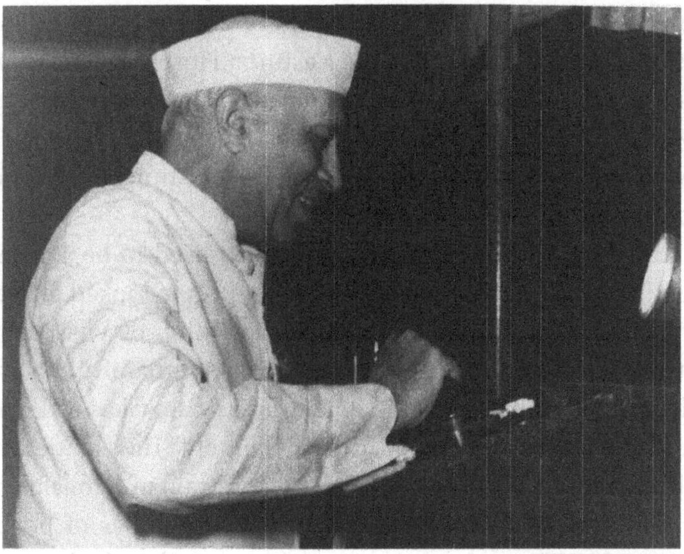

Pt Jawaharlal Nehru inaugurating the BHEL plant in Bhopal

in joyful hues. The positive impact included freedom of work and livelihood, enhanced opportunity of stable employment, thereby reducing the dependence on the unpredictability of agriculture; safety at work with the availability of modern medical facilities; increase in the sources of amusement, and most importantly, the development of a sense of 'individuality' which was very necessary to break away from the shackles of traditional taboos and social mores, which hung around the collective psyche of the populace like the proverbial albatross around their necks.

New sets of people, who came in from all over the country, brought along with them their own cultures and life-styles; different languages; dressing styles; food habits and the like became a melting-pot for the evolution of a brand new way of life, really an amalgamation of slices of life from all over the country.

Iconic institutions within BHEL were for many years to

come, the pride of the city and were counted amongst the best. Medical institutes like the Kasturba Hospital, educational institutions like the Carmel Convent School for girls, the Jawahar Lal Nehru School and Career College were landmarks, metaphorically and literally, which most old-timers will fondly recall.

There was a time when English films used to be screened only in Natraj theatre located in BHEL. People looked forward for famous cultural events like the celebration of Vijaydashmi at the BHEL Dussehra ground, the Durga Ashthami and Navmi celebrations at the Kalibari in Piplani area, Vishwakarma Puja in the factory premises and inside the plant etc. The eighties kids will still remember the joy-ride on the toy-train in Kamla Nehru Bal Udyan, which still attracts a sizeable number of people. The weekly haat or vegetable and fruits market, had its own charm. BHEL had its vast, well maintained tree-canopy areas and green-belt areas, which also acted like oxygen generators to the ever-expanding city of Bhopal.

Of late, the large PSU culture is dying a slow death. PSUs were conceived to generate maximum employment, while at the same time provide social welfare even to non-employees who by virtue of their being a part of the place, have contributed and sacrificed for the establishment of the factory.

Private corporations with their media savvy and often pretentious Corporate Social Responsibilities (CSR) plans cause more harm than good to the soul of a city. Environment friendly mega industrial undertakings like BHEL in the proximity of a city give a new dimension to the city's life and build up a syncretic, tolerant and pan-Indian culture, which was the aim of our nation builders in the first place.

FOUR

BHOPAL'S PRESENCE IN BOLLYWOOD

'...a writing, with images in movement and with sounds.' This is the famous French film director Robert Bresson's cryptic description of cinema. Ever since its arrival in India in the late Nineteenth-century, the moving and talking pictures – the movies – have enthralled and captivated the imagination of people in myriad ways. Slowly but steadily, Bollywood spread its wings, to provide an increasingly enhanced audio-visual experience over the years. There was never a dearth of good stories to be told through the medium of cinema, and many excellent and memorable movies have been made to great national as well as international acclaim, in all the prominent Indian languages.

As offshoots, full-fledged and flourishing regional language film industries have come up in Marathi, Bengali, Punjabi, and of course, Tamil, Telugu, Kannada and Malayalam languages. In fact, the Indian film industry is today the largest in the World, producing more films than even Hollywood each year. The technical expertise has also jumped by leaps and bounds over the years and we now routinely produce films with as much technical finesse as Hollywood.

Bollywood, has manifested India's soft-power in the arena

of diplomacy worldwide. Attracting talent from various streams of creativity, it produces films that captivate audiences not just in India but the world over.

Bhopal too has, amongst other things, had its share of men and women who have proved their mettle in Bollywood. A quick research throws up surprising results and brings up names of several members of the Bollywood fraternity who have their roots in, or are connected to Bhopal in some way. These include such celebrated names as Annu Kapoor, who is a typical mohalla-lad born in the Itwara locality in the old city. Annu had to quit school early in life due to his family's difficult financial situation. The well-known actress, Jaya Bhaduri, though born in Jabalpur, did her schooling at the St. Joseph's Convent here. The film and television actor, Rajeev Verma, a household name now, is from Bhopal. Rajeev acquired a degree in Architecture from the Maulana Azad National Institute of Technology in Bhopal, before making a career in films.

The maverick penman, Javed Akhtar, who graduated from Saifia College, unabashedly declares his love for Bhopal and admits that he is more attached to Bhopal than to Lucknow, his ancestral home. He has often spoken of his years in Bhopal as being some of the most formative ones of his life, and some of his closest friends still live in Bhopal.

In the late eighties and early nineties, for most of us, Sunday mornings were reserved for the immensely popular television series 'Ramayan'. Sunil Lahiri, who played Lakshman in the show, was from Bhopal. Not many are aware that Sunil and his brother were first to shoot a film titled 'Phir Aayee Barsaat' in Bhopal.

Saif and Soha Ali Khan's great grandmother, Sajida Sultan, was the second daughter of Nawab Hamidullah Khan, the last Nawab. That makes Saif Ali Khan the *de jure* Nawab of Bhopal through inheritance.

The veteran actor, conspicuous for his baritone and forceful dialogue delivery, Raza Murad, grew up in Bhopal and often shares fond memories of the vibrant *gully* (by-lane) culture here. Rumi Jaffery, who has directed films like 'God Tussi Great Ho' and 'Gali Gali Mein Chor Hai' etc. has demonstrated his love for the city by shooting his debut directorial venture here. The model-turned-actor, Shahwar Ali, has an unmistakably Bhopali demeanour.

Many films that have been shot here over the years – In Custody, Rajneeti, Aarakshan, Lipstick-Under my Burqa, Bhopal has become the filming destination of choice for many directors.

FIVE

CRUMBLING GATES TO ETERNITY – THE DARWAZAS OF BHOPAL

'Your offspring shall possess the gate of his enemies.'

Thus says the Bible (Genesis 22:7). This is a part of the blessings Abraham received from the Lord, bestowing him with the control of the gates of his enemies' cities, so that he could enter and conquer them without much effort. City gates were conventionally built as an opening in the fort walls for controlled ingress and egress of people and goods. Over a period of time, apart from their intended use, the gates also became symbolic of the display of the king's power and glory. In addition to providing protection, city gates were places of central activity.

The first mention of a city gate is found in Genesis 19:1. It was at the gate of Sodom at which Abraham's nephew, Lot, greeted the angelic visitors that came to his city. Over a period of time, city gates, depending on their historical circumstances, became *sine qua non* or something essential in their scheme of things, for empire builders.

Thus, when Dost Mohammad Khan laid out the plans for establishing the city of Bhopal some three hundred years ago, he included a number of gates along the outer fortification

The Dakhil Darwaza – Gate of the Taj Mahal Palace in Bhopal

walls, and some within the city that demarcated the areas to be occupied by royalty from those that were to accommodate plebeians. One of the first to be constructed and the oldest surviving gate is the Jumerati gate, which is located along what old-timers would refer to as the 'Laila Burj'. The credit of protecting and preserving this precious monument goes to a group of shopkeepers – both Hindu and Muslim – led by Samad Dada Islammiya Hotelwale and Qayoom Javed.

Running almost parallel to the Laila Burj is the 'Patrawala Burj', which terminates at the Budhwara Darwaza. Laila Burj further meanders to the Peer gate. It is said that the women of Bhopal used to pour boiling oil on enemies who attempted to enter the city during the Great Siege of 1812-13 from the top of this darwaza. A little ahead, towards Royal Market, stands the Imami gate. The darwazas of Bhopal were mostly named after days of the week – Itwara, Mangalwara, Budhwara, Jummerati etc.

Some of the most magnificent darwazas, like the Dakhil

The Jumerati Gate

Darwaza at the Taj Mahal Palace, the Lal Darwaza near Model Ground, and the Regiment Gate, which is the entrance to the Sultania Infantry Lines, were constructed later by erstwhile ruler Shahjehan Begum, the Islami Gate at Shahjehanabad and the Gate at Bagh Farhat Afza were constructed by Sikander Jahan Begum. The youngest of all the darwazas is the Shaheed Gate or the Bhopal Darwaza.

Some historians are of the opinion that since construction of statues was prohibited in Islam, most of the aesthetic sensibilities of the rulers were applied to the constructing of the darwazas. However, it must be said the darwazas of Bhopal, even though attempting to emulate the Indo Saracenic style of architecture, lack the finesse and ornamentations of the Persian and Mughals darwazas.

The darwazas were constructed with an aim of more than just an access control method. Some still stand upright – absorbing, since ages, the bustling activities around as citadels of history, with the chronology of the past embedded in them.

SIX

DAR-UL-KOHALA - THE CLUB INDOLENT

In the early twentieth century, many intellectuals, sensing the danger that a highly mechanised society could wreak havoc on mankind, began to redirect the essential basis of their *oeuvre* towards the virtues of leisure. The Victorian neo-classicist English painter John William Godward's series of painting celebrating *dolce far niente* (pleasant idleness), became a bestseller at art galleries in Paris and London. Then, in 1935, Bertrand Russell in his book, *In Praise of Idleness and Other Essays,* stirred the hornet's nest by citing such gems as:

> 'I want to say, in all seriousness, that a great deal of harm is being done in the modern world by belief in the virtuousness of work, and that the road to happiness and prosperity lies in an organised diminution of work...', and, '...the time you enjoy wasting is not wasted time.'

This was followed by Charlie Chaplin's irreverent magnum-opus, 'Modern Times'. But, the idea of this radical thought first came from Søren Kierkegaard, the first existentialist philosopher, way back in the late nineteenth century, when he asserted that, '*Far from idleness being the root of all evil, it is rather the only true good.*'

Looking at the general advancement in the infrastructure

Jigar Moradabai

and the fast pace of life in Bhopal today, who would have imagined that not so long ago, there existed a club here, which not only encouraged idleness, but also practiced it to boot. This club, aptly called the 'Dar-ul-Kohala', which literally means 'a place for the indolent'. Here, the famous dictum 'An empty mind is the devil's workshop' was systematically deconstructed.

Mushairas, where shayari is recited, and patiabaazi, in which the participants expound languorously on anything and everything under the sun, have always been an integral part of the Bhopali culture. The people who organised and were at the centre of these seemingly 'ungainful pursuits', had a nonchalant, devil-may-care attitude and a discernable contempt for accepted societal norms.

Observing this unique phenomenon, the famous Urdu poet, Jigar Moradabadi, who was a rage in Bhopal during the 1930s and 1940s, had the mischievous brain-wave of creating an institution that celebrated idleness and coined the name, 'Dar-ul-Kohala' for it. The charter of the club was absolute for its members, and was quite the theatre of the absurd, with such farcical rules as accepting a pillow as membership fees, a stipulated timing of 9 pm to 3 am, not allowing people to sit or stand, seniority based on the geometrical position of the members etc. i.e. a member who is lying can order about the member who is sitting or standing etc. Once when there was a minor fire due to the charcoal falling from the hukkah, nobody got up to douse the fire, and a passerby had to do the job!

This idiosyncratic entity dissolved by itself after Jigar left Bhopal, leaving behind him another iconoclastic chapter in Bhopal's history.

SEVEN

FAIZ AHMAD FAIZ – THE SECULAR SUFI FOR ALL TIMES

'Mujh se pahli si muhabbat mere mehboob na maang...
aur bhi dukh hain zamaane mein muhabbat ke siva.'

No other Urdu poet or shayar from the sub-continent evokes as much strong emotions as Faiz Ahmad Faiz (1911-1984) does. If you come across scalding angst and a strong undercurrent of revolutionary messaging disguised in subtle undertones of love, in a ghazal or nazm, otherwise brimming over with romance – you have unmistakably stumbled upon an imprint left by Faiz Ahmad Faiz.

Faiz has been sung by nearly all prominent ghazal singers, from Iqbal Bano, Nayyara Noor, Farida Khannum, Mehdi Hasan and Gulam Ali. His *qat'aat* (verse) *'Kal raat teri bhooli hui yaad aayee...',* formed the backdrop of the most famous and perhaps the longest running Pakistani TV series, *'Dhoop Kinaare'* in the mid-eighties, that was also hugely popular in India.

Significantly, unlike an overwhelming pathos and futile nostalgia one finds in most of his predecessors and contemporaries of Urdu poetry – Faiz, through his writings bequeathed his readers with a reassuring and affirmative message and hope in the face of oppression, injustice, pain, despair and frustration...for example, *'hum mehnatkash jagwalon se jab apna hissa maangeinge ...'* or *'bol ki lab āzād haiñ tere....'*

A citizen of the world, Faiz was always in sync with the global movements taking place in his time that resisted oppression, tyranny and injustice for a new world order. Noam Chomsky, the great American linguist and political thinker says Faiz was, '*...prescient in catching the mood of disillusionment with the decolonised post-colonial states.*' Whether it was the Palestinian Intifada (*Mere Dil Mere Musafir*), the anti-apartheid movement in South Africa (*Aa Jaao Africa*), the partition of India (*Subh-e Aazadi*), the Iranian students struggle of 1959, the McCarthy era of repression of dissent in the United States, the European student uprisings in the 1960s, the Algerian freedom movement (Faiz's moving tribute titled *'Hum jo tareek raahon mein maare gaye'*), the Arab-Israeli War of 1967 (Sare-*vadi-e-sina*), writings on Bangladesh (*Hum ke thahre ajnabi*) etc.

Faiz's Bhopal connection is not unknown. Even though Faiz was never popular with the establishment and royalty, he was loved and respected by the hoi polloi – the masses – in the erstwhile principalities and protectorates, notably those of Bhopal and Hyderabad. He was always a people's poet '*...sab taaz ucchaale jayeinge, sab takht giraye jaayeinge.*' It was only in April 1981 that Faiz came to Bhopal for the first time on the invitation from his long-time admirer and friend, Fazal Tabish, a well-known Urdu writer and poet himself, who was the then Secretary of the Madhya Pradesh Urdu Academy. It turned out to be a memorable visit. Faiz was welcomed by Atal Bihari Vajpayee in New Delhi. The event in Bhopal was rightly named *Jashn-e-Faiz,* in which prominent Hindi and Urdu writers, poets and thinkers like Shamsher Bahadur Singh, Dr. Qamar Raees, Gyan Ranjan, Akhtar Sayeed, Uday Prakash, Naseer Parvaaj etc. came together on a single platform. Here, Faiz was felicitated in the programme *Shab-e-Naghma,* where the nazms and ghazals of Faiz were sung by the Bhopal-based singers.

The evocative film, *Muhafiz* (*In Custody*, 1994) by Ismail Merchant, which was incidentally shot in Bhopal, utilised Faiz's poetry to great effect, managing to embed it as the soul of the film. All the *nazms* and *ghazals* used in the film, barring one, were Faiz's published work. Since the city of Bhopal formed the backdrop of the film, the iconic Bhopal landmark, the Taj-ul-Masajid played an important part, where one of Faiz's famous nazms was effectively depicted in the final, climactic moments of the film. The 'crown among mosques' was a backdrop and also a significant character in this scene, symbolic of the great legacy that will not be easily forgotten.

Famous poets and writers have always been judged in the light of their ideological and religious leanings. Few, though, have been as stratospheric as Faiz Ahmed Faiz, who rose above any such labelling. But, certainly, some of the writings of Faiz irrefutably intertwine religion and revolution. Derivatives from Islamic scriptures are powerfully portrayed so as to create a very positive and throbbing *la dolce vita* or slice of life. His works reverberate with the spiritual and mystical aspects of Islam known as 'Tassawuf' or Sufism. He was also referred to as 'Malamaati Sufi' or the blameworthy Sufi. His nazms like *'Hum dekhenge...'*; *'...irani tulba ke naam'* etc. are full of Islamic allegories and metaphors.

Faiz was one of the founding members of the Communist Party of India, and the leftist literary movement which culminated into the formation of the All India Progressive Writers' Association. He was also the first Editor of 'LOTUS', an Afro-Asian journal which essentially promoted Left wing writings. Not surprisingly, he is presumed to have been an atheist. But religion, particularly Quranic piety, was always uppermost in his thought process. Qateel Shifai, another great Urdu poet, once asked him about the movements in Islamic literature in an interview, Faiz's quick response was – *'In my opinion, the literary movements of Muslim writers in Muslim countries are a part of Islam.'*

Though, in Faiz's biography, *The Way It Was Once,* Ali Madeeh Hashmi, his grandson disagrees. He writes:

> '...Faiz's intrinsic creative value lay in his ability to keep alive, an awareness of the problems that assail victims of oppression and injustice on universal scale... his philosophy rises above ideological restrictions...the ideological contours of his poetry have faded'.

But, Bhopal has seen the deference of Faiz towards spiritualism through his silence and, for once, not through his poetry!

Faiz visited Bhopal once again in the winter of 1983, for a programme organized by Madhya Pradesh Kala Parishad, just few months before his death. Manzoor Ahteshaam, a prominent Urdu/Hindi writer from Bhopal, recalls an interesting and touching moment during the poetry recitation session, on the terrace of the Kala Parishad, in honour of Faiz. Just when the *Daavat-e-sukhan* (the invitation for reciting poetry) was offered to Faiz that evening, the maghrib Azaan was invoked from the Moti Masjid. Manzoor says that he was awe struck when Faiz froze at that moment and did not utter a single word during the entire invocation of the Azaan. As if on cue, among the audience, too, there was pin drop silence. This reveals another interesting aspect of Faiz's personality. Even though he never himself believed in the dogmas and rituals of a religion, he was sensitive to the religious sentiments of everyone around him. He never forced his viewpoint and beliefs on any one, leaving it to his poems to do the job.

Faiz could well earn the sobriquet of a 'Secular Sufi', being relevant and contemporary even now, more than ever. As P.B. Shelley has said: *'Poets are the unacknowledged legislators of the world.'*

EIGHT

THE VANISHING HILLS OF BHOPAL

'...This is another great difference between our civilisation and yours. You admire the man who pushes his way to the top in any walk of life, while we admire the man who abandons his ego.'

In his book, *Seven Years in Tibet,* the Austrian mountaineer Heinrich Harrer eloquently and succinctly sums up in this one, short paragraph, how Tibetans have always understood that conquering the ego is the ultimate achievement, and how this very personal achievement can alter one's perspective on everything, and that the ability to understand this compels them to accord the utmost respect to what nature has bestowed on them, rather than accomplishing worldly feats as proof of personal achievement. The book, in which he recounts his experiences in Tibet between 1944 and 1951, spanning the years between World War II, and the Chinese People's Liberation Army's invasion of Tibet in 1950, was also made into a much-acclaimed, eponymous movie.

Some countries have learnt from the destruction caused to their natural surrounding by way of development. The best example is of the crooked street (Lombard Street) in San Francisco. While it was being constructed in 1922, the original

An old photograph of the Upper Lake

plan was to reduce the hill's steepness by over twenty-seven per cent, but the city planners prevailed upon the engineers to keep it in its natural form. They perhaps may have been swayed by the ancient Aztecs who ruled the present day California and were big time nature worshippers. But, ironically, in most of the developing world, it is still an anathema to compromise development to keep intact their natural landscape. Interestingly, even the mythical Govardhan Parvat near Mathura is now reduced to merely a hundred feet which seems to airbrush its mythological description of a precipitous mountain.

Topographically, Bhopal is primarily spread over five hills: the Arera, Shyamala, Idgah, Neori and Katara hills. There are two other minor, less conspicuous hills: the Shahpura or Danish hill and the T.T. Nagar hill, which are possibly secondary spurs that came up at the junction of the Shyamala and Arera hills.

For the last three decades, those observing the growth of the city have been alarmed to notice that it is in serious danger of being deprived of its spectacular verdant hills. In the early eighties, the city was more or less clearly demarcated by the five major hills over which it is spread. Through careful and consciously planned architecture, the relatively flat or

Hills of Bhopal seen in the distance, with Fatehgarh Fort in the foreground

plateaued areas were generally allocated for the residential, market-squares and similar zones that would host a larger population. The hills were designated for features that would house a comparatively sparser population, like government offices, art centres and sometimes exclusive residential enclaves. Utmost care and meticulous planning went into keeping the forest cover and the rain-water catchment areas and their feeder rivulets undisturbed and intact.

But, in more recent times, incessant digging and soil erosion, dynamite-blasting and levelling of natural topography in order to build roads and complementary structures – bridges, culverts, pipe-lines etc. to service the ever-burgeoning demand of residential colonies on the hills, has produced a massive erosion of natural contours of the hills. This, in-turn, has either seriously damaged or completely destroyed large chunks of the natural catchment area of the Upper Lake – a drainage system that is the life-line of the local ecosystem, along with the substantial green cover that Bhopal and its surrounding areas have been endowed with. This catchment area comprises of minor, rain-fed rivers and rivulets that circumvent the city and drain into the lakes, significantly, the Upper Lake and keep the water-levels consistent.

Thoughtless and often, incompetent planning by city

South T.T Nagar while it was being developed in 1956

planners and an unholy nexus between the powers that be and the builder-developer lobby, has ensured a steady and rapidly increasing destruction of the environmental and ecological balance in and around Bhopal. Blockage and plugging of naturally flowing rivulets and large-scale felling of trees, compounded by unchecked flattening of hills and hillocks to accommodate residential and commercial buildings, roads and ancillary services, are not only altering the weather pattern for the worse, but are also slowly and surely eroding the tranquil beauty of the city forever.

We have already witnessed the vanishing of the Aravali hills in and around Delhi, and the rampant destruction of the stunning, prehistoric granite rock-formations in the Deccan Plateau near Hyderabad, to cite just two examples, which were a result of reckless construction and quarrying, and which have altered the weather patterns of both these cities. It is now time for us, the citizens of Bhopal, to send up a joint prayer to the heavens and rise in a single, consonant and reverberating voice to let our city be....

If we do not, then, as the poet Andrew Marvell has said:

'But at my back I always hear
Time's winged chariot hurrying near;
And yonder all before us lie
Deserts of vast eternity.
Thy beauty shall no more be found.'

NINE

HIRA HAIRCUTTING SALON – THE FIRST HAIRCUTTING SALON IN BHOPAL

The ancient traditional profession of the 'Nau' or 'Nai' in our culture has gone through several changes along with the metamorphosis of the social order over time. It was perhaps one of the most intimately interactive of all professions, partly because of its prerequisite that two people, not related or associated in any other way, have to share personal space. In Hinduism, no ritual is complete without an active role played by a barber, beginning with the *mundan* in the early stages of one's life, right up to the *shraadh* ceremony conducted after one's demise! From mythological accounts and folklore to Bollywood's masala films, the 'Nai' continues to be omnipresent.

In earlier times, barbers had small makeshift stalls in the bazaars and haats. These open-to-sky, wayside spas performed basic ablutions like cutting trimming and dyeing hair, shaving, providing head and body massages, etc.

Many nais also doubled as spies or the 'kissa-go'. The latter were practitioners of an honourable profession of storytelling, 'dastan-goi' or 'kissa-goi', which was an art that was perfected with practice. The nais invariably had an innate sense of repartee and rhetoric, which are the basic requirement for an accomplished kissa-go. Bhopal, in the not-too-distant past, had barbers who were also famous kissa-go (storytellers). Old timers can still recollect the name of Lalji Bhai, who made it a point to cater to clientele from noble families and learn their tehzeeb and the sophisticated articulation of their language. He always dressed in the typical Bhopali 'pyjamah-kameez' with a 'sadri'. Even though he was illiterate, he could narrate the entire history of Bhopal, right from Dost Mohammad Khan to anecdotal incidents from the lives of the Nawabs.

Lalji Bhai is also credited with establishing the first modern hair cutting salon in Bhopal, called the 'Hira Hair Cutting Salon' (Reference: *Sirf Naqsh-e-Qadam Rah Gayae,* by Shyam Munshi), sometime around the early forties in the Chowki Talaiya area. It was later shifted to Sultaniya Road, and eventually fell victim to the ravages of time and modernisation and was shut down. Gems like Lalji Bhai have now become mere punctuation marks in the evolution of Bhopal as a modern City.

TEN

HUM PARDESI PANCHI BABA

(Nirguni Bhajan rendered by Kan-phate Sadhus at Kumar Gandharva's cremation)

It was a typically humid but pleasant monsoon evening in Bhopal, in July 1987. I, a gawky teenager, sat wide-eyed and dazed, at the residence of Ashok Vajpayee, author and poet of repute and a Hindustani classical music aficionado, who was Secretary to the Culture Department at the time. The presence of so many literary and cultural giants under one roof was at the same time intimidating and exhilarating to me. I did not realise then that I was one of the privileged few who have had the golden opportunity of listening to an artist of the stature of Kumar Gandharva sing in an informal and exclusive private 'baithak'.

Kumarji, as he was affectionately called, was at his vibrant best that evening, and was perhaps more relaxed than he would probably be at a public concert. He sang some 'Tulsi ke pad' exquisitely, followed by some of his most memorable, and now immortal 'Nirguni bhajans', originally written by Kabirdas: '*Ud jayega hans akela...*,' '*Naiharva hum ka na bhave...*,' '*Kaun thagava nagariya...*,' etc. That truly divine evening, when I heard the maestro sing in alternate stretches of high-pitched but magically sonorous bursts, and low, soft and lilting 'taans' in that

Kumar Gandharv – deep in riyaaz

verandah, fragrant with the scent of blooming *chameli* blossoms, will remain etched in my memory forever.

1987 saw Kumar Gandharva perform at the iconic Bharat Bhavan in Bhopal, in some of the most celebrated series of literary and classical festivals organised at the Vagarth and Anhad (respectively, the literary and music sections at Bharat Bhavan).

Born in North Karnataka, aptly called the cradle of Hindustani classical music, as Shivaputra Siddharamayya Komkalimath in April 1924, Kumarji began training in Hindustani classical music under Pandit B.R Deodhar at an early age. His mastery over technique and musical acumen were so deep and rapid that he himself began teaching at the school before he had turned 20. By his early 20s, he had earned his nom de plume – Kumar Gandharva – and had started to garner great praise from audiences and critics alike.

Then, out of the blue, fate dealt an unkind hand. Kumarji was struck with tuberculosis, and was told by doctors that he would never be able to sing again. For the next six years, Kumarji endured a torturous period of illness and silence. Doctors advised him that trying to sing could prove fatal, and gave him little hope of recovery.

Gradually though, aided by excellent care from his wife Bhanumati, and the discovery of streptomycin as a treatment for tuberculosis, which he began to take, Kumarji recovered and began to sing again. However, his voice and singing style would always bear the scars of his illness: one of his lungs had been rendered useless by the disease, so he had to adapt to singing with a single lung.

This challenge compelled him to evolve his own unique style of 'gayaki'. The explorer, maverick and rebel of circumstance that Kumarji innately was, enabled him to redefine the contours of Indian classical music and to evolve a new style of singing that, to an extent, broke the traditional shackles that bound a singer by limiting him to the specific type of gayaki of a 'Gharana'.

He rose like a phoenix from the ashes of his conventional musical training, and soared above all his contemporaries to mesmerise a wide cross-section of music lovers through his newly acquired, ingeniously creative and distinct rendering style. His music started to appeal to the common music lover, who may not have understood the fine nuances of Hindustani music, but had a keen ear for good music. He thus, helped more people discover classical music. Kumarji explored and adapted the singing traditions passed on by wandering hermits, folk-singers and gypsies, and the yogis of the 'Nath' sect and the 'Kanaphatiya sadhus', whose bhajans he adored.

Kumarji was one of the founding trustees of Bharat Bhavan, and has contributed immensely towards creating its music section: *Anhad*. It is because of his inspiration that *Anhad*, to this day, continues to give equal importance and encouragement to *Pandavani* and Malwa folk-performers and singers as it does to classical heavyweights. Kumarjis last public performance was at Bharat Bhavan on 16 December 1988, where he sang Surdas ke pad. He passed away on 12 January, 1992.

'Reins completely loose, galloping in ecstasy and yet contained in melody and time.' This is how the noted Kannada author U.R. Anathamurthy describes Kumar Gandharva's art.

ELEVEN

LYALL BOOK DEPOT – BHOPAL'S OWN LIBRAIRIE GALIGNANI

Apart from the Eiffel Tower, the Notre Dame, and the Louvre, there is another little gem of a landmark in Paris, the *Librairie Galignani*, which claims to be the oldest bookstore in Europe. Parisians do not boast about it, but do acknowledge it with pride when it is enquired about. It was established in 1801, three years before Napoleon Bonaparte became the Emperor of France, and is located in the historical, upmarket Rue de Rivoli.

In India, way back in the 1950s, a dreamy-eyed nineteen-year-old, determined to carry forward the family business of books, arrived in the recently declared capital of the newly formed state of Madhya Pradesh – Bhopal. He was conscious of the fact that he could no longer return to his hometown, Lyallpur, which was now in Pakistan. This young man was Krishna Chandra Rakheja, who opened a multidisciplinary bookstore in Bhopal in October 1956. The bookstore was named Lyall Book Depot, in honour of the family business which had its origin in Lyallpur.

In the years to come, the bookstore would become an iconic milestone for Bhopal. It was multidisciplinary in that it catered to academic requirements of engineers, doctors,

Krishna Chandra Rakheja

lawyers and accountants with its vast collection of professional books and at the same time, it also took care of the requirements of college students who usually did not have much money to spend on books with its stock of used books which cost very little. Furthermore, the bookstore satisfied the hardcore, book-loving intelligentsia with its well-stocked book titles, both Indian and foreign, on eclectic subjects like philosophy, the arts and culture etc. The first book to become a bestseller at Lyall was Jawharlal Nehru's *The Discovery of India*.

Any bibliophile who has grown up in Bhopal in the four decades since the sixties, will definitely have some anecdote to share about Lyall or its owner. Frequent visitors would spend hours skimming through books, reading blurbs and generally taking in the heady ambiance that only a good bookstore can provide. Renowned personalities who were regular visitors included names like M.N. Buch, B.V. Karanth, Ajit Jogi, Javed Akhtar, and a bevy of senior bureaucrats and police officers. Very often, the road opposite would be jam-packed with parked Ambassador cars, with a *lalbatti* and CPZ number-plates (CPZ was the identifier for government vehicles in M.P. at the time).

In my second-year of college, I, too, used to frequent the store and vividly remember the slim gentleman, with a slightly stern, but comforting demeanour, always dressed in an immaculate light-coloured shirt and dark trousers. Before the era of Amazon and Flipkart, Lyall Book Depot was the only place in Bhopal where you could find any book you wanted. I remember buying a copy of *The Transcendence of the Ego,* by

Lyall Book Depot, the iconic bookstore of Bhopal

Jean-Paul Sartre, which my father needed urgently to complete a paper he was writing on Sartre.

The store carried an old world charm, the ambience being that of a library oozing with the erudition and wisdom of the authors – eager to spill over from the shelves. It had that familiar invigorating aroma, very much like petrichor emanating from old books, newly arrived publications, teak shelves and the pheromones of its visitors. It is often said about Galignani of Paris that the books there are not just products; they are, in fact, objets d'art, laden with aesthetics and pearls of wisdom. Without exaggeration, the same was true with Lyall. This store was run like an institution where the relationship between the customer and the storeowner was that of convivial bonhomie! He never had the fawning attribute of a salesman eager to sell his wares and treated all and sundry with a dignified nod of acknowledgement. His son, Vikas, has loyally followed in his father's footsteps and has augmented the honourable business of books by establishing a successful publishing house.

(*Note: Sadly, Lyall Book Depot was completely gutted in a devastating fire in December 2022, marking the end of a glorious era.)*

TWELVE

PUTLIGHAR – MINAR-E-BHOPAL

The architecture of buildings and the way in which spaces within them are utilised conveys mystical, esoteric, cultural, religious and symbolic messages. The 'Minars' (or Minarets) have been somewhat of an architectural enigma, and have drawn analysis from many academic disciplines like psychology, politics, sociology, and the fine arts etc. Minars, it is now understood, were first conceived from four phallic symbols present in a pagan temple that existed in Damascus in pre-Islamic times. Throughout history, phallic architecture has, through consecutive civilisations, been associated with the 'phallic symbols of male domination, power and rational instrumentality.'

In Islamic architecture, minarets and domes have come to accumulate numerous Freudian interpretations, same as the Obelisk in ancient Egypt, the Shivling in the Hindu belief-system, Hermes in the Roman civilization, and Priapus, the Greco-Roman deity etc.

The 'Minar-e-Bhopal' was once a part of the huge industrial complex which Shahjehan Begum had started building in August 1892 in a vast stretch of land just ahead of Shahjehanabad. This complex was, for some unknown reason, called the 'Putlighar'. These days, often mistakenly taken to be

The historic Putlighar in Bhopal

the remnants of a mosque, the minar has been, quite wryly, described by a travel blog as:

'...a bit to the north-east of the Taj Mahal Palace is another intriguing-looking old architectural relic, the Putlighar Minar, apparently a former minaret, but now abandoned and standing alone. It has a scary-looking spiral staircase on the outside, without handrails or anything, and with several steps already missing.'

This minar was the first mill in Bhopal that used a forty horsepower motor for ginning cotton to removing the seeds from the fiber, for producing cotton bales. It gave employment to people, and depending upon the season, also doubled as the place where the knotting and braiding grass into bundles was done, so that it could be used as cattle-fodder. Sometimes, it also served as a flour mill.

The most conspicuous part of this industrial complex is its chimney – the Minar-e-Bhopal – a name apparently coined by some zealous traveler writing about his travels because of its resemblance to the architectural style of Minarets in Iran. The structure of the chimney perhaps has suggestive phallic connotations, and could have probably been inspired by Jules Breton, a French realist artist who advocated the adoption of phallic architecture in late nineteeth-century Paris, and who is thought to have suggested that the Vendome Column at the Venom Place in Paris be adapted into a factory chimney!

The Minar-e-Bhopal may have been intended for a very different purpose, though after the passage of such a long time, historical analysis and modern research do suggest that it could be a symbol of dominance and power quite akin to the Qutub Minar in Delhi, and the Chand Minar in Daulatabad.

THIRTEEN

A SUNDAY WITH R. K. LAXMAN

One of the abiding reasons for my deep affection for the city of Bhopal is that it was here that I not only met, but was blessed enough to be able to spend an entire Sunday interacting with someone whom just not I, but the entire thinking population of the country, loved and admired – the legendary cartoonist, illustrator and humourist, R. K. Laxman, the iconic 'Common Man' himself!

This delightful episode goes back to about two decades, when Laxman was in Bhopal at the invitation of the BHEL Cultural Centre to deliver a lecture. Nothing had prepared me for this overwhelming experience. What I had anticipated would only be a brief, 10-15 minute impersonal, formal, tight-lipped interview...turned out to be a day long, vivacious, no-holds-barred conversation. I was pleasantly surprised when, contrary to his reputation as an erudite recluse, he readily accepted my invitation to my home that evening after his formal engagements were over. So, a major part of this interaction took place in my own home. I still do not believe this stroke of luck....

While waiting for Laxman to arrive at Sanchi Bhawan, the BHEL Guest House, I was filled with that journalistic determination for a 'line-up'. When he arrived, accompanied with his wife, Kamla, there were the brief and obligatory introductions along with an exchange of a great deal of

R.K. Laxman spending a relaxed evening at my home

pleasantries. We then proceeded for the lunch that the Cultural Centre was hosting in his honour. The conversation gradually picked up, and Laxman recounted his Indore visit the previous day in great detail and with his quintessential wit. Describing the arrival of the presiding guest for the event at which he himself was the chief guest, he turned to me and asked with childlike innocence what the difference between a chief guest and presiding guest was!

I could feel the inherent honesty that Laxman had, which automatically seeped into everyone around him. His unreserved, razor-sharp and electric brilliance would compel anyone to question all mundane and worldly situations, actions and reactions that we are engrossed in while living our everyday lives. I observed that Laxman had a childlike innocence and curiosity within him. With a mischievous glint, he asked me to see what the foreigner at another table was reading. When I told him it was Gabriel Garcia Marquez's *Strange Pilgrims*, Laxman told me he was fascinated with Maequez's *One Hundred Years of Solitude*. He narrated another interesting incident, when he was invited to be the chief guest at the Sir J. J. School of Art in Mumbai to deliver the keynote address. It was quite ironic, he said, because during his student days, he had applied for admission to this very institute, but had been flatly refused an entry. Alluding to this, he said in his speech that evening, 'If I had been accepted and had graduated clutching a diploma in art, walking down the portals of the J. J. School of Art (he mimicked a Victorian English accent here), I would have most likely been languishing in some corner of an advertising agency, drawing visuals for foods, bearing the name 'crunchy- munchy vita biscuits'!

Surprisingly, though R.K. Laxman could make any gathering burst out into peals of laughter with his wit, humour and instant repartee, the pensive and brooding eyes behind his library-frame glasses betrayed his outward demeanour – they reflected the many bad hands dealt by life that his spirit must have taken, in order to be tempered into the diamond that the man now was. Those eyes clearly revealed where the vertical lines of worry and parallel lines of surprise on the forehead of the 'Common Man' come from.

As most of us know, the 'Common Man' was the immensely popular and unforgettable caricature by R.K. Laxman, which represented the collective middle and poor class of the country, and pointed out one specific situation or incident, either political or social, that was affecting the country at that particular time, from the front page of *The Times of India*, every morning.

Later that evening, after we had retreated to my home for the evening, the conversation continued over his favourite drink, Old Monk rum. Laxman became reflective. He told us how Kamla, his wife, was his memory, calendar, diary and itinerary, all rolled into one. It was a pleasure to listen how he met Kamla, who also happens to be his niece; the description of his mother's smell, the awesome personality of his father, his fascination for cane furniture, his extreme hatred for 'the obvious things in life', and of course, his Nietzschean disdain for God: *'I don't believe in God, God believes in me.'* We indeed covered quite a gamut of subjects in an animated yet amicable atmosphere that evening.

It became difficult for me to create an ambience in which I could shoot-off my formal questions for the interview I was to do, amidst his constant hilarity and constructive sarcasm. But I did manage to formally interview Laxman, an achievement which I am proud of. I reproduce the interview below:

Me: What in your life has affected you most, which prompted you to choose cartooning as a profession?
R.K. Laxman: I didn't choose cartooning, cartooning chose me. I learnt it from the ambience in which I was born. Children first learn to draw, then they learn to write. But for me it was drawing all the way from age three. I have been illustrating for my brother throughout. No institution teaches a man to be humorous. I have subconsciously learnt the essence of the human feature called caricature.

Me: What are the types of personalities that attract you?
R.K.L: Politicians don't work for the nation, they work for me! When I started, it was the time of Second World War, the time of Winston Churchill, Stalin, Hitler, and Mussolini. Freedom movement personalities like Gandhi, Nehru, and Patel. After independence, Indira Gandhi, for quite a long time. Narsimha Rao being the most sketchable. The greatest problem I faced was when Rajiv Gandhi took over as prime minister, he was just too handsome to make a caricature off. I was afraid that soon I'd be out of my profession if he fulfilled all the promises he had made, but I was lucky he faltered in the end.

Me: In one of your interviews you said that a cartoonist is the saddest person...?
R.K.L: Do I look sad? (laughs). Cartoonists are not the saddest but the most tormented people. A cartoonist has to choose from

the gristly mill of everyday newspaper headlines. Cartooning is always an agonising, painful and torturous business. The muse of cartooning does not appear so easily.

Me: Can a cartoonist manifest an ideological bent or approach through his cartoons? Can it be encased in an ideology?

R.K.L: Cartooning is an art of complaints and disapproval. It's an art of irony, paradoxes and opposing forces of ridiculous contradictions. If a cartoonist manifests an ideaology, he will be a propagandist. Cartoonists are not builders and destroyers of society, but they look for faults in society. Even if I ever live in utopia, I would still look for lacunae.

Me: Apart from a political cartoonist you have been a short story writer, fiction writer, and also TV serial director. What do you find the most relaxing?

R.K.L: I draw sketches of Ganapati. There are forms of Ganapati in the entangled roots; it is so clear and recognisable. Suggestive, so I've nine or ten of them. Along with it my friend, the crow, they get sold very well. Those are my relaxing business. If I get tired of them what do I do? I repair clocks, I've got quite a few of them broken, remove the whole thing, put it back, oil it, the joy of seeing them, get up at One o' clock at night and look at it and the blooming thing has stopped at twelve 'O' – clock (laughs). I even model with M-seal. But now I don't find time at all, I've taken on too much of work, not political but, I do calendars, I do, for example, ICICI advertising promotional things, BPL, they come to me, I freelance on all those things. Illustrate books on management, somebody writes, Sharu Rangnekar writes the book on management and (laughs) I illustrate them. Then I regularly do for an American magazine called *The Leader*, also for an American newspaper weekly called *India Abroad*, I send sketches of Indian life. Where do I get time for anything?

Me: In your autobiography, *The Tunnel of Time*, if I may comment on it, I presume, it must be something like *The Malgudi Days,* as you perceive them. Is it nostalgia? A positive one though....

R.K.L: It's nothing to do with *Malgudi Days.* See, I'll tell you, my brother and I were born in the same place, gone through the same experiences, walked through the same streets, met the same people. He converted it into fiction and I've done my bit as an impression. He's got a verbal reaction; I've a visual reaction of the same hut, of people and so on. But in this *Tunnel of Time* my experience in England, TS Eliot, Graham Greene, Presley, Bertrand Russel, I met them, Atlee in Labour Conference. My brother has never met all those people, I've met. I've written about that. You might like that.

Me: As it generally happens with all creative geniuses – it's nearer to a work of fiction than a chronology of events?

R.K.L: I've mentioned in the initial stages this is not an autobiography in the normal sense. Then I'd become so self-conscious, I won't be able to carry on. I've no diary, no calendar, I don't even wear a watch, this watch is of my wife's, what you see (laughs). And I don't record anything, don't keep old letters and refer to them. I depend upon my memory for what it is worth. I've written, on, JJ School of Arts, meeting Nehru, everything has come, but I hardly mention any names. How I walked into *Times of India* after resigning from *Free Press Journal,* there's a slight tension there, and my neighbour was Bal Thackrey, we both sat and did cartoons for six months. All that I never mentioned, whom I saw, who my editor was, name of the editor Mr Frank Mores, was there someone else? No. Some people were eager to know, but I never said because they are not important in my life (laughs).

FOURTEEN

REMEMBERING MISS AUER

Since colonial times, India has seen extremely sagacious, dedicated and strong British women who made India their home, and who stood up for and devoted themselves to noble causes for the betterment of the Indian masses. The most notable ones are of course, Annie Besant who is known for the Home Rule Movement that is believed to have set the stage for the independence movement in India, and who was by far the most prominent Englishwoman involved in the Indian freedom struggle; and Madeleine Slade or Mirabehn as she was christened by Mahatma Gandhi, whose ardent follower she was. Since 1925, she always stood by his side during all the freedom movements he initiated and helmed, she had given up her elite lifestyle to follow and practice the spartan Gandhian way of life.

In the legacy of Annie Besant and Mirabehn, Bhopal too, has been fortunate to have had an extraordinary Englishwoman, who made Bhopal her home and dedicated herself completely in kindling young hearts and minds in the field of education, which was her area of expertise, for over three decades. 'I blow my candle light, but don't blow out the stars!'. A fine poet, as the preceding line demonstrates, and a gifted teacher, Iris Cynthia Philomene Auer, M.B.E. (1904-1998), founded the All Saints School in Bhopal with a mere eight students in 1980, and which today has evolved into the All Saints Group of Institutions. Miss

Miss Auer

Auer had taught Kaiser Bia Zaman, scion of the Kurwai state, in England and came to Bhopal in 1967 on her request. With the All Saints School she inspired generations of students with her value system. She was honoured with the Member of the Order of the British Empire (M B E) for her contribution towards education, in 1989.

I first met Miss Auer one balmy evening at the Kurwai House on Idgah Hills, when I had gone to meet Zia, who along with her elder sister Maryam, was among the first Indian students of Miss Auer's. Zia was a talented young woman and together we had started the Bhopal Chapter of GROUND (Group for Nuclear Disarmament) in 1987. At the time, I was deeply into Russian literature, so when I first saw Miss Auer, sitting elegantly on a cane chair, she reminded me of a Grand Duchess! I soon developed an admiration for her *joie de vivre,* her perfect Queen's English and her razor-sharp intellect.

In all my adolescent haughtiness, I would try to flaunt my knowledge of English history. To my surprise I found that Miss Auer could put certain historical events and milestones in perfect logical perspective with great élan. Once while discussing Churchill, who had led England to victory in the Second World War, I almost belittled the English people for having dislodged his Conservative Party and voting in a Labour led government under Clement Atlee after the War. Miss Auer interjected me and said, 'No, we did the right thing; Churchill was our leader during the War, we couldn't have elected him when we had peace.'

...A wise advice for all of us today!

FIFTEEN

SHAKEELA BANO BHOPALI – THE FORGOTTEN QAWWALI QUEEN

The year was 1951. It was just two years after the sun had set upon the feudal history of the 250 years of uninterrupted existence of the Bhopal riyaasat, though the aura and the trappings of regality still remained undiminished. During a festive occasion a musical soiree was organised at the Ahmedabad Palace. It was customary for young and budding singers and musicians to be introduced at such soirees under the strict patronage and supervision of their teachers – the Ustaads. The audience was members of the aristocratic families of Bhopal, a few remaining Britishers and music connoisseurs; the ambience was somewhat heavy with the futile, overhanging nostalgia of the days gone by! Nawab Bhopal, Hamidullah Khan was the guest of honour.

A young singer, all of nine years old, started singing. The song was the latest popular number originally sung by the noted playback singer Shamshad Begum from the Hindi film 'Bahar': *'Dunia ko laat maro, duniyaa salaam kare, mud mud salaam kare, jhuk jhuk salaam kare....'* Suddenly, there was a flutter in the audience... gesticulating and enacting every word of the song, the little singer had started to kick in the direction of the ex-Nawab sitting in the audience! Even though the

Bhopal State had been merged with India, the protocol towards royalty was still subconsciously in place and kicking in the direction of the ex-Nawab was certainly not acceptable.

But the little girl got away scot-free, mainly because of her talent and her confident performance that evening. This little girl grew to be Shakeela Bano, who was of Pathan descent and had inherited the nonchalant attitude and great sense of self-worth that the Pathan women of Bhopal typically possessed. After Shakeela had garnered much public adulation and popularity in Bhopal, the suffix 'Bhopali' was added after her name, to make her the inimitable Shakeela Bano *Bhopali.*

What Begum Akhtar, the queen of *gazal* singing was to Awadh, Shakeela Bano was to Bhopal. Shakeela's sense of her own self-worth was very strong, as mentioned above, and it manifested itself in her demeanor, conduct, and in her political views. This confidence showed in her performances on stage. Though unlike Begum Akhtar, whose popularity was limited to aficionados of the more refined and rather eclectic form of singing – the *gazal*, Shakeela Bano's *qawwali* was popular across board – from aristocrats and connoisseurs of music, to the common man on the street.

In the 1950s, Shakeela went to Bombay to try her luck in films, and soon became a craze over there as well, with her films like *Jagir, Dastak, Shradhanjali* etc. doing good business. At the same time, she remained popular as a *qawwal.* Some gems in her repertoire include such hits as *'Milte hi nazar tumse, hum ho gaye deewane; Peene waale meri ankhon se piya karte hain; Sainyan doli leke aaye tere dwar,* and *Ab yeh chhod diya hai tujhpe* amongst others. It is said that film producers would re-release their films that had flopped earlier, after adding a *qawwali* or two by Shakeela and this would turn the fortunes of their films, making them successful. Although the first qawwali that was recorded in a female voice was that of the famous

Shakeela Bano Bhopali

Nurjahan, *Aahen Na Bharin Shikve Na Kiye* (Lyricist Naqsh Lyallpuri from the film Zeenat -1945), Shakeela continued to remain the first female qawwal to maintain the musical genre of *qawwali.*

In my assessment, her comparison with the famous Egyptian Singer Umm Kulthum, who dominated the Middle Eastern music scene for close to five decades, is more apt than with Begum Akhtar. Like Kulthum, Shakeela too faced tough competition from established female singers of her time, and instead of performing for a more exclusive audience, both Kulthum and Shakeela performed mainly for the general public, thus expanding elitist classical and traditional genres of music into the popular realm.

Unfortunately, Bhopal, her birth place also became the death-knell for Shakeela. She was exposed to the lethal methyl isocyanate gas in the Bhopal gas disaster in December 1984, while visiting a relative. She could never recover from the after effects of the poisonous gas, and after a long period of hospitalisation, compounded by neglect by family and fans over the years, died a painful and lonely death in 2002.

Perhaps the overarching presence of the five Begum Nawabs, spanning over almost two-hundred years of rule has dwarfed many prominent and illustrious female personalities. Shakeela Bano was one of them. Why do we have such amnesia when it comes to taking care of the people who have consolidated our cultural heritage and legacy? Shakeela Bano was not an exception, countless others musicians, writers, singers and painters have had much worse fate.

In her own words:

'Un ko fursat kahāñ jo ye socheñ
bāno imsāl kis vabāl meiñ hai'

(Where does anyone have the time to think; what calamities have befallen Bano?)

SIXTEEN

BHATSUAR – THE BHOPALI JUGAAD

If we were to go with the famous Hindi adage – *kahin ki eent, kahin ka roda; bhanumati ne kunba joda,* attributed to Bhanumati, the wife of Duryodhan, then certainly 'Jugaad' as a concept must date back to the Mahabharata!

The jugaad approach to innovation has become so popular that Jaideep Prabhu has authored a book: *Jugaad Innovation: A Frugal and Flexible Approach to Innovation for the 21st Century.* Jugaad is actually a quintessential instant, impromptu and improvised solution to a situation or thing, which comes out of sheer cunning creativity and through the use of whatever resources are available at hand. *'A frugal, flexible and inclusive way that taps into the native ingenuity of millions of Indians, across social and economic groups,'* says Prabhu in his book. But the most accurate description comes from a blog: 'Jugaad is an ancient Indian cultural belief and daily practice that anything is possible. It is the divine union of the impossible and the possible, a magical mixture of ingenuity and locally sourced ingredients.'

Over the years, jugaad has also been applied to improvise motor vehicles. The undulating terrain and a severely inadequate public transport system, prompted Bhopalis to come up with their own jugaad – the wildly famous Bhatsuar.

The Bhatsuar – an example of classic Bhopali jugaad

Its body resembled that of a big, fat pig and it made an unrelenting, ear-splitting noise of bhat...bhat...bhat... when its improvised engine, assembled from a motley collection of parts from all types of derelict vehicles, was jerked into life. The name *bhatsuar* was derived from the fact that its ungainly shape resembled that of a bloated pig (*suar* in Hindi) and the constant drone of bhat...bhat...bhat... while being driven. The carriage accommodated around 12-15 passengers and was made from metal sheets stapled together in a haphazard manner. Its roughly triangular body rested on three wheels. The basic but huge handlebar gear-shift that operated three forward and one reverse gears. It had a precarious brake-pedal. It was fuelled by diesel, but I strongly suspect that it was mostly cheap kerosene from the government ration shops that was used instead. The *bhatsuar* may have been an unlikely public transport marvel, but it was also a big-time air-pollutant. Over the years, this eye-sore of a vehicle eventually phased itself out, with the arrival

The Bhopali Jeep

of better options of public transport that were less damaging to the environment and more convenient for people.

Another typical Bhopali jugaad is the still ubiquitous Bhopali jeep. The romance of Bhopalis with this rustic machine goes back to when the thirteenth and the last Nawab of the Bhopal state, Hamidullah Khan. When he was sworn-in as the Nawab, he ordered a fleet of eighteen automobiles from Nash Motors in the USA, and had them all customised for shikar. He continued his love affair with these mean machines and during the Second World War, further added to his fleet of shikar vehicles the Austin Champ Jeep, one of which still adorns the entrance of the Noor-Us-Sabah Palace Hotel.

Hamidullah was a Don Juan kind of strapper who was considered to be a trendsetter. Many amongst Bhopal's nobility tried to emulate his lifestyle. Those were the days of large landholdings, predominantly covered with forests and sprawling grasslands that swarmed with large game. It became a fashion statement of sorts for members of the nobility and the *noveau riche* of the Bhopal state to drive down to their farmhouses in their jeeps and return home with a shikar. This jeep would typically be a left-hand drive, with two huge fuel canisters and a hammock-like sack hanging from the back end.

This was called the jhola, which was made of jute or nylon, and was used to ferry the hunted game back.

The Bhopali jeep kept on being innovatively modified, mostly by master-mechanics like Mohammad Zameer, also fondly called 'Nirale'. His family has run a motor repairing garage since 1946, and still has a deluge of customers who want alterations to their jeeps. The emphasis is on preserving an antique look, with peeling paint and bullet marks to give it an elegantly rough demeanour.

The Bhopali jugaad survives, and how!

SEVENTEEN

THE 'BHOOT BANGLA' TALES – BHOPAL'S OWN GHOST STORIES

There are at least a dozen places in and around Bhopal about which spooky tales abound, and where people are said to have experienced paranormal activities. Such juicy gossip is now the warp and weft of the fabric of the city's life. For example, the Raisen fort is rumoured to contain the mythical 'Paras Patthar', which is supposedly guarded by djinns (genies). The area around the infamous Union Carbide plant, the Dow Industrial Area complex, is said to be haunted by the ghosts of the innumerable people who died in the tragic gas disaster in December 1984.

Another fort which, though situated some distance from Bhopal, the Shivapuri fort, is rumoured to be the abode of the spirit of its builder, the Maratha king Vir Khanderao, which is said to be unable to let go the king's hedonistic lifestyle while he was alive. It is also supposed to be guarding an enormous treasure buried somewhere in the fort. Residents of the nearby settlements swear by the belief that anyone who happens to witness the music and dance soirees that this ghost put up on full moon nights, is fated to die soon after.

Then there is the legendary Bhoot Bangla in Bhopal, scary and spine-chilling tales of which are very popular. Earlier known

The Taj Mahal Palace in Bhopal – haunted by history

as the Wahid manzil, it was located in the Lal Ghati area on the way to the airport. Vivid recollections of many spooky ghost-sightings in the decrepit, unoccupied building can be heard from old timers. Apparitions in grotesque shapes and sizes, terrifying, screechy and piercing sounds and voices, deep echoing laughter coming out of nowhere, made for horrifying, but nonetheless intriguing, accounts of the denizens of the netherworld. Sometime ago, this (ill)famous Bhoot Bangla of Bhopal was razed to the ground by city administration.

In her book, *Memoirs of a Rebel Princess,* Abida Sultan, the daughter of the last Nawab, narrates an incident that she believed was her close encounter with the supernatural. It was while attending the annual mela (fair) at the ladies' club which she patronised. This mela was organised in a very old haveli (mansion). By the time it got over, it had started getting dark. As she prepared to leave, she felt the need to go to the makeshift toilet that had been put up in the cellar. But since it was not very clean, she decided to use an isolated backyard of the haveli instead. Despite having been warned about the presence of 'churails' in the backyard, Abida dared to go there all by herself. While driving back to her palace, the Rahat Manzil, on the road along the lake, she suddenly heard some whistling, whispering voices taunting, coming from the back of the car. Abida writes:

> 'I passed my hand behind the rear seats and all over the dark foot-rest area in the back and found it empty. I was stunned and aghast. Just then, a hundred shrill voices began shrieking...followed by clapping and peels of mocking laughter.'

Like all the erstwhile Islamic principalities, particularly Lucknow, Hyderabad and Delhi, Bhopal also assimilated the tales of Djinns and fairies from Persian and Arabian folklore and interbred these with the local tales of 'bhoots', 'pishaach' and 'churails'.

EIGHTEEN

THE *BHOPALI ZUBAAN*

'If you talk to a man in a language he understands, that goes to his head.
If you talk to him in his own language, that goes to his heart.' said Nelson Mandela.

'A language is not just words. It's a culture, a tradition, a unification of a community, a whole history that creates what a community is. It's all embodied in a language...'as the great American linguist Noam Chomsky has surmised on what language signifies. However, if the civilisational parameter of a culture is its language, then a more nuanced word for language would be the Persian term: *Zubaan*. Etymologically, it means the spoken language of a specific place, but accurately, it means a spoken language that has absorbed the essence of the culture and society and their continuing evolution within a civilisation.

Due to the overarching reach of Islamic dynasties throughout the sub-continent in the medieval period, Farsi (Persian) remained the court language over a very long period of time. There was the *zubaan-e-nizam* (language of the administration) and the *zubaan-e-majhab* (language of the religion). Then there was the language spoken by the hoi polloi, the *zubaan-e-aam*, which carried the typical ethos of the hubbub of everyday life. All three of them combined make for a rich oral tradition.

The language tradition of Bhopal has a very interesting history. Before the city was founded in the mid-seventeenth century, the Gond tribe ruled almost the entire hilly regions of Central India for about four centuries. Over time, the Gonds developed social, cultural and political interactions as well as matrimonial alliances with prominent Hindu and Muslim royal families of those times. Because of this, the tribal race gradually evolved into a more sophisticated ethnic group which was heavily influenced by the language and life-style of their contemporary Mughal and the Rajput clans. Thus, it is thought that the Gond ruling class adapted themselves to speaking Persian. The ordinary tribesmen, however, stuck to speaking in their own native dialects – *Gondi* and *Korku* (a dialect derived from Tamil and Kannada, and spanning a cultural connection between many tribal groups). But due to the incessant appropriation of their culture and language, the Gond kingdoms and their languages soon got subsumed by other, more prevalent languages of the time, thus vindicating Chomsky's observation that: '*...when a language disappears, a lot is lost. A language is a repository of cultural wealth. Each language is a way of understanding and interpreting the world.*'

Later, after the establishment of the Bhopal State by the Afghans, Farsi remained the *zubaan-e nizam* utill about 1857, when the then Nawab, Sikandar Jahan Begum changed it to Urdu, which was heavily influenced by Persian. Arabic continued to be the *zubaan-e-majhab*. Being a relatively new administrative setup, the Bhopal State had an eclectic and assimilatory culture; the farsighted Nawabs encouraged people from all faiths and all parts of the World to settle here so as to acquire the best talent into their state. It is also thought that some Afghan families spoke only Pashto, the native Afghani language and were often called the *Kharya,* which was a not-so-acceptable term. Fazal Tabish, the well-known author-poet from Bhopal, has mentioned this in his novel, *Voh Aadmi,* which is inspired by his own life and times in Bhopal.

The language of the common populace of Bhopal continued to be a mishmash of Pashto, Turkish and Hindi (not Hindi as we know it, but a potpourri of 'Khariboli', 'Brajbasha' and 'Avadhi' – a mixture which the Sufi poet Amir Khusro called 'Hindavi'). This, I presume, later evolved into the typical Bhopali '*zubaan*', or in the racy liveliness, popularly called *bakr,* which is replete with words like 'tuppar' or 'thatte' for roof, 'tum-tum' for the horse-driven 'tonga', or 'chhaliya' for betel-nut, 'kavelu' for roof-tiles, etc. It continued to evolve, while being polished consistently and growing richer with the constant infusion of fresh words from Marathi and Chhattisgarhi, after the state of Madhya Pradesh was etched out of the Central Provinces and Berar in 1956.

Remember the rib-tickling twang: '*ese kese pese, miyan*', immortalised by Jagdeep as Soorma Bhopali in the movie *Sholay*?

NINETEEN

BHOPALI CUISINE – EVOLUTION AND INFLUENCES

In comprehending the history of mankind, it becomes amply clear that no civilisation is complete without its prototypical cuisine, staple food and festive fare. Quite a bit is known about the gastronomic tradition of Bhopal. Dost Mohammad Khan loved his roast guinea fowl and roast duck. He was known to have never eaten sweetmeats of any kind, nor encourage his soldiers to eat any. It appears that he may have combined the high-protein meat diet of the Afghans with the locally available and predominantly eaten, grain and vegetable-based diet of the original inhabitants of the area.

If we were to study the evolution of a food culture specific to Bhopal, we would not identify a specific, unique, *Bhopali* flavour or palate. We will instead discover that Bhopali cuisine is a collection of flavours influenced by many cuisines that have been tweaked by either adding or removing particular ingredients, or by altering cooking methods to better suit local conditions and availability of ingredients.

Since the time modern Bhopal was founded, many regions have implicitly and often ambiguously, affected the taste and look of food in Bhopal. It is an amalgamation of influences from Hyderabadi and Lucknowi cuisines, with touches of the

Afghani, Malwa, Nimaari kitchens, and interestingly, even the food of primitive tribes like the Korkus and the Gonds!

Traditional cuisines have always been affected strongly by the climate and soil of the particular region, the social and financial status of the people living there, the norms and regulations of caste and tribe. Thus, the Gonds and Korkus tribes' staple, made from two types of millets, *kodo* and *kutki*, finds an echo in today's exotic dishes like 'mundiya ka pech' and 'chusela'. A residual Afghani effect can be seen in the 'bade ka kebab', 'khade masala ka gosht', 'bakre ka paya', and the typical old Bhopal biryani, which intriguingly, is served during breakfast! This biryani does not require the elaborate and precise cooking method or a nuanced use of spices, and is very light on the stomach.

The Arab and Central Asian soldiers that came to Bhopal brought with them the famous *Dilli ki nalli nihari*, the *Sulemani chai* (which became so popular that it was rechristened as the *Bhopali Sulemani chai*), haleem or khichda, the Bhopali filfora etc. The Nawabs' kitchens liberally used traditional Afghan recipes, along with a sprinkling of Lucknawi and Nizami food. Invariably, some of their best *khansamas* came from Lucknow and Hyderabad. But ingenious tweaks to recipes by the Bhopali chefs, for example, using only star anise (chakra phool) instead of *garam masala*, and not using the *dhungar* (smoking) method, imparted these dishes a distinct, new flavour. It made them taste very different from their original avatars from the then renowned fine cuisines of Delhi, Rampur, Lucknow and Hyderabad.

The most popular dish from the kitchens of the Bhopal Begums was the *kalia razala,* which is mentioned in the book, *The Cooking Delights of the Maharajas*, by Digvijaya Singh, the Raja of Sailana. Typically, Nimari food like the Bhopali 'pohe' with sev, and 'fariyali khichdi' have also become popular. But by far the most underrated, yet immensely popular dish eaten by the poor and the rich alike is the *Bhopali tukde.* This is nothing but leftover pieces of *roti,* dried in the sun and then steamed with pulses.

Apart from this, Bhopal also enticed people, even foreigners, to indigenise their rituals and cuisine. The Bourbons of Bhopal, who are indelibly connected to the history of the city, also adopted many local rituals and modified their dietary habits. Indira Iyengar, a Bourbon descendant, mentions in her book *The Bourbons and Begums of Bhopal: The Forgotten History,* a dish similar to the *Bhopali tukde.* She describes the '*Malidha* festival', which was a ceremony that was held on 3rd December every year, on the occasion of the Feast of St. Francis. *Malidha* is an Urdu term for anything that is crushed before being eaten. For this, very thick *puris* were made from dough that was kneaded with ghee. These thick *puris* were then crushed by hand and made into *malidha,* which was then blessed by the priest, before it was consumed.

Indira also mentions a mouth-watering dish which was eaten after the prayers on Maundy Thursday during the Christian holy month of Lent. This is the *besan ki roti* (bread made from chickpea flour) and *baingan ka bharta* (a kind of mash made from roasted eggplant). The beauty of this dish was that it maintained the sanctity of the holy month of fasting by observing the virtue of frugality, as not a drop of ghee was used in the making of this dish.

Mumtaz Khan, ace fashion designer, and a connoisseur of and writer on Bhopali Culture says that there is a reason why in most of the old Bhopal families sweet and savoury food is eaten together. For example:

> 'nukti (motichoor) with khaare (savoury snacks), Zarda (sweet saffron rice) with pulao or biryani, chana (chickpeas)

> with chironji (Ilaichi daana) etc.' He mentions that 'Nawab Hamidullah used to keep channas in one hand and chironji (Ilaichi dana) in another for Iftaar during Roza, waiting for the 'tope' (cannon) to fire, which is an announcement to break the fast. Immediately after that he used to mix these and eat them. He further had this peculiar habit of mixing the zarda with biryani. A famous khansama from Hyderabad is believed to have become so exasperated with this habit of the Nawab that he left the palace swearing never to return.'

All the dishes mentioned above have now found its patrons from the star hotels to the 'dhabhas' and shacks in and around Bhopal.

TWENTY

THE FIRST NEWSPAPER AND CINEMA HALL OF BHOPAL

Recently, while reading a review of the much acclaimed book, *Hicky's Bengal Gazette: The Untold Story of India's First Newspaper,* by Andrew Otis, I started ruminating about the history of the newspaper in Bhopal. A bit of research and passing references in some write-ups on Bhopal lead me to two important developments that occurred during the early thirties which were notable enough to make an interesting story. Newspapers and cinema halls are also a part of salient features that contribute towards determining social developmental indices of cities.

Surprisingly, Bhopal, despite being a feudal protectorate, was a notch above many territories being directly administered by the British during the Raj. By all accounts, the Bhopal Begums were the *first-among-equals* when it came to performing their sovereign duties such as education along with health and revenue reforms. It was Shahjehan Begum who started a government newspaper, *Umdatul* in 1871. The effect of this was gradual but heady. Nawab Hamidullah Khan, with his liberal and modern outlook encouraged all avenues which had the potential of exposing his people to the stimulating and informative progress that the outside World was witnessing

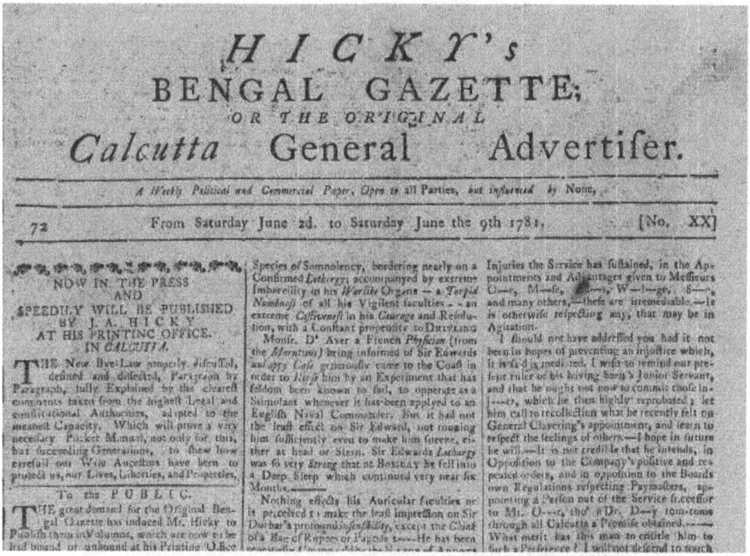

HICKY's
BENGAL GAZETTE;
OR THE ORIGINAL
Calcutta General Advertiſer.

A Weekly Political and Commercial Paper, Open to all Parties, but influenced by None.

72 From Saturday June 2d. to Saturday June the 9th 1781. [No. XX]

NOW IN THE PRESS
AND
SPEEDILY WILL BE PUBLISHED
BY J. A. HICKY
AT HIS PRINTING OFFICE
IN CALCUTTA.

THE New Bye-Law properly diſſected, defined and diſſected, Paragraph by Paragraph, fully Explained by the clearest comments taken from the highest Legal and constitutional Authorities, adapted to the meanest Capacity. Which will prove a very necessary Pocket Manual, not only for this, but succeeding Generations, to shew how carefull our Wise Ancestors have been to protect us, our Lives, Liberties, and Properties.

To the PUBLIC.

THE great demand for the Original Bengal Gazette has induced Mr. Hicky to Publish them in Volumes, which are now to be had bound or unbound at his Printing Office

The first newspaper to be printed in India

in all spheres. This he did even at the cost of rubbing the British colonial administration the wrong way on one hand, and fomenting dissent within his own people, on the other.

It was Nawab Hamidulah, who, as the head of state, gave the Bhopal region its first newspaper, *Nadeem,* in 1933, which was not an establishment gazette like *Umadatul* but an independent newspaper. It came out in the official language, Urdu, which had been proclaimed the court language by Nawab Sikander Begum way back in 1858. Sikander Jahan considered Urdu to be closer to the people than the more intellectual and scholarly Farsi (Persian). This was quite a revolutionary step in a time when even the British went with the Mughal tradition of holding court proceedings in Persian.

However, after the merger of the Bhopal State with the Indian Union, *Nadeem* continued its glorious run. It continued to be published by Hakeem Syed Qamrool Hasan, an eminent citizen of Bhopal. He was assigned this responsibility by the

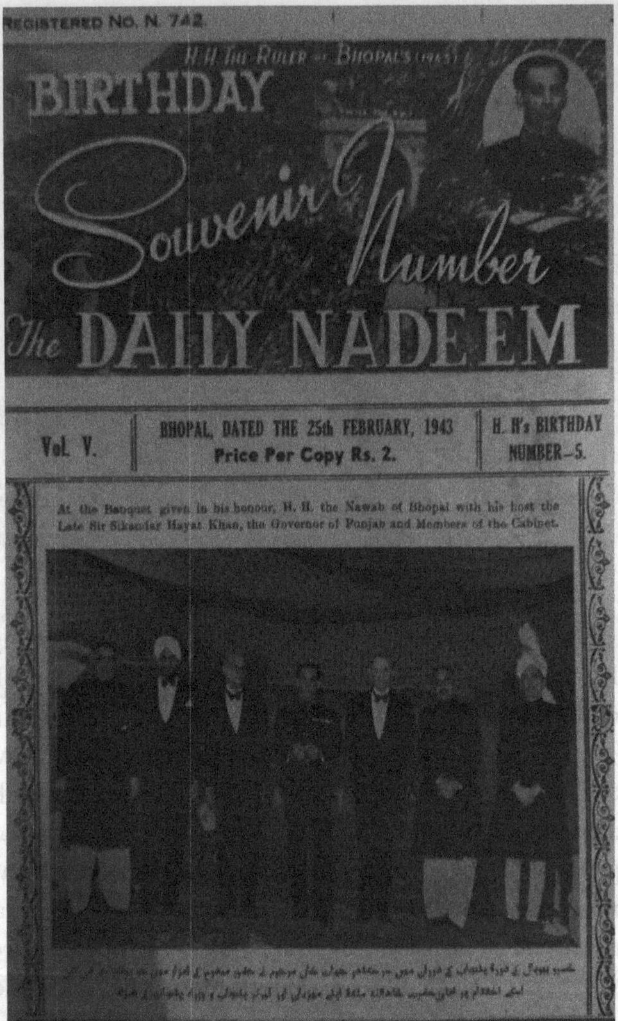
REGISTERED NO. N. 742

H.H. THE RULER OF BHOPAL'S (1943)

BIRTHDAY Souvenir Number

The DAILY NADEEM

Vol. V.	BHOPAL, DATED THE 25th FEBRUARY, 1943 Price Per Copy Rs. 2.	H. H's BIRTHDAY NUMBER—5.

At the Banquet given in his honour, H. H. the Nawab of Bhopal with his host the Late Sir Sikandar Hayat Khan, the Governor of Punjab and Members of the Cabinet.

Cover and Pictures Printed at the Rajal Press, Chawri Bazar, Delhi.

An issue of 'Nadeem', the first newspaper to be published in Bhopal

Nawab himself. After Qamrool Hasan, his son Arif Hasan kept the family tradition going, and is the current owner and publisher of *Nadeem.* He proudly states that *Nadeem* is not only the first newspaper in any language to be published today from Madhya Pradesh, but it also holds the enviable record of being the longest continually running Urdu daily, still going strong today as the *Rozana Nadeem*. Elders in-the-know from the old city area recall the peculiar voice modulation of a particular hawker of this newspaper, who was blind, and whose unusual call was impatiently awaited each morning.

I used to wonder why movie halls were called talkies in the olden days. When movie halls came into existence, they only screened silent movies. It was only after the first Indian 'talkie' – the first Indian feature film with sound, *Alam Araa* – released in 1931 that the term 'talkies' became popular. In the late thirties, after talking movies had made their debut, there was a picture hall in the Itwara area of the old city area of Bhopal, which was called 'Tatta talkies'. It was called this because it was in fact a largish shanty, made from used wood, sacks and tin-sheets, which in the local jargon were called 'tattas' and 'phattas'. A ticket cost just one *ānā* (which was 1/16th of a rupee), and one had to bring his own mat to sit on while watching the movie. And quite oddly, though it was called a 'talkies', it only screened silent movies! Nevertheless, it is this one of a kind 'Tatta talkies' which holds the claim of being the first cinema hall in Bhopal.

Interestingly, the first newspaper of Bhopal was started by a king but the first picture hall was started by the hoi polloi, the commoners. This is a spectacular sociological message!

TWENTY-ONE

THE *HAMMAM* IN BHOPAL – AN ENDURING LEGACY

Etymologically, the word 'hammam' means 'bath' in Arabic. The concept of a hammam gained large-scale popularity with the Turks, who refined and extended it to include public bathing stations which had specialised and elaborate structural engineering design and architecture. These later set a trend and became the hallmark of all 'Turkish Baths' in Europe, the Middle East and India.

The idea of public bath-houses originated in ancient Greece, one of the oldest civilisations, but remained limited to hip-baths. The Romans developed this concept further, to include almost all those features that are now found in Turkish baths all over the world. These were built in an architectural style known as *Çamberlitaş*. This is a unique set of intricate water-duct designs and made of special building materials with thermostatic properties for temperature control. This fascinating feat of human ingenuity made possible a continuous and unprecedented refinement for luxury and comfort. The Turks could also have incorporated Islamic elements and Unani (Greek) bathing techniques in the hammams, after being influenced by the Byzantine empire, which they had captured.

Mostly seen as a Turkish import, the hammam formed a

mandatory part of the palaces of the rulers during the Sultanate era, the Mughals and later, the splinter Islamic and Hindu kingdoms in India. It was also adopted by the Rajputs and the Marathas. It imbibed many attributes of the Islamic culture, too.

While there is no dearth of hammams in India, nearly all of them are vestiges of the grand ruins of the splendour of forts and palaces of the past, which, sadly, are now in various stages of decay. Bhopal boasted of many hammams in earlier times, particularly within the palaces of the nobility in Islamnagar and the more famous one near Peer Darwaza, but all of them were meant exclusively for the members of the royal household.

Another continuum that Bhopal as a city has kept with its past history is a 300-year-old still functional, hammam, which is still being run by a determined family of barbers who trace their ancestry to a trusted 'hajjam' of the first Nawab, Dost Mohammad Khan. Called Hammu Khalida, he received the hammam as a gift from the Nawab, for his adroitness as an expert masseur and for having valuable knowledge of exotic medicinal herbs and healing oils. It was he who opened this luxury, hitherto the domain of nobility and rich business households, to the common people.

Located in the ramparts of the old fort opposite the Kilol park, this traditional hammam, earlier called the 'Hammam-e-Qadimi,' and now rechristened as the Royal Qadimi Hammam. Mohammad Jameel, its present owner, inherited it from his father Abdul Jaleel and grandfather Abdul Rashid. It is essentially a steam-bath spread over an area of about five thousand square feet, consisting of four large rooms.

The first room is the waiting room, modestly furnished in the old living-room style, and maintained at a moderate temperature. The second is a prep room for the actual bath. It is relatively warmer than the first, and here customers are acclimatised to take on the hot bath which is to come next.

The Royal Qadimi Hammam of Bhopal

An interior view of Royal Qadimi Hammam

The third room is the steam-room, in which steam percolates out through perforated openings in the walls. The fourth room is where the temperature crosses 60 degree Celsius, and where the masseurs scrub your body with a special pumice stone from Ajmer, before massaging it with oils mixed with herbs. It takes almost 30 to 35 quintals of firewood and eight days to start the hammam, with a recurring need for another 3 to 4 quintals of wood every day to keep it running. The hammam opens only for six months in a year – from Diwali up to Holi.

The most captivating and impressive part is that despite the paltry income that it generates and the daunting challenges the owner faces in terms of managing to procure the firewood, stiff and unfair competition from the fast mushrooming modern and chic spas and salons, the paucity of trained masseurs, and with the younger generation reluctant to take up the family business, this family is fighting to preserve the connection with a past culture and a bygone lifestyle.

TWENTY-TWO

THE *PANCHAKKI* OF BHOPAL

When President Trump, withdrew the participation of the US from the 2015 Paris Agreement on Climate Change initiative, and accused India of seeking 'billions and billions and billions', by not agreeing to ratify the laid down proposals and procedures for the implementation of global climate change norms, patriotic fervour gripped most of us in India. One could not but go back in time to reminisce about how self-sufficient, environmentally friendly and sustainable methods and devices were largely used for catering to everyday requirements of energy, fuel and mechanical power, in the past.

One such simple but highly effective device was the *Panchakki,* or the water-mill. Before large-scale electrification had been accomplished, most daily chores were done manually, including grinding of various grains in milling stones to obtain a variety of flours. These tasks were mostly left to the women folk to do. One of the limitations of grinding on the household milling stones was that they could not cater to the occasional massive requirement of *rasad,* or rations for the troops, and for supplying to mass gatherings.

Sultan Jahan Begum, is credited to have initiated the establishment of the first mechanically operated flour mill around 1890. Considering the condition of other feudatories

The actual mechanism of the Panchhaki

during that time, it was quite a modern decision and a remarkable feat of engineering which used the flow of water to generate mechanical power. This *panchakki* was located on the banks of the Lower Lake, in a huge room just adjacent to the present Kamla park area. It was officially named the 'Hamidia Flour Mill', but was popularly known as the *panchakki* in local jargon. The remains of the water inlet can still be seen, but the *panchakki* has been gobbled up by today's municipal pump house.

This *panchakki* had two massive millstones, each with a span of about four feet. Since much earlier, excess water in the Upper Lake used to be released into the Lower Lake via an underground tunnel. It was at this interflow that the kinetic energy generated by the rapidly cascading water was arrested by directing the flow towards a wheel which would start rotating from the energy, and in turn cause the millstones to rotate and grind against each other. Through another contraption, an operator could engage or disengage the millstones with the touch of a handle. The installation of the *panchakki* was considered a welfare measure, which further prompted many more public welfare initiatives taken up by the rulers.

The building that housed the Panchhaki

Perhaps, it is high time that conservationists took note and rallied behind the option of going back to such simple, effective, low-cost and renewable, environmentally friendly means to harness natural power, so that it can be put into use for the benefit of mankind.

TWENTY-THREE

MAJMAGIRI – THE MEDIUM IS THE MESSAGE

In an era when there were no modern means of communication, how was a product marketed and how was curiosity and value created for it?

'The medium is the message' is a phrase coined by Marshall McLuhan, a Canadian professor, in the early sixties. McLuhan proposed that a medium itself, not just the content it carries, affects the society in which it plays a role, not only by the content delivered over the medium, but also by the characteristics of the medium itself. A medium embeds itself in any message it transmits or conveys, creating a symbiotic relationship through which the medium influences how the message is perceived. The idea generated fervent intellectual and philosophical debate at the time.

However, much before the advent of television commercials, billboards, radio jingles, or the Internet, this philosophy was being practiced more or less every day in the haats and bazars, and in other forums such as community gatherings, etc., in most parts of India, and Bhopal was no exception to this.

The allusion is to the vibrant culture of a crude, home-grown, but extremely effective way of 'product marketing', called 'Majmagiri'. A crowd or gathering of people, means *majma* in Urdu. Majmagiri can roughly be described as the activity in which a seller would extoll the virtues and benefits of his product through an elaborate and over-the-top, dramatic, song and dance routine, or a sleight of hand performance to prove the veracity of his fake and essentially useless merchandise to prospective buyers.

Many types of fake, exotic commodities and remedies, like purported aphrodisiacs, hair-growth oils, talismans, trinkets and artefacts were sold this way. The crowd-pulling strategy was decided impromptu and would target the focus group from amongst the assemblage. The seller would burst into a euphoric song describing the effectiveness of his product to the gathering, or make children shriek in delight through his buffoonery or scare them by putting on grotesque masks. Majmagiri was an art acquired through the age-old 'ustad – shargid' (teacher – pupil) tradition.

Shyam Munshi in his book on Bhopal, *Sirf Naqsh-e-Qadam Rah Gaye...*, describes some popular and rather intriguing items that would be on sale, including cataract curing lotions for old men, aphrodisiacs that were pitched by displaying photographs of virile-looking wrestlers, talismans, whose effectiveness was proved by apparent scalding with hot iron tongs through sleight of hand etc.!

More often than not, such items purchased by gullible customers would land them in serious trouble. But unlike today, no one pressed charges or dragged the seller to 'consumer courts', and the seller would happily continue to spin his yarn to sell his product! It is important to understand here that it was not the products that were important, but the ceremony that went behind convincing people to fall for buying these clearly counterfeit products that formed the crux of the unique phenomenon of majmagiri.

TWENTY-FOUR

REMAINS OF THE BYGONE DAY – THE TRIBAL CULTURE OF BHOPAL

Two seemingly unconnected and inane events triggered in me the desire to explore the tribal past of Bhopal. A visit to the haats in the BHEL area, and the sound of distant drumbeats around midnight, raising to a crescendo, just after the first spell of rains recently. It was very much like the 'Drums of the Night' in the famous 70's album Mandingo III. The drum beats were not new; I have been hearing them almost on all occasions that celebrated nature and the weather pattern, way back in the eighties from my Professors Colony residence. A close poet friend, Dr. Rajendra Dhodapkar, once remarked that he can still smell the distinct and peculiar acrid aroma of the forests in the populated Arera hills. Maybe a poetic rhetoric, but Bhopal does transmit tribal civilisational elements.

Long before the kingdom of Bhopal came into being, the land was inhabited by the aboriginal tribes of the Gonds, the Korkus and the Bhilalas. As mentioned elsewhere in this book, after Raja Bhoj and before Dost Mohammad, which would be sometime between the 11th CE and the 17th CE, Bhopal, as we know it today, consisted of many small Gond principalities, as well as an independent clusters of villages with a distinct tribal

A sample of Tribal Art

Art depicting a Tribal Drummer

culture. The elite of the tribe, who were known as Raj Gonds, were influenced by the Rajput and Muslim cultures. Rani Kamlapati was a Gond queen. They adopted many practices and rituals that were hitherto unknown, and were considered insignificant and meaningless in the predominant Gond culture. But the Gond masses still continued to be hunter-gatherers, and at best practiced collective *Jhum* (slash and burn) cultivation. Individual ownership of land was an aspect unknown to them.

So, it is worth mulling over what are the urban signposts or the continuity of the earliest tribal moorings of our city.

The sound of drumbeats is one of the most representative and known features of a tribal culture. We know that it is generally used as a means of communication by sending coded messages during festivities, processions after a triumph, or during social or religious rituals. People staying on the outskirts of the city can sometimes still hear some of these

The Mandingo -III Album

and if one is discerning enough, the nature and purpose of the drumbeats can also be deciphered. The haat culture of Bhopal – the throbbing hubbub of a living tradition can still be seen intact in certain places in the city. It is not the government allotted spaces and stalls that I am talking about. It is the old-style exchange of commodities and farm produce, both barter and paid, that still works on interpersonal trust and comfort.

Colourful tribal art, mainly paintings, on road-facing walls all over the city is another example of sharing of cultural space with native inhabitants of the land. Some prominent buildings in the city have been designed with tribal architecture as an inspiration. A fitting example is Bharat Bhavan, the world-renowned multi-arts complex located beside the Bada Talab, with a pervasive, underlining theme of 'open-to-sky-spaces', designed by the iconic architect Charles Correa.

But alas, if we were to search for living specimen from the Gond tribe, we would be hard-pressed to find any. Only a few Gond families, based in the Gondipura village located in the Berasia tehsil near Bhopal can be tracked down, who are leading a truly tribal life, probably the only settlement still attached to its tribal roots, and seemingly unruffled and uncontaminated by modern civilisation as yet.

Like the sub-title of the album '*A Story of Survival*,' In Mandingo III with its music titled: Invocation to the Gods, Watching and Waiting Battle, War Dance, Celebration etc., the leitmotifs of the residual elements of Bhopal's tribal culture, the distant drum beats, the haats and the paintings, all seems to send a coded musical, celebratory and pictorial messages, respectively, to the present civilisation to learn from its past.

TWENTY-FIVE

THEATRE IN BHOPAL – NO ROYAL PATRONAGE!

'All the world's a stage...', the clichéd yet relevant monologue from Shakspeare' *As You Like It* reiterates the mere transitory and metaphorical existence of human beings on earth, quite akin to the brief lifespan of characters in a stage-play.

India is the only country which has witnessed the evolution of the dramatic arts and theatre over the last 5,000 years or so. Beginning with the Sanskrit treatise on drama and stagecraft, *Natya Shastra*, attributed to the sage Bharat Muni, and believed to have been compiled between 200 BCE and 200 CE, India has seen the steady growth of the dramatic arts over the centuries, into aesthetically profound, modern and innovative present-day theatre movements and groups like the Parsi Theatre, 'Naya Theatre' founded by the late drama virtuoso Habib Tanvir, the Indian Peoples Theatre Association, and the Rangmandal at Bharat Bhavan in Bhopal, to name a few. It is also important to acknowledge the continuity that folk theatre of a myriad hues provided to keep stagecraft alive over the years, by weaving various dramatic genres together.

Interestingly, there is no evidence of theatre in any form being patronised during the rule of the Begums in Bhopal.

Celebrated Theatre personality, B.V. Karanth

Habib Tanvir, founder of the iconic 'Naya Theatre'

Dance in Bhopal, in any form, was always considered to be a decadent art since the time of the Begums. However, a few old-timers mention the arrival of the renowned Kathak dancers Kalkadeen Maharaj and Bindadeen Maharaj, the grandfather of Birju Maharaj sometime around 1902. They stayed in the palace as State guests. Not much is known about their purpose of visit though. Dance as an art form though, got a covert approval since Nawab Hamidullah took over.

In the corresponding years, other princely states are known to have supported the dramatic arts. In Delhi, for example, the Mughal era saw the *Raas Leela* (a musical, dramatic enactment of the divine dance that Krishna is said to have performed with the Gopis) started by Emperor Jahangir, took the shape of a full-fledged dance drama during the reign of the later Mughals, complete with structured notes and sequences. In Lucknow, Nawab Wajid Ali Shah fine-tuned the dance drama 'Radha Kanhaiyya Ka Kissa' with the mystical elements of

The 'Parsi Theatre Company'

Sufism. He has rightly been acknowledged as the 'first playwright of Hindustani theatre'. In the South, in Tanjore, the Bhonsle kings had written and staged dramas inspired by the 'Jan Natak' and folk traditions like the 'Yaksha Gaan' and the 'Bhagvad Mela'.

In fact, if one reviews the artistic and cultural landscape of Bhopal from the time the city was founded, until the early 20th century even cursorily, what emerges is a highly staid, vapid and suffocating scenario. With the brief exception of the rule of Shah Jahan Begum, the aesthetic sensibilities, if any, were overwhelmingly overshadowed by the drudgery of religious and royal ceremonies.

It was only in the late 1930s, when the first travelling Parsi theatre company arrived and performed in Bhopal, that the seeds of an enduring love for theatre were sowed in the hearts of the people here. Later, Madanlal Kapoor, father of film actor Anu Kapoor, became the owner of this company and based it in Bhopal and utilised the talent of local artists.

However, the golden period of theatre in Bhopal was yet to dawn. That started with the formation of the iconic 'Naya Theatre' by the master of stagecraft – Habib Tanvir in 1959, along with tribal artists from Chhatisgarh. Groundbreaking plays like 'Agra Bazaar', 'Charandas Chor', and 'Mor Naam Damad' etc., set high theatrical standards which are difficult to emulate even today.

The pinnacle of the theatre movement in Bhopal came with the formation of the Rangmandal, the stage and theatre wing of Bharat Bhavan, in 1982. Under, B.V. Karanth, its first Director, Rangmandal emerged as the fulcrum of innovative theatre styles, with brilliant stage directors like Fritz Benevitz, Ratan Thiyam, Barry John and Bansi Kaul patronising it. Because of Bharat Bhawan being a quasi-government institution, Rangmandal attracted both – budding and established talent – from all over, and gained popularity worldwide.

But what could have been the reason for the lackadaisical approach by the Begums towards this particular art form. It could be the prevailing social mores which recognised this form derisively as 'nautankibaaz'. It also appears that the Begums in their overzealousness to consolidate their rule missed out completely on the elements or symbols of hedonistic pleasure.

TWENTY-SIX

SWEET, UNHEARD MUSIC

'*Heard melodies are sweet, but those unheard are sweeter,*' said John Keats.

Unlike the principalities of Lucknow, Gwalior, and Rampur etc., where history would remain incomplete without paying tribute to their glorious musical legacy – the state of Bhopal remained relatively backward in the realm of music. The attitude of the Nawabs of Bhopal towards patronage to music, vocal or instrumental, was at best lukewarm, and if not discouraging, then certainly, indifferent. During the consecutive rule of the four Nawab Begums in particular, public musical soirees and dance performances by *nautch* girls etc. were as good as prohibited. For a very short period of time during the rule of Shahjehan Begum, before she was radicalised by her consort Siddiq Hasan, there may have been a few sporadic performances by prominent musicians and *tawaifs*.

That said, the state of Bhopal did house some illustrious classical 'gharanas' and nurture some now lost forms of singing. Apart from classical singers like Pandit Bacchu Maharaj, Ustad Bhura Khan, Ustad Masita Khanand, and *quwwals* like Sadiq Quwwal and Rashid Quwwal etc., there existed a rather unique group of women singers called the *Mirasans,* who were patronised by the female nobility of the time. This is not

A representation of the Mirasans

surprising, considering that the Begum Nawabs were known for encouraging woman-centric activity.

The distinct identity of the mirasans was their code of conduct, which strictly forbade them to perform to a male audience. In the days when nautch girls and tawaifs were considered an integral part of society, the mirasans lived, sang and performed only for women audiences, to the extent that the accompanists that played the musical instruments at their performances were also female. An amazing aspect of their restrictive patronage was that they managed to create a connoisseur class among their patrons that truly appreciated and understood the intricacies and fine nuances of classical and traditional music. Their style of singing generally revolved around feminine and soft-hearted aspects of life. Some evocative renderings on longing and separation from the beloved – *virah* – are attributed to them.

Another famous name which could keep its strictly female audiences enthralled was that of Putli, a transgender, or *Khwaja Saraah,* who was famous for her renditions of the *thumri,* embellished with perfect *murkis* and *khatakas* (stylish vocal intonations in Indian classical and folk music). Putli is said to have held public performances of her own in the early twenties.

Their form and genre may have been lost in the annals of time, but just like the unheard sweet music in John Keats's *Ode On a Grecian Urn,* the lilting songs of longing by the mirasans, and the playfully coquettish *thumris* by Putli shall reverberate hauntingly in the minds and souls of music lovers, always.

TWENTY-SEVEN

PATTIABAZI IN BHOPAL

Imagine the wooden platform like stretchers that throngs of people sat on in the lanes and by lanes of the bustling Khorasan, in the misadventures of the bumbling *Mullah Nasruddin* and his donkey. You will probably be surprised that almost similar milieu existed in Bhopal. This was a unique phenomenon called 'Pattiabazi'. This was actually a medieval era, public forum for gossiping and 'time-pass', as idling without anything constructive to do is called in India.

Common households could not afford to have exclusive spaces for receiving (predominantly) male visitors, which was necessitated by the purdah system, which was essentially the sequestering of girls and women from male family members and outsiders. Most of the socialising would take place outside the house, in the by-lanes and other available open areas. A few slabs of stone or wood, called the 'pattia', placed strategically so as not to block the flow of people in the streets and adequate for seating a small gathering of men, were ubiquitous in Bhopal of the old. These often evolved into permanent structures. These were usually made of rectangular, polished slabs of rock, placed on a support at each end, or simply cemented into the outside wall of houses, making a bench-like structure.

People from all walks of life would congregate on these pattias, just to kill spare time at hand by indulging in banter or to discuss serious issues like statecraft and administration; to attend mushairas or to solve knotty social issues; to gossip about a clandestine love-affair or to ignite the sparks of a far-reaching political revolution; discuss sports or to seek settlement of disputes – making the practice of pattiabazi an integral part of the Bhopali tehzeeb. The pattiabazi culture of Bhopal was also inextricably intertwined with 'kissa goi' or 'dastaan goi' (storytelling), and eventually impacted on the traditional style of kissa goi narration. These days, some experiments are being done, in which the age-old pattia tehzeeb of Bhopal is being performed as 'pattia-goi'.

Though it was mostly a circumstantial ingenuity, the architecture for utility of available space was very similar to that in old city of Cairo, where a rectangular open space was called 'Tahtabush'. It was an exclusive space for men to receive male guests or a sitting area to welcome common guests. Dr. Meera Dass, then member INTACH in a paper titled *City with a Past – an Account of the Built Heritage of Bhopal,* writes:

'The 'pattias' (Hindi for platform in the front of a house used as a sit-out) of various buildings matched each other in an ordered manner. People spread out on to these pattias in the evening and these become centers of daily social intercourse and gossip.'

The most famous pattias of yore were the ones at the houses of Syed Zahoor Hashmi and Pandit Khushilal Vaidh at Atta Shuja Khan, Feroz Khelon ki gulli pattia at Budhwara, Jumerati chauraha pattia, pattias at the shops of Bhaiyya Ezaz, Nadra Medical Hall, Sharma ji tailor-master ki dukaan etc. People would gather at these pattias after finishing their daily chores, and indulged in pulsating, animated conversation and ubiquitous *chai* until dawn. Famous personalities of Bhopal, like Dr. Shankar Dayal Sharma, Khan Shakir Ali Khan, Maulana

Saidullah Khan Razmi, Pandit Chaturnarayan Malwi etc. have spent their long hours at the pattias.

Pattiabazi no longer exists, because of road expansion and the dissipating social ethos. Shyam Munshi, in his seminal book *Sirf Naqsh-e-Qadam Rah Gaye* rues that if the culture of pattiabazi had been kept alive, the worst communal riots after the Babri Masjid demolition would never have happened in Bhopal.

TWENTY-EIGHT

TRADITIONAL ATTIRE OF THE ERSTWHILE STATE OF BHOPAL

The traditional urban attire of men and women of erstwhile Bhopal was an amalgamation of the Mughal and Afghan way of dressing. It was also highly influenced by whatever current fashion was trending in the Lucknow royals' wardrobe, particularly for women's wear. Later, in the early twentieth century, it drew greater inspiration and took on elements from traditional Turkish attire, as is evident from the wide use of the Turkish cap – the 'fez' – and the still-popular ladies 'kaftan'.

Shyam Munshi, an authority on life-style of the bygone culture of Bhopal has elaborated about traditional garments and their everyday use. He describes four predominant types of male dresses in use by the nobility and the common people. The first was the combination of a white 'churidar payjama', 'mulmul kurta', 'sherwani' and the 'safaa' as headgear, primarily favoured by the elite nobility. However, the relatively well-to-do commoners also wore these and sometimes, replaced the sherwani and safaa with an 'angarakha' and 'turki topi'. Another combination was simple payjama with a sherwani, a working-class dress.

Most white collar kachcheri (office) goers devised a more

Mumtaz Khan's sketches of traditional Bhopali dresses for Men and Women

practical, comfortable and uncomplicated outfit. This comprised of something between a *churidar* and a simple payjama and went by the name of 'roomaalidar payjama', aptly also called the 'Bhopali payjama'. It was worn in combination with a *Qameez* (shirt) and a coat. The *shalwar qameez* was introduced by the Pathans, and the roomalidar payjama ensemble is one of its many avatars. The trader class generally wore a dhoti with a simple kurta and a coat and topped these with 'kalf lagi pagadi' (starched turban), much like their counterparts in the India of late nineteenth and early twentieth century.

Traditional attire of the women in Bhopal can be compared with the exquisite and eclectic costumes famously worn by Meena Kumari in *Pakeezah*, or Madhubala in *Mughal-e-Azam*, tweaked by a few alterations and some ingenious tailoring. The 'Liba-o-poshaak', now commonly known as the 'Bhopali Joda' had a unique grace and functionality to it and was worn across all sections of society, women from the nobility as well as the common ladies. This dress consisted of three parts: the 'churidar payjama' which was almost skin-tight up to the ankle, a 'kurta' that again, was body-hugging with many complex creases up to the waist, then falling downwards in a loose cupola-shaped encirclement. The third part was the 'dupatta', an embellished, almost six-yard long piece of fabric, worn in two folds over the chest, and thrown back over the shoulders.

The renowned fashion designer from Bhopal, Mumtaz Khan, who is an authority on the Bhopali libaas, and during a long conversation mentioned some interesting aspects of this. He says it is more popularly called the *Bhopali Kurta* or *Turki kurta*:

'This most prominent and now popular attire was evolved from the Turki kurta by the Begums which conformed to the tenets of Islam, which state that the curves of the body should not be visible, and wherever the body parts were vulnerable to be visible, they must be covered with pleats. In addition, they wore a five-meter long *dupatta,* which was used not just to cover the entire body but was also to style the dress. This form of attire was made more prominent by the famous singer Shakeela Bano Bhopali, who kept this fashion alive.'

About the evolution of the Bhopali pyjama, he says that the traditional pyjamas had broad *mohri* (flair at the foot) which would get soiled by the red soil of Bhopal, and the Bhopalis could be identified immediately on spotting the soiled mohris, and would be made fun of. Gradually, the mohri became narrow with *churis* (folds) and only a stretchable cloth called *Ureyb* could be used to make this payjama. He also mentions about the elaborate use of abhrakh (mica) in making safas. The fabric was prepared by mixing abhrak with starch by the ladies of the house. This was further crushed to make the unique trail of the 'Bhopali safa'.

Sometimes, noble women chose to wear a 'seedhe palle ki saree'. The relatively humbler class of women wore the more affordable 'lehnga-choli', and the 'lughra' or 'chunni'. Another interesting tailoring ingenuity was the often bright ochre-coloured 'labaada', created for women of the upper crust, which was nothing but lehnga and choli sewn together as a single piece, for everyday use.

The elaborate and fancy ceremonial regalia of the Bhopal royalty was juxtaposed with the more humdrum dresses of the ADCs and courtiers – a bandgulla or Jodhpuri coat with gold trimming, a light-blue 'safa' and a gold 'turra' (crest of feathers on the turban) which was a traditional Rajput symbol of nobility. Today, designers like Mumtaz and Niloufar are well- known in the country. They have mastered their craft by developing and nuancing the patterns of the traditional attire of Bhopal.

TWENTY-NINE

THE TWO MYSTICS OF BHOPAL

'*The Lamps are different, but the Light is the same,*' says Rumi. Bhopal has evolved through an era of obvious wisdom, which can be ascribed to particularly two spiritual men, who lived here during the early nineteenth century. These two saintly men, though living in complete isolation and solitude–quietly, but effectively, managed to infuse and spread spiritual knowledge from their respective religions. In the present day, the syncretic culture of Bhopal that has emerged over the years as a result of the teachings of these great saints, has helped the city remain largely peaceful and tolerant in the face of religious polarisation and turbulent communal tensions that have gripped other parts of the country periodically.

This high level of tolerance, mutual respect and camaraderie between people of two different religions can be largely attributed to Sant Shree Sheetaldas, who was a Hindu 'Sadhu', and Hazrat Shah Ali Shah Rahmatullah Alaih, a great Muslim Sufi saint, who lived in roughly the same era in Bhopal. Sant Sheetaldas lived near the Upper Lake in today's Kamla park area, in what is now called the 'Sheetaldas ki Bagiya.' Hazrat Shah Ali Shah lived on a small, isolated island in the Upper Lake, which is also called the Takia *Tapu. The island houses* his tomb and carries great religious and archaeological significance.

Little is known of how these two spiritual souls disseminated their spiritual knowledge, but together, they held 'Satsangs' (spiritual gatherings), alternatively at their respective abodes in the city, in their mystical quest for answers to life and death. They also nurtured deep sense of respect and brotherhood towards each other. Although they lived as per the teachings and tenets of their own religious scriptures, they are said to have spent time together every day, sharing a common *chillum* (an earthen receptacle for smoking marijuana). It is said that after Hazrat Shah Ali Shah died, Sant Sheetaldas not only gave-up smoking the chilum, but regressed into a state of complete silence. Thus, living another axiom by the Sufi poet Rumi that "Silence is the language of god, all else is poor translation".

This tradition was carried forward by such famous Peers as Shah Rauf Ahmad, Peer Abu Ahmad, Hazrat Shah Sharf Uddin Hussaini Chisti , whose dargah at the base of the Raisen Fort is a very popular and spiritual destination for the seekers from all communities.

THIRTY

WHAT'S IN A NAME?

Have you ever wondered who named our rivers, hills and mountains? Poets have pondered over and historians have researched on this, but the most plausible answer has emerged from an academic movement, referred to as the 'People's History' or 'History from Below'. Thus, 'History from Below' seeks to take as its subjects ordinary people, and concentrate on their experiences and perspectives, contrasting itself with the stereotype of traditional political history and its focus on the actions of "great men". New Histories – The Free Online History Magazine elaborates:

> 'Most obviously, the central principal of 'history from below' represented a seismic shift from previous engagements with the past, widening the field of historical actors and paving the way for developments including gender history, subaltern studies and the democratisation of historical knowledge in the years which followed. The group was formed in 1946 by a new generation of Marxist historians including Eric Hobsbawm, E. P. Thompson and Christopher Hill, along with non-academics such as A. L. Morton and Brian Pearce.'

Interestingly, Bhopal has had a long tradition of naming gullies, mohallas and similar parts that are abuzz with the everyday hubbub of city, by the utility or functions that the area performed. Carrying forward an age-old oral tradition, these have been named by ordinary people and in their own vernacular languages, thus retaining their characteristic lisp and tenor along with a solid historical base. So, there still exist places with names like 'Gulia Dai ka mohalla' and 'Kali Dhoban ki gulli'!

Even the Darwazas, and later the mohallas in the Shahar Panah (walled-city) were named mostly after the days of the week, like Itwara (for Sunday), Somwara (for Monday); Mangalwara (for Tuesday); Budhwara (for Wednesday); Jumerati (for Thursday) and so on.

Before this, when Dost Mohammad built the Fatahgarh fort and named it after his wife Fatah Bibi, he, too, named the six gates of the fort, quite conveniently, after the days of the week. This was also because villagers and Korku tribals would come into the fortified city to sell their goods and produce in the *haat*, organised at each of the darwazas on the day of the week it was named after.

Another interesting aspect of such functional names was that even though they might have been derived from elite sources, their intonation quickly got distorted to make them fit into the everyday parlance of the place. Thus, a *mohalla* called 'Atta Shuja Khan', in which 'Shuja' means valiant, became 'Atta *Suje* Khan', in which 'Suje' means 'swollen'! Similarly, 'Pipariya Paeenda Khan' became 'Papriya *Penda* Khan', and 'Narwar Khan Dera' got distorted into 'Narwar *Khandera*'. Many other were named after the profession or category of people who inhabited there. Some of them were Ahirpura, Kumharpura, Malipura, Kasaipura, Bhangipura etc.

But these were the people who named or renamed their workplace, but what about new Bhopal which still has prosaic names from a bureaucrat's files of areas as '*das number*, *gyarah* number, *chhe* number etc. and horrifyingly even '*sadhe-gyarah* and *sadhe-barah* number'. It's high time we gave some honourable names to such places. It reminded me of a facetious fact told to me by my colleague who returned from a deputation to Namibia. He said that due to the lack of imagination and perhaps even convenience, the Namibians name their children as Joseph One, Joseph Two and so on.

THIRTY-ONE

BHARAT BHAVAN - THE PROFOUND MUSE

Few bureaucrats have the ability, the vision and the opportunity to create history; fewer have the aegis of the political dispensation of the day, and still fewer are the ones who have all of these factors going for them at the same time. Just like the concept of the 'poet philosopher king' proposed by Plato, a poet-bureaucrat is a gift to the people he is destined to serve. Ashok Vajpeyi, the man, the writer and the bureaucrat, fits perfectly into the third bracket.

Since its inception in 1956, Madhya Pradesh has seen stalwarts in the field of politics, but it has been fortunate in having had a succession of outstanding, highly capable and truly committed bureaucrats, in equal measure. These exceptional administrators have not only artfully chiselled the destiny of the state, but still stand as role models for generations. Names like R.C.V.P Noronha, M.N. Buch, S.C. Behar and Satyanand Mishra belong to this distinguished group. I have written about the theatre and music scenario in Bhopal of the past elsewhere in this book, and we know that there was not much happening in the field of arts and culture until as late as the 1960s.

Bharat Bhavan and Ashok Vajpeyi are two entities that are inextricably linked to each other, so, one evening during

The inauguration of Bharat Bhavan, etched in stone

his recent visit to Bhopal, I requested him to talk about how the idea of establishing a one-of-its-kind multi-arts complex originated, how the concept was fleshed-out and developed, and how subsequently, the iconic institution called Bharat Bhavan came into being. He explained the entire history behind this profound muse with a demeanour of a detached yogi, highlighting his own cameo in the entire episode only where necessary!

Initially, after the formation of Madhya Pradesh, most of the governance was centred on the development and consolidation of the new state and Bhopal as its capital. There was no separate ministry for culture; it functioned as a department under the Ministry of Education, headed by a Deputy Secretary. The few existing institutions for arts and literature, like the regional Lalit Kala Parishads – the Abhinav and the Sangeet Kala Parishads – came under the purview of this department.

Ashok Vajpeyi first arrived in Bhopal in 1973, as Deputy Secretary to the Department of Culture. Before the idea of Bharat Bhavan came up, Vajpeyi, all of 32-years old then, had already created a name for himself when he organised a hugely popular and successful event, 'Utsav-73' that was conceived and executed singlehandedly by him, with the support of the MP Kala Parishad, and which eventually went on to become an annual feature. This was a gathering of the outstanding and revered musical luminaries of Indian classical music of the time, like Pandit Krishna Shankar Rao, Ustad Amir Khan, Ustad Abdul Haleem Zafar Khan, Ustad Amjad Ali Khan etc.

Under Vajpeyi, the Department of Culture established the Ustad Alauddin Khan Academy with its two wings – the 'Dhrupad Kendra', under the dhrupad virtuoso Zia Fariuddin Dagar, and the 'Chakradhar Nritya Kendra', mentored by Pandit Kartik Ram. These two centres have since produced illustrious artists in the classical Hindustani vocal tradition of dhrupad, and the classical Indian dance form of Kathak, respectively.

The concept of Bharat Bhavan as a multi-arts complex, incorporating various art forms to showcase the plurality of India's culture, was first considered during the deliberations that took place to mark 25 years of India's Independence, in 1972. It was proposed by Pupul Jayakar, popularly known as the Czarina of culture, who was advisor to the then Prime Minister, Indira Gandhi, on matters of art and culture. It was proposed that each state of India should have an institution to promote and propagate the arts, which would be partly funded by the central government. However, it was only Madhya Pradesh that whole-heartedly embraced the proposal and eventually made it a reality.

Arjun Singh, the Minister of Education between 1972 and 1977 sent a note regarding this to P.C. Sethi, the Chief Minister of the state at the time. Sethi allotted an eight-acre piece of land on the edge of the Bada Talab, adjacent to the Chief Minister's official residence in Bhopal, for the construction of this institution. By now a known name in the field of

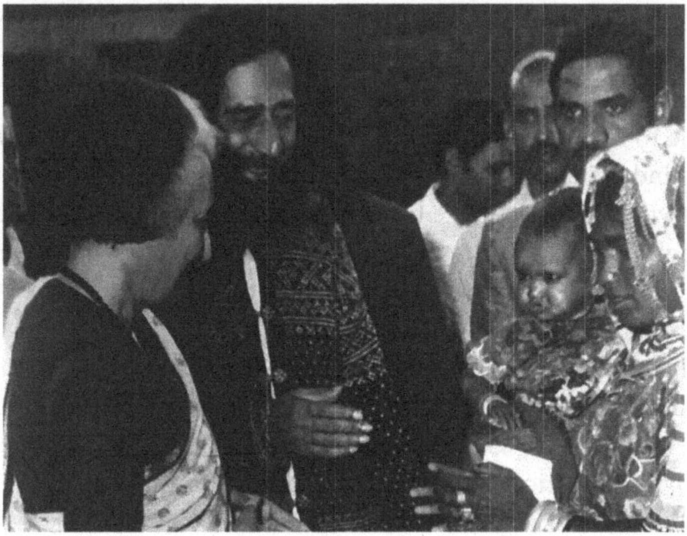

Indira Gandhi, the then Prime Minister during the inauguration of Bharat Bhavan on 13 February 1982

culture, Ashok Vajpeyi became a natural and obvious choice to be included in the eminent committee that was formed to spearhead the establishment of Bharat Bhavan. This included R.C.V.P. Noronha, the Chief Secretary, M.N. Buch, Secretary, Urban Development and Ashok Vajpeyi, Special Secretary, Culture. The charter was to create a permanent abode for cultural pursuits, and to develop a platform which would be a permanent forum for artistic and cultural activities, not only for the state, but for the entire country.

The Bharat Bhavan Nyas Adhiniyam, 1982, received the formal assent of the state Governor on the 27 October 1982. Under this, Bharat Bhavan was to have four distinct, yet intersecting wings: 'Rangmandal' for theatre and the dramatic arts; 'Roopankar' – the fine arts and painting wing; 'Vagarth' – the section for Indian poetry, and 'Anhad' – the wing devoted to Indian classical music and dance.

The Rangmandal was to aim at not just staging plays, but perpetuating continuous practice, by making its members overall participants in the theatrical experience, who would then be able to find new dimensions in their pursuit of acting. The idea behind Rangmandal was not limited to promoting dramatic activities, but also looked at creating a theatre revolution which would connect with the ambience that includes all aspects of the art. The emphasis would be on the development and enrichment of local theatre in all its genres. Over the years, it has been proved that the strength of the stage-play is in its being indigenous, and therefore, the nature of theatre should be local but its soul should be Pan-Indian. At Rangmandal, popular theatrical genres and their production are still relevant, and is done using modern sensibilities.

Roopankar is the apex museum of fine arts in the state, and is operated, and hypothecated by artists themselves. It is supported by artists from all over the country and it is they who curate the collections themselves. Roopankar houses works of select artists who have made important contribution in the field of contemporary painting and allied arts, with each artist's collection exhibited in a systematic, chronological order. Roopankar debunks the myth that being contemporary is just being urban, and therefore offers equal space and opportunity to folk and tribal arts as well.

Invoking the great Indian tradition of the concept of incorporating the *vak* (sound) and *arth* (meaning) in the memory of the great poet Kalidas, the library dedicated to Indian poetry – Vagarth at Bharat Bhavan had the definite purpose of recapturing and preserving human eloquence.

India's poetic tradition, which has been in existence for over two millennia now, is one of the richest in the world. Its contemporary scenario too is active and vigorous. The goal of Vagarth is to collect and preserve all forms of poetic expression,

Team Bharat Bhavan (From R to L):
B V Karanth, Ashok Vajpeyi, Arjun Singh,
Vijaymohan Singh and J. Swaminathan

past and present, whether spoken, written or printed, available through manuscripts, printed books, sound recordings on tapes and disks, etc. It has a department for poetry in all major Indian languages, formed in consultation with prominent contemporary poets or language experts.

Activities undertaken at Vagarth are poetry recitation sessions, organising enriching studies, symposium and workshops related to poetry; acquisition and publication of poetry collections; promotion of the translation of world poetry into Indian languages; recording the works of all important poets in their own voices and preparing digital playback formats of these (this was done on cassette-tapes and record discs earlier); inviting prominent poets to come and live in Bhopal as poet-in-residence; organising appropriate activities for the consolidation and preservation of the poetry tradition in consultation with the advisory board.

Music is an ancient form of expression, an imperishable

repository of our ethnic memory and uniqueness, our specific sense of country and the human condition and the constant dynamic change it goes through. Anhad, the music wing of Bharat Bhavan, is an effort to restore this tradition and its extremely rich present with its all-pervasive splendour, variety and possibilities, so that it can become a permanent and reliable centre of good taste, exploration and experimentation. It also aspires to be an active medium of interrelationship and exchange between the scriptures and people.

The architect chosen for the planning and execution of the building of this one-of-its-kind edifice was the much acclaimed Charles Correa.

'When Shyama Charan Shukla became Chief Minister he wanted the site to be shifted, because Chief Minister's residence was close-by and he thought if something more majestic and imposing came up, it might dwarf the CM's residence....' Therefore, the site was ordered to be shifted to a location within the campus of Motilal Nehru Vigyan Mahavidyalay, facing the Chota Talaab, ostensibly because Charles Correa wanted a waterbody to be an integral feature of the design. Laughing in his inimitable style, Vajpeyi said, '...but luckily, Shukla's Government fell soon after, so the original site was given back for the project.'

Vajpeyi also recalled that when, finally, an independent Department of Culture was formed, delinking it from the Education Ministry, he proposed two important decisions to be taken by the Chief Minister, who was also had the Department of Culture. One, that the existing Lalit Kala Academys be merged with Bharat Bhavan, and two, that the building be constructed not by the Public Works Department, but by the Bhopal Development Authority which was under the Department of Urban Affairs. The then CM, Arjun Singh also raised a very pertinent and farsighted concern, saying, 'Bharat

Bhavan cannot be run as an adjunct of the government, it has to have its autonomy, and asked Vajpeyi as to how this could be done. On Vajpeyi's suggestion that it be governed by a trust, Arjun Singh countered that his cabinet might not agree to it, and asked if the suggestion could come directly from the Prime Minister's office? Upon this, Vajpeyi spoke to Pupul Jayakar, who assured him that not only would she put in a word to the PM, she would also write a letter to all concerned, backing the creation of a trust. With this, Bharat Bhavan was converted to a trust by a resolution passed by the Cabinet of Ministers. A proposal to appoint life-trustees was also mooted in order to ensure continuity of the ideas and purpose by those who had originally conceived it. The three life-trustees appointed were Arjun Singh, J. Swaminathan and Ashok Vajpeyi.

Bharat Bhavan was inaugurated on the 13 February 1982 by the then Prime Minister Indira Gandhi, who in her inaugural speech, said:

> '...long time ago, it was my dream that such Bhavans should be built in every state, so that the worthiness in this country which is in the villages, in the hills, in the forests, in the desert, can be given an opportunity to get out, flourish. How can those people who are in the cities, who though consider themselves educated, are actually separated from their roots, how we can reunite them with their roots.'

Another outstanding feature initiated at Bharat Bhavan was the effort towards 'redefining the contemporary', by the painter J. Swaminathan and theatre personality, B.V. Karanth. This was hitherto only a concept that had never actually been implemented anywhere.

Vajpeyi further elaborated '...by incorporating, the notion of the folk and the tribal within the notion of the contemporary...

this is the only museum in the country even today, after almost forty years, where the urban, the folk and the tribal are all seen and displayed as a part of the contemporary.'

This was indeed the rare instance that a bureaucrat was not only given the credit for accomplishing an important feat, but was also being showered with high praise by members of the Legislative Assembly, while speaking in favour of the bill during the debate for the creation of the Bharat Bhavan trust, in the assembly.

In fact, Vijaymohan Tiwari, an MLA from Manjholi, is on record saying:

> 'Perhaps it has happened for the first time in the history of our country that an administrative department has handed over an institution created by them to the public, just like one would hand someone a rose. The man responsible for achieving this, if I may put it in the words of Muktibodh, is Ashok Vajpeyi, who has handed over this rose to the people of Madhya Pradesh, and Madhya Pradesh is proud of this.' (from *Bharat Bhavan – Bhulne Ke Virudh Ek Dastavez*).

In its undiluted existence of eight years, until 1990, the four wings of Bharat Bhavan had created a record of sorts, the prominent milestones being: more than fifty all India painting exhibitions organised at Roopankar, besides, nineteen international exhibitions, thirty-three artist camps, seven tribal and folk-art collection drives etc., to list a few. It houses 4,386 folk and tribal works of art as well as 702 urban ones, making it one of the largest painting archives in the country. Eminent artists whose works have been exhibited at Roopankar included names like M.F. Hussain, Satish Gujral, Tyeb Mehta, V.S. Gaitonde, to name just a few.

Rangmandal produced 42 stage plays under 17 directors, with 831 shows, and 43 theatre workshops. It also established the first professional theatre repertory in the country.

Similarly, Vagarth hosted 40 Hindi poets of various generations under its 'Samvat' series.... A World Poetry Festival featuring 26 poets in 25 languages from 21 countries was organised as a tribute during the centenary year celebrations of Jawaharlal Nehru. A flagship magazine – 'Poorvagrah' is also published under its ageis.

Anhad has the distinction of organising over 1,800 hours of live classical and folk music concerts, notable being the 'Parampara' series, featuring senior masters of music and dance. Sarangi mela – a first of its kind festival-cum-seminar, featuring more than a hundred sarangi players from all over the country and a number of other music exponents.

A true art aficionado, who happened to become a bureaucrat, thus gave an enduring legacy to the country, at a juncture when art and culture were not even a consideration. Vajpeyi created a collective muse, which changed the cultural landscape of Bhopal forever, and because of the extension of which to the entire country – the enduring elements still vibrate and thrill the people of this city. The subtle ways in which Bharat Bhavan of the yore refined the aesthetic sensibilities of the youth of that generation was not only transforming, but was also highly evolutionary. It taught one to discern between good and bad art, and genius from mediocrity in personality enhancing insights into literature, art, theatre, cinema and music. Not many know that the harmonium was not allowed inside the precincts of Bharat Bhavan. Until 1990 at least, I do not remember seeing a singer use the harmonium during a concert. The political dispensation after 1990, however, decided to amend the charter of Bharat Bhavan in an effort to convert its perceived 'elitist' and 'highbrow' reputation to more accessible, more inclusive participation.

THIRTY-TWO

HOCKEY CHRONICLES – FROM THE 'KHAPOTE' TO OLYMPIC GOLD MEDALS AND BACK

'Ashockey of hockey', the newspapers screamed after a recent debacle by our hockey team, hinting that our team was one to be reckoned with in the not-so-distant past! Bhopal's contribution to Indian as well as international hockey has been significant.

It was only in 1909 that Bhopal was exposed to the game of field hockey when the first hockey tournament – the 'Inter-State Forces' was organised at the Kali Parade Ground, located near the now infamous Union Carbide chemical plant. The tournament was free for public viewing, and it was after this that the common masses opened up to this game with missionary zeal. Soon, by 1915, there were at least five major hockey clubs in the city – the 'Sikandariya', 'Ikatdariya', 'Bhopal Heroes', 'Nooria' and the 'Bhopal Police' clubs. These were modestly funded by admirers and players alike, and attracted throngs of young men towards the game.

The cost of Rs. 2 for a hockey stick and a ball was prohibitive at the time, so enthusiasts would chop off tree branches that were roughly shaped like a hockey stick and would further prune these into proper shape. These improvised sticks were called

The Indian-Hockey Team at the Berlin Summer Olympics in 1936, where they won the Gold Medal

'khapote' by the locals. The ball was fashioned out of tanned hide which was stuffed with cloth and sewn closed, to make what could be called a prototype of the modern-day hockey ball. Their uniform too was hilariously indigenous – the Bhopali pyjama, folded up to the knee and tied up, to look like bloated shorts, and the kameez tucked into these make-shift shorts, to look like a T-shirt.

Most of the hockey players from Bhopal who went on to achieve glory on the international hockey scene were nurtured in the 'hockey nurseries' which had mushroomed and thrived in the narrow, constricted lanes of the old city, like the 'mehndi wali gali', 'hathi khana maidan', 'khirniwala maidan' etc., with the home-made 'khapote' as their prized possession.

There is an interesting tale, which is also mentioned by Shyam Munshi in his book, *Sirf Naqshe Qadam Rah Gaye*, about an old woman who, in her own small way, contributed towards the development of modern hockey in Bhopal. Simply referred to as 'budhiya' (old woman) and familiar to all hockey lovers of the time, this old woman was actually a rag picker, who managed to retrieve broken and discarded

The Indian Hockey Team at the Helsinki Summer Olympics in 1952, where they won a Gold Medal

hockey sticks and worn out balls from the garbage she rummaged through. She would then refurbish the gear as best as she could and sell it back to players at a modest, affordable price. Her little business is said to have grown over time, so much so that she could eventually give up rag-picking and start dealing exclusively in hockey related items.

Fortunately, hockey in Bhopal remained a game of the masses, unlike polo and cricket, which took on a glamourous and somewhat elitist mantle. It, however, had to wait until 1930 for royal patronage. Although in her memoirs, Princess Abida Sultan has haughtily dismissed hockey players of Bhopal as being '*drawn mostly from the underprivileged class of Barru Kat Muslims...*', her father and cousins were funding various hockey clubs and had established the 'Bhopal Hockey Association' in 1931.

Nawab Rashiduzzafar Khan – himself a competent hockey player – founded the famous 'Bhopal Wanderers' club in 1930 and started the prestigious tournament, the 'All India Obaidullah Khan Gold Cup' in 1931, an annual tournament which continues to be held to-date. It was through this club and this tournament that Bhopal gave the World two famous players – Ahsan Mohammad Khan and Ahmed Sher Khan – who participated in the Summer Olympics in Berlin in 1936, under the captaincy of the iconic Major Dhyanchand and won the gold medal for (pre-independence) India. At the 1952 Summer Olympics in Helsinki, four players from Bhopal Akhtar Hussain, Habib-Ur-Rahman, Latif-Ur-Rahman and Anwar Ahmad Khan played for the Pakistan team, as they had migrated after 1949.

Later, Inam-ur-Rehman and Aslam Sher Khan, two players from Bhopal represented independent India at the Olympic Games of 1968 (Mexico City, Mexico) and 1972 (Munich, Germany) respectively.

From the humble 'khapote' to royal patronage, and from heady Olympic gold medals to a largely side-lined and neglected game, Bhopal has witnessed the part intoxicating and part depressing, but surely turbulent journey of field hockey on the domestic and the world-stages. But hopefully, the seeds sowed in the 'hockey nurseries' are still buried and lying dormant, and perhaps only need a bit of nourishment and encouragement to bring back the golden days of Indian hockey in Bhopal and indeed, the world over.

BIBLIOGRAPHY

Islam and Power in Colonial India: The Making and Unmaking of a Muslim Princess – Barbara Metcalf

Beete Din Bhopal Ke – Khalid Mohammad Khan

Daastaan-e-Bhopal – Khalid Mohammad Khan

Woh Aadmi – Fazl Tabish

Sookha Bargad – Manzoor Ahtesham

The Bourbons and Begums of Bhopal: The Forgotten History – Indira Iyengar

Begums of Bhopal: A Dynasty of Women Rulers in Raj India – Shaharyar M. Khan

Memoirs of a Rebel Princess – Abida Sultan

The Gohur-i-Ikbal (An Account of My Life) – Sultan Jahan Begam, Nawab of Bhopal, (1858-1930); Translated from Urdu by Payne, C. H.

Bhopal Connections: Vignettes of Royal Rule – Shaharyar M. Khan

Sirf Naqsh-e-Qadam Rah Gaye... – Shyam Munshi

Vintage Bhopal – Ashok Shah and Gita Subherwal

The Taj-ul-Ikbal Tarikh Bhopal (The History of Bhopal) – Shahjahan Begum, Nawab of Bhopal (1938-1901); Translated from Urdu by Barstow, H. C.

Hayat-I-Qudsi: Life of the Nawab Gauhar Begum Alias the Nawab

Begum Qudsia, of Bhopal – Sultan Jahan Begum, Nawab of Bhopal, (1958–1930)

A Brief History of the Bhopal Principality in Central India – William Hough

History of the Paramara Dynasty – D. C. Ganguly

The Rise and Establishment of the Bhopal State – O.P. Malhotra

BhopalNama

Writing a City